Foucault and Managerial Governmentality

In the last two decades there has been an explosion of research inspired by Michel Foucault's suggestion of a new concept, 'governmentality'. The distinctive feature of modern governmentality is that across all sorts of fields, rule is predicated upon the active subject as the vehicle through which—and by which—power is exercised. The appeal of governmentality is that, whether we are considering the workplace, the school or welfare regimes, it opens up new ways of looking at familiar institutions.

Foucault and Managerial Governmentality is about Michel Foucault's concept of governmentality. The novelty of this concept is that it looks at the ways that populations and organizations are imagined in ways that premise collective gains through expanding individual freedoms. Specifically, how are technologies of freedom devised that improve the overall performance—health, productivity or parental responsibility—of a given population?

Understanding the operation of technologies of control is a simple enough task, argues Foucault, but also one that blinds us to the increasing prevalence of technologies of freedom. *Foucault and Managerial Governmentality* aims not just to locate this concept in Foucault's wider research project but to apply it to all sorts of management techniques. By applying governmentality to questions of management and organization we will also develop Foucault's original, somewhat sketchy concept.

This book has three innovative narratives: an awareness of the historicity of the concept; the application of governmentality to specific forms of management, which means that we escape the temptation to read any and all forms of technology and organization as an expression of neoliberalism; and, finally, the interviews with Peter Miller and Nikolas Rose which provide unique intellectual and personal insights into the development of the governmentalist project over the last thirty years.

Alan McKinlay is Professor of Human Resource Management at Newcastle University Business School, UK.

Eric Pezet is Professor in Organizational Theory and Human Resource Management at the University of Paris Ouest Nanterre, France. He is co-founder of the international research centre, Paris Research in Norms, Management and Law (PRIMAL).

Routledge Studies in Management, Organizations and Society

For a full list of titles in this series, please visit www.routledge.com

This series presents innovative work grounded in new realities, addressing issues crucial to an understanding of the contemporary world. This is the world of organised societies, where boundaries between formal and informal, public and private, local and global organizations have been displaced or have vanished, along with other nineteenth century dichotomies and oppositions. Management, apart from becoming a specialised profession for a growing number of people, is an everyday activity for most members of modern societies.

Similarly, at the level of enquiry, culture and technology, and literature and economics, can no longer be conceived as isolated intellectual fields; conventional canons and established mainstreams are contested. **Management, Organizations and Society** addresses these contemporary dynamics of transformation in a manner that transcends disciplinary boundaries, with books that will appeal to researchers, students and practitioners alike.

Recent titles in this series include:

Foucault and Managerial Governmentality

Rethinking the Management of Populations, Organizations and Individuals

Edited by
Alan McKinlay and Eric Pezet

Routledge
Taylor & Francis Group
New York London

First published 2017 by Routledge

711 Third Avenue, New York, NY 10017
2 Park Square, Milton Park, Abingdon, Oxfordshire OX14 4RN

Routledge is an imprint of the Taylor & Francis Group, an informa business

First issued in paperback 2018

Library of Congress Cataloging-in-Publication Data
A catalog record for this book has been requested

ISBN: 978-1-138-91566-4 (hbk)
ISBN: 978-0-367-02655-4 (pbk)

Typeset in Sabon
by Apex CoVantage, LLC

Contents

About the Contributors

Jose Bento da Silva is an assistant professor of organization studies at Warwick Business School. Jose is an organizational theorist interested in the historical emergence of the modern enterprise and in the origins of capitalism in the sixteenth and seventeenth centuries. Jose's research is mainly historical and centred on the case study of the Jesuits' international development between 1540 and 1773. Through the case of the Jesuit organization, Jose has been uncovering the organizational traits of early modernity and historicising modern managerialism.

Jose holds a PhD in business studies from the University of Warwick and two bachelor degrees (Engineering and Philosophy). Prior to joining academia, Jose worked in the corporate and non-governmental sector for 15 years.

Nelarine Cornelius is Professor of Organizational Studies at Queen Mary, University of London. She was previously Professor of HRM and Organization Studies at Bradford University School of Management, where she held posts including Associate Dean Research and Director, Bradford Centre for Business in Society. Nelarine's research is in the area of contemporary and historical aspects of business and society. Her work has appeared in many international journals, books and book chapters. She held visiting posts including Senior Honorary Research Fellow, Kings College Hospital Medical School, Visiting Professor, McGill University, and Visiting Researcher, École des Mines de Paris. She is currently Visiting Professor at the University of Paris, Nanterre and Distinguished Visiting Professor, University of Lagos. She is Fellow of the British Academy of Management, Royal Society of Arts and Principal Fellow of the Higher Education Academy UK. She is a founding member of Paris Research in Norms, Management and Law.

Steven J. Gold, PhD, directs General Education at the Art Institute of California, Orange County, USA. His writings on Richard Rorty and Business Ethics were published in *The Journal of Business Ethics* and the journal *Philosophy of Management*. Currently he is part of a research team studying 'wisdom' and *in extremis* decision making in the US Army, the first section published in the *Journal of Military Psychology* and the second forthcoming. Dr. Gold edited collections on Ethics and Public Policy, Critical Legal Studies and Political Theory. For two decades he pioneered online learning and published a range of articles on digital technology and distance education. Dr. Gold is a freelance martial arts writer, co-authoring books and publishing features on traditional Chinese, Filipino and Brazilian martial styles.

Mark Haaugard is Professor of Political Science and Society at the National University of Ireland. He has written and edited many books on power, including *The Sage Handbook of Power* (2009), with Stewart Clegg. He is editor of the Sage *Journal of Political Power*.

Keith Hoskin is Professor of Accounting at the University of Birmingham, England. He seeks to re-think our historical-theoretical framings of changing ways of thinking and acting and modes of veridiction. He adopts a 'bottom-up' approach combining archaeologies of shifting patterns of statements and discourses with genealogies of shifting practices, and the enabling of different modes of subjectivation and objectivation. He has published across the fields of accounting, management and the histories of education and translation, where he edited and contributed to the Greek and Latin section of the de Gruyter *Translation* encyclopedia. His current projects include analysing the interplays of 'accounting', 'managing', and the constituting of subjects and states in different eras: before and after writing, in imperial China, in the European sovereign and administrative state, and in the era of the governmental management of the state, and the corporate commercial and financial management of 'economic truth'.

Alan McKinlay is Professor of Human Resource Management at Newcastle University Business School. He has published extensively on business and labour history, industrial relations and how Michel Foucault's work can be used to understand long-run developments in management, organization and work. His most recent book, with Philip Taylor, is *Foucault, Governmentality, Organisation: Inside the Factory of the Future*.

Alistair Mutch is Professor of Information and Learning at Nottingham Trent University. His research interests span organization theory and history, and he is widely published in both domains. His historical work has appeared in leading journals such as *Social History* and *Scottish Historical Review*, and his organizational work in journals such as *Organization Science* and *Organization Studies*. His *Religion and National Identity: Governing Scottish Presbyterianism in the Eighteenth Century*, bringing Weber and Foucault to bear on archival material, is published by Edinburgh University Press (2015). He has been an associate editor of *Organization* and is a member of the editorial board of *Academy of Management Review*.

Paolo Quattrone is Professor and Chair of Accounting, Governance and Social Innovation at the University of Edinburgh Business School and Dean of Special Projects for the College of Arts, Humanities and Social Sciences. Before joining Edinburgh, he was Professor of Accounting and Management Control at IE Business School, Madrid and Reader in Accounting at the Saïd Business School, and Official Student (i.e. Fellow) of Christ Church. A truly international scholar, he has conducted research and taught at the Universities of Catania, Kyoto, Madrid *Carlos III*, Manchester, Oxford, Palermo, Siena, Stanford and Luigi Bocconi of Milan. His work addresses questions related to the emergence and diffusion of accounting and managerial practices in historical and contemporary settings. He is particularly interested in researching the relationships between material accounting visualizations and decision making, strategizing and governance.

Eric Pezet is Professor in Organizational Theory and Human Resource Management at the University of Paris Ouest Nanterre. He is co-founder of the international research centre, Paris Research in Norms, Management and Law (PRIMAL). His research is developed from a critical management perspective, specifically about the embodiment of the organization, management history and the genealogy of practices. There is a particular interest in governmentality, especially how people are governed in organizations, how knowledge helps in the government of others and self, and what it means to be autonomous in organizations.

Nancy Richter works as a project leader at Alexander von Humboldt Institute for Internet and Society (Berlin/Germany) in the area of Innovation and Entrepreneurship since March 2014. She completed her PhD in the field of Economics and Social Sciences at the Bauhaus-Universität Weimar and deepened her studies in the history of modern management at the University of St. Andrews (Scotland) and at Edith Cowan University in Perth (Australia). Her research interests include work and organization studies, management history, entrepreneurship and innovation management studies.

Scott Taylor, Reader in Leadership & Organization Studies, Birmingham Business School, University of Birmingham, UK. My primary research theme is the individual and collective human experience of work and workplaces, in all its variety and richness, approached through critical interpretive analysis of qualitative data. I have conducted research funded by the UK Economic and Social Research Council, the British Academy, the British government, and two UK universities. From this I've published more than 20 research papers in peer-reviewed journals in management and organization studies, sociology, and social research methods, 10 book chapters, one co-authored book, one edited textbook, one edited practitioner-oriented collection, and numerous occasional papers. I work in higher education because I want to contribute to understanding management, work, and organization through both research and teaching/learning, with each informing the other, to encourage more humane working contexts and practices. I am currently analysing datasets relating to women's experiences of masculinized professions such as politics and brewing, and am school director of undergraduate programmes.

Part I

Introduction

1 Governmentality

The Career of a Concept

Alan McKinlay and Eric Pezet

Introduction

> 'How to govern oneself, how to be governed, how to govern others, by whom the people will accept being governed, how to become the best possible governor'.
>
> —(Foucault 2007: 86)

Of all the many concepts Foucault developed, deployed and abandoned—or neglected, governmentality has proven the most fruitful in terms of sparking innovative historical and empirical research. Foucault did no more than sketch the concept of governmentality in a series of lectures and seminars in 1978–79. Unlike his other College de France lectures, the governmentality lectures were not intended for publication, nor did they offer a foretaste of a forthcoming book. To say the least, then, governmentality was a concept in the making (Lemke 2001). Our concern in this chapter is twofold. First, to outline the debates about where governmentality is located in the long-run of Foucault's thinking and politics. Broadly, although Foucault was clear that governmentality reflected a continuation of his concerns with power, knowledge and practice, several commentators suggest that he was on his way towards the ethical turn of his final years. On this reading, the final, ethical Foucault had not abandoned his earlier concern with power so much as rejected it completely. Strategy plays a curious role in governmentality: paradoxically, governmentality rejects any top-down, centralised notion of power and strategy the better to emphasise the dispersed nature of modern power and the near ubiquity of strategic thinking in all manner of settings. Third, Foucault consistently referred to his concepts as part of a toolkit. Strangely, neither Foucault nor subsequent governmentalists made much effort to develop any methodological guidelines. It is a strange toolkit indeed that comes with no instructions. We will collect Foucault's few scattered comments on methodology and interpret governmentalist research to uncover more general methodological instructions.

Governmentality has four clear principles. First, governmentality involves the development and deployment of specific strategies and forms of knowledge to tackle particular problems. Governmentality is practical: how to think about and improve, if not solve, a given social problem. Second, governmentalist strategies are predicated upon increasing individual freedom while reducing the role of, say, the state or management. Third, governmentalist strategies are legitimised to the extent that they are rendered neutral, rather than furthering a particular vested interest. Fourth, governmentalist strategies develop credible ways to define, monitor and assess a population so that specific types of individuals can be targeted for intervention. The efficiency and effectiveness of representation and intervention has to be open to evaluation and contestation (Foucault 1980). Here, 'government' does not refer to the institutions of the state but to those activities that aim to shape the conduct of others in a certain direction. This open definition starts from practices, not institutions, and is consistent with what Foucault calls his ascending form of analysis. In an important sense, Foucault's use of 'government' is an implicit acknowledgement that his previous research on 'discipline' could—and was—too easily read as a form of control that downplayed, if not neglected, resistance. Government, by contrast, is predicated on the assumption that the governed will always adapt, resist, subvert or ridicule the practices of governing, to some degree. 'Government', as Maurizio Lazzarato (2009: 114) aptly puts it, establishes a 'strategic relation between governors and the governed whereby the former try to determine the conduct of the latter, and whereby the latter develop practices in order "to avoid being governed," to minimise being governed, or to be governed in a different way . . . or else to govern themselves'. Such forms and moments of counter-conduct open up new possibilities, perhaps fleeting, to remake oneself.

Politics without the State?

Foucault's two lecture series of 1978 and 1979 are about the distinction between state and civil society or, rather, how that distinction has been defined and acted upon. In the decades since Foucault's lectures, our understanding of neoliberalism has been refracted through the experience of the Thatcher, Kohl and Reagan regimes and their successors. Above all, neoliberalism has become equated with a veneration for the market and obsession with reducing the role of the state to the bare essentials of maintaining the security of the population and the minimum regulation necessary for markets to function. Foucault's radical act was to take neoliberalism seriously as a philosophical and political project, rather than just as an ideological cover for the basest of ruling class interests. Foucault's understanding of neoliberalism differed from progressive commonsense. Unlike classical liberalism, neoliberalism regards the market as defined by competition rather than exchange. Foucault invokes the construction of *homo oeconomicus* as the libertarian vision of neoliberalism: the individual is remade—or remakes himself—as a *permanent* entrepreneur, irrespective of the social context. The central figure of this new order was to be 'homo oeconomicus, everyone is cast as and becomes, willingly or not, "an entrepreneur of himself"' (Foucault 2008: 232). Only by maximising the freedom of this fictive, but enormously powerful, figure in *every* domain can the individual and social good be max-imised. Classical liberalism, by contrast, regarded the individual as a perma-nently *social* actor whose sociality vied with narrow economic rationality when placed within a market. Economic rationalities can, do and should determine all individual and social action (Foucault 2008: 240).

Neoliberalism involves the marketization of social relations far beyond even the broadest definition of 'the economic'. Famously, Thatcher pro-claimed that 'economics are the method: the object is to change the soul'. Indeed, the audacity of neoliberalism was that it wants not just to remake social relations but that individuals should view themselves as entrepreneurs and their actions as enterprising. Note that it was not just that individuals were encouraged to think of themselves *as if* they were entrepreneurs but to actually *be* ever more enterprising selves. Think of the ways that key catego-ries of social democracy have been expunged while those of liberal democ-racy have been transformed: citizens have become tax payers; workers have become consumers of their own employment. In turn, this produces citizens as consumers, fathers who economise their thinking about their family life. What better type of individual to demand a polity that delivers efficiency and extended consumption for the individual, irrespective of the collective? Lois McNay (2009: 56) has observed that changing the ways that politics is imagined through classic liberal concepts of individualism and freedom has profound implications for resistance and political opposition: 'If individual autonomy is not the opposite of or limit to neo-liberal governance, but rather lies at the heart of disciplinary control through responsible self-government, what are the possible grounds upon which practical resistance can be based?'

Foucault's reading of neoliberalism suggested that it was not about the withdrawal of the state from the social but the re-imagination of its role: directly, to marketise its own activities; indirectly, to produce proxies of quality or efficiency to make marketization possible in domains where the state was long assumed to be a direct provider. Again, it was not the with-drawal of the state that was the radical promise of neoliberalism so much as its redefinition of the state's purpose as parallel, if not prior, to the market (Gane 2014). This was not about the withdrawal of the state from the mar-ket but a different kind of *active* role in making and extending markets: as broker, guarantor and client. The state's relationship to the market was not simply to correct market imperfections or to avert failures, to *react*. Rather, the neoliberal state had to initiate and constantly be seeking to expand mar-kets into areas previously considered inherently exempt from market forces: 'One must govern for the market, rather than because of the market' (Fou-cault 2008: 121, 145). The hallmark of the neoliberal state was not that it withered away but that it actively sought to increase the scope and salience of market forces.

The question then becomes how to use individual freedom to construct and maintain social order? This is the problematic at the heart of liberal government: how to accept, or manage, the risks inherent in freedom. To govern liberally is to maximise the individual's freedom to choose, a freedom that also expects the individual to understand and accept the risks—and perhaps to meet the costs—of poor choices. At once, this is government that is ambitious, always tempting hubris, in its search for ways of allowing individuals greater self-government the better to secure collective order. Paradoxically, neoliberal government expresses itself as both massively ambitious and humble. Neoliberalism reversed the conventions of mid-century social democracy. Where the state had intervened to correct market failures, neoliberals proposed the reverse: that markets should be used to correct not just institutional but also social failures. It was not that institutions were correctives to market excesses but that the social should be subordinated to the market or, more accurately, that the social itself be marketised. There is no social relationship that cannot be understood through economic rationality. Such an understanding is the precondition to increasing the importance of self-management. It is axiomatic that whether as citizen, worker or partner, the individual is active in making her own life, not a passive cultural dope. An optimistic reading of governmentality is offered by Tiziana Terranova. The spaces, both temporal and spatial, that are necessarily created—or abandoned—by neoliberalism need not necessarily be colonised by its logic. Rather, such milieu 'would also be open to other individuations, less stabilised and more unruly, capable of individuating new transnational and translocal subjectivities. There is thus a fundamental ambivalence to the notions and categories invented by liberal/neoliberal governmentality that can open up onto different existential universes or forms of life' (Terranova 2009: 242).

The governmentality lectures are best read as provisional rather than rounded, definitive statements. Equally, Foucault's lectures, much more obviously than his books, reflect contemporary, often pressing, political concerns. Managing capitalism through the state had proved an impossible burden for social democracy while Marxists' visions of capturing the state maintained the anti-democratic instincts of vanguardism. There are also other, deeper lineages of anti-statism, suggests Foucault, in both liberal and conservative traditions. The strategic gain of governmentality is that it refuses to render the state unique: an object to be questioned, vilified and eroded. Rather, the state subjects itself to new governmentalist strategies and ways of organising. The insistence that the state does not exhaust the possibilities of politics is to expand the spaces for collective action and resistance. Governmentality, in other words, represents Foucault's conceptual effort to repoliticise the social to shift progressive political strategy away from an obsession with capturing the state.

Stewart Elden's (2016: 103) forensic study of Foucault's thinking in the final decade of his life concludes that it is facile to enlist Foucault as an apologist of neoliberalism that could be glimpsed only in the faintest outline in the late 1970s. At most, Foucault was struggling to historicise the first stirrings of a new political order. His provocations, however, have allowed others to grasp the novelty and audacity of the neoliberal project as opposed to a throwback to laissez-faire capitalism. Governmentality was a restatement of this abiding concern to dispel any lingering notion that any and all social and institutional change can be traced back to a single class dynamic. Foucault does not offer a critique of neoliberalism as an ideology; indeed he is respectful of its inventiveness and shrewd appeal to opinion makers. Foucault's question is how does neoliberalism imagine itself working? Again, Foucault was careful to stipulate that he was more concerned with how governors *imagined* governing rather than the actual practice of government.

Distinguishing between liberalism and neoliberalism was about the limits of government and, ironically, the transformative power of the state. Neoliberalism was not about restoring a lost world of laissez-faire capitalism but about how governments produced unlimited markets, at least in theory. The greatest good for the greatest number cannot be delivered by the state but can only be realised through maximising the freedom of all. Of course, Foucault was hardly original in pointing to the importance and infinite forms of political power beyond the state. To do so, however, is not to argue that the state has become apolitical. Equally important, argues Eric Santner, Foucault does not register that the emergence of the modern state is paralleled by the rise of a mass citizenry, an entirely new popular force that has effects on all forms of politics. Santner points to 'the new modern form (of the flesh): *masses of busy bodies*'.

> Biopolitics is always mass politics in the sense of dealing with the massive presence of a sublime object—the virtual reality of a fleshy mass—now circulating in and agitating the life of the People, which means in turn, that political economy, the domain that Foucault came to see as a central site of biopolitical administration, acquires a certain sacramental dimension, the aspect of a 'mass'.
>
> (Santner 2016: 90)

Governmentality leaves little space for mobilisation through political parties; it implies the ephemerality, if not futility of collective action; all of which leaves only identity politics as the only possible form of resistance. Wendy Brown's (2015: 62) lament for the untimely death of *homo politicus* and the demos identifies the hallmark of neoliberalism as the expansion of the market into the daily fabric of the social world:

> With neoliberalism, the political rationality of the state becomes economic in a triple sense: the economy is at once model, object, and project. That is, economic principles become the model for state conduct, the economy becomes the primary object of state concerns and policy,

and the marketization of domains and conduct is what the state seeks to disseminate everywhere. . . . 'Economy' is also detached from exclusive association with the production or circulation of goods and services and the accumulation of wealth. Instead, 'economy' signifies specific principles, metrics, and modes of conduct. . . . Again, neoliberal political rationality does not merely marketize in the sense of marketizing all social conduct and social relations, but, more radically casts them in an exclusively economic frame, one that has both epistemological and ontological dimensions.

In fact, it is perfectly plausible to argue that there is no sharp break in Foucault's thinking: governmentality expresses nothing more than disciplinary power by other means and unconfined to the total institutions of the prison, the hospital and the asylum. To be sure, the oblique techniques of maximising individual choice do not involve confinement, but even total institutions are predicated upon some degree of individual agency and a moralising mission. Equally, neoliberalism mobilises incentives and sanctions around individuals who are *obliged* to choose, free to invoke those lures and deterrents, much like the recidivist prisoner knowingly risks calibrated punishments for his infractions.

For Foucault, the knowledge of power is hidden in plain sight. That is, he creates his own 'surface archive' based on the debates inside expert communities or public debates. He is insistent that the arts of governing are not hidden in 'spontaneous, blind practices' but are the subject of careful, clearly defined debates that produced abstract knowledges and principles (Foucault 2001c: 313–14). To enter a 'deep' archive is to trace how this governmentalist logic was translated into the everyday routines through which power acts and is experienced. The deep archive is a secret place where only *real* historians live. Foucault did not do deep archival research, but this was not so much a weakness as a methodological choice. Foucault's 'archive' is not a special repository where secrets are hidden. Rather, Foucault's archive is not found so much as constructed from forms of public knowledge. Indeed, the public nature of knowledge is what defines it as knowledge. For it is the public nature of knowledge that allows it to be subject to scrutiny by experts, policy-makers, citizens and those subjected to its gaze. Foucault is, in this sense, the most shallow of empiricists. Perhaps we can hear something of this in a quite different context: an aside by Foucault about why he turned to classical ethics to best express his hopes for contemporary, ethical self-governance.

A long time ago one knew that the role of philosophy was not to discover what is hidden but to render visible precisely what is visible; that is to say, to make appear what is so close, what is so immediate, what is so instantly linked to ourselves that because of all this we do not perceive it.

(Foucault 2001a: 1601)

True, Foucault emphasised that his purpose was to understand 'the level of reflection in the practice of government', by which he meant 'the way in which this practice that consists of governing was conceptualized both within and outside government, and anyway as close as possible to governmental practice' (Foucault 2008: 2). To say the least, we may certainly quibble about whether Foucault really approached, even distantly, 'governmental *practice*'. The point remains, however, that he was interested in the reflections of practitioners rather than their experience. It is futile to ask gaolers or prisoners or doctors or patients about the logic of penology or medicine as a form of knowledge. Hermeneutics may tell us about how people act, how they experience life in institutions, but not about the logic of those practices or institutions. Indeed, it is precisely this space that post-Foucault governmentalist research has explored. This instinct to work on the *surface* of things is central to Keith Hoskin's chapter. Hoskin writes in two registers. First, he attends to the *precise* meaning of modes of governing as rendered in the definitive French versions of Foucault's lectures. But there is much more to this chapter than mere exegesis. Rather, Hoskin's surface reading of the French texts restores the centrality of 'managing' and 'cost' to Foucault's outline of governmentality, something that is obscured in the English translation. Second, using the original French texts restores cost accounting as central to Foucault's elaboration of managerial governmentality that pivots on the relationship between security and risk. Over three lectures Foucault builds his distinctive ascending analysis of management, accounting and governmentality. Foucault's account of contemporary governmentality, Hoskin explains, does not look to the state but to the application of some form or other of accounting to activities beyond the market. This is a significant revision to earlier genealogical studies of management that concentrated on discipline.

Governmentality points us towards how the articulation of meta-languages of political theory are translated into expert knowledge and routine practices. Dispositive represents a key phase in the development of Foucault's thinking. A dispositive is constructed to address an urgent problem. A dispositive is 'an ensemble of strategies of relations of forces which condition certain types of knowledge and constituted by them' (Foucault 1977: 299). A dispositive comprises 'the network which is arranged between elements', such as discourses, institutions, architectures, regulations, laws, administrative procedures, science or philosophy. Dispositives are composed of technical and institutional arrangements, discursive and non-discursive elements, and deployed at different dimensions of the social to achieve certain objectives. Those power and knowledge relations imbricated in a dispositive evolve over time. A dispositive is a historical construct: the elements within a given dispositive can only be understood historically. In organization studies, the promise of dispositive is that it defers 'attention from the organisation as an entity to a larger social field, without reducing the former to a given, even more fundamental entity (eg society), dispositional analysis elucidates conditions for organising and organisational processes. . . . It questions the perception of organisations as closed entities that primarily limit and control behaviour, even as it problematizes a sharp distinction between inside and outside the organisation, and between the individual and the collective' (Raffnsoe et al 2014: 3). The notion of dispositive stresses interconnectedness and entanglement and favours the logic of entailment over that of causality.

Giorgio Agamben (2009: 1–2) highlights the vital importance of dispositive as a technical term for Foucault and one that is closely related to governmentality. To say the least, Foucault provides an open-ended concept, for the elements of a dispositive can comprise just about anything: from discourses to buildings to laws to administrative practices. So, a dispositive is composed of technical and institutional arrangements, discursive and non-discursive elements, used at different social locations for specific purposes. There is no need to establish a meta-language or practices that link all these disparate projects together. Indeed, quite the reverse, for Foucault is at pains to argue that each project has to be understood in its own terms and cannot be reduced to some overarching logic or class interest. Agamben's close reading of Foucault's texts and interviews that discuss dispositive and governmentality acknowledges that Foucault never clearly defined dispositive but suggests that it has three elements: any discourse, practice or institution can combine to comprise a dispositive; that the dispositive always has a clear strategic function and is located in power relations; and it 'appears at the intersection of power relations and relations of knowledge'. The common translation of dispositive as 'apparatus' defines the term almost exclusively in technical terms: 'to manage, govern, control, and orient, in a way that purports to be useful, the behaviours, gestures and thoughts of human beings' (Agamben 2009: 11–12). The danger is that Agamben's technical definition diminishes the strategic dimension of dispositive. Practically, the term points to the links between the urgency of a situation, the need to develop a strategy and strategic targets, the devices required for the strategy to be pursued and the mustering of conceptual and administrative capabilities. The sense of emergency that triggers innovation in power and knowledge is vital. Urgency entails an evaluation of risk and a prioritisation of immediate action. Now, strategy involves consideration of existing institutions and practices, of how to cope with inadequate resources and conceptual and administrative uncertainties. A dispositive has a specific purpose with a defined objective. A dispositive is not intended to be a universal panacea. Nor need this sense of urgency or strategic assessment be shared by all. Gilles Deleuze goes further. For Deleuze, a dispositive affords visibility to objects through knowledge and power relations. Crucially, each dispositive generates or eliminates objects (Deleuze & Lapoujade 2007: 339). Dispositives operate through knowledge, power and self. A dispositive, argues Deleuze, is creative: 'lines of subjectivation (ie increasing gaze on certain actors) seem particularly apt to trace paths of creation' where 'a line of subjectivation is a process, a production of subjectivity in an apparatus'. A dispositive, for Deleuze, necessarily involves knowledge, power and self: that by increasing—or reducing—the gaze on certain actors the dispositive creates trajectories of subjectivation (Deleuze & Lapoujade 2007: 341, 345).

Governmentality studies the ways that the subject is created and the techniques that are applied to this subject as they become this subject. The subject can be studied from the perspective of how that knowledge that defines her is elaborated and contested by various experts and how that expertise is expressed in institutions and practices. Finally, even in the most extreme settings, the individual is not only shaped from the outside. To problematise is to establish relationships between the subject and practices. To problematise is to create an object of thought and to define a subject: the fool, the delinquent (Foucault 1984: 670). Problematisation is to establish a set of questions from which actions on individuals and the social can be understood, legitimised and contested. Three dimensions structure action: the representation of the individual or of the social, the knowledge that underpins this representation, and the expert debates that legitimise this knowledge. Only through knowledge can the individual or the social be described. To problematise is to give knowledge the status of truth. And only through this truth can practices directed at the individual or the population be legitimised. Methodologically, specific forms of problematisation can be studied through their constituent relationships. 'Knowledge is not made to understanding, it is made for cutting' (Foucault 1998: 380). We cannot look for the cause of a specific form of governmentality in the interests of motivations of individuals, institutions or classes. Yet a defining characteristic of governmentality is that political choices are rendered neutral and technical. This is the peculiar invisible nature of governmentalist power that *is* everyday routines and practices. Banal and invisible, governmentality presents information as unconstestable, except in the merest detail (Roberts 1991: 359). The paradox of governmentality is that it is inversely related to power. The power of accounting, for instance, is greatest when focused on those 'who are subject to the visibility that it creates and the constant surveillance that it makes possible' (Roberts 2001: 1553).

Mark Haugaard's chapter conducts a dialogue with Foucault about power. Haugaard's close reading of Foucault's programmatic, sometimes enigmatic, remarks on power maps these onto central social theories of power. Haugaard hears echoes of Steven Lukes' three dimensions of power in Foucault, together with a fourth dimension, subject formation. The fourth dimension refers to the ontology of the subject of formation, a dimension to be interrogated genealogically. Foucault's distinctive contribution here, argues Haugaard, is that truth becomes a matter for the human sciences rather than theology. Institutions become places of experimentation, not only places to store the sick or delinquents or children or workers. Knowledge is taken seriously as the stuff of power. It has almost become a truism that Foucault was careful to avoid specifying a general theory of power, always insisting that power could only be understood in specific forms. Power does not have an origin. So, although one can discern the motives of actors in specific contexts, these do not express the wider or deeper interests of, say, profession, class or race. If Foucault was clear that his project was to study power in situ, then there was little point in defining power in the abstract. Quite the opposite: to provide an abstract definition of power would be misleading if not counter-productive. That power is masked in routine has long been a commonplace of the social sciences. Foucault's argument is subtly but vitally different. Power is not hidden behind routines but *is* routines. The commonplace, the taken-for-granted *is* the very stuff of power. Here, we have to recall that Foucault was not only, and certainly not a consistent, historian of the disciplinary, administrative powers that seep into, indeed make, everyday life. Foucault was a curator as much as he was a historian, ready to juxtapose images in order to highlight radical differences between, for instance, sovereign and disciplinary power. Oblique interventions are much more efficient and consistent with liberal freedom than prohibitions and direct control. Governmentality is, importantly, to restate as much as it is to reformulate Foucault's approach to power. Sovereign power was manifest and comprehensible in its spectacular, public displays of kindness or in its awful duty to inflict pain. Disciplinary power, on the other hand, *is* the mundane practices of everyday life. So, power is 'always a way of acting upon an acting subject or acting subjects by virtue of their acting or being capable of action. A set of actions upon other actions' (Foucault 1983: 220). Such an open-ended formulation, compounded by uncertainty over historical periodisation, is not a definition that can be easily pressed into analytical service. Or, as Patrick Joyce puts it, how can we best analyse all those many complex systems of rule that 'make power *work*' (Joyce 2010). Different governmentalist programmes may be related but this is always a contingent relationship; each programme is irreducible one to another. In practice, governmentalist programmes share common themes: individual responsibility, self-reporting and self-awareness; measurement of individuals and populations; a desire by authority to efface itself by withdrawing from routine decisions in favour of risk assessment.

In contrast to his disciplinary studies, the governmentalist Foucault emphasises the indirect, oblique nature of the cues, incentives and sanctions used by neoliberalism to manage individuals through their own freedom. Acting on the conduct of conduct is to establish and sustain the conditions and incentives to act in certain ways, rather than to enact constraints and sanctions. One of Foucault's few doctoral students, Jacques Donzelot (1979), charts the ways that the family became a target to be monitored and managed as a population and at a household level, as a bulwark against civil unrest. Donzelot illustrates the long-term making of a dispositive in response to a crisis or a seemingly intractable social problem. Each intervention is accompanied by a sense of urgency. For Donzelot, such a crisis was not reducible to class interests but common to all, governors *and* governed. Under the Ancien Regime, the father's power was underwritten by the sovereign to whom he returned obedience. Through the mid-eighteenth century this compact was gradually broken. Wealth was now based on production rather than rank and the population must now be managed, peace and order maintained. The family must be incorporated into society. The family must be socialised: fathers encouraged to remain at home, children educated. The family is cast as the bulwark against civil disorder. Youth education becomes an issue, across the classes. For Donzelot, the family becomes the target of government, an object of knowledge *and* a means of government. Competing forms of expertise arose from public health officials, philanthropists and educationalists. This shift was registered in law. The father's domestic rule was no longer absolute but could now be removed by the courts. Motherhood becomes the source of morality and family socialisation. This intervention was productive in that it expanded from the family to education, housing and health. Again, given the scale of this problem, interventions can only be efficient to the extent that they produce self-management (Deleuze & Lapoujade 2007: 345; Agamben 2009: 11–12).

The dispositive addresses the population rather than the individual. This shift of analysis does not amount to a change of scale, because the population is not an aggregate of individuals, but an entity with its own characteristics. Mediating instruments inscribe both representation and intervention. Representation in that they define external objects to be subjected to examination and experimentation. Representation entails robust categorisation, thresholds and measurement techniques with sufficient agreement to allow debate within a given expert community. Representation can be more or less abstract; more or less precise; more or less useful. 'We shall count as real', argues Ian Hacking (1983: 146), 'what we can use to intervene in the world to affect something else, or what the world can use to affect us'. Just as microscopes are much more than 'black boxes with a light source at one end and a hole to peer though at the other', so mediating instruments are techniques that construct new objects to be studied and experimented (Hacking 1983: 189). A mediating instrument must first act as 'an epistemic resource' to allow its conceptual development or as the basis of intervention in the social (Morrison & Morgan 1999: 30–31). Dispositives go beyond the individual and focus on the population and allow the formation of collective entities. At this level, they are not a means of individualising but rather of creating effective governmental institutions. Two levels of dispositives co-exist for the population: on the one hand, the dispositive of policing, which ensures the repression of disorder; on the other, the economic dispositive, which ensured the maximum welfare of the population (Foucault 2007: 353–354). The former is a prerequisite of the latter.

Expertise, Experts and Governmentality

Nikolas Rose has written extensively about the spread of the 'psy' disciplines' authority across disparate domains. Practical and theoretical processes of definition and division are central to the 'psy' disciplines and their exhaustive efforts to codify human subjectivity and behaviour. This was not just to render individual subjectivity and behaviour intelligible in some abstract sense, but to arrange it into statistical arrays the better to make it calculable, predictable and manageable (Rose 1988: 195). Once the basic principles and mechanisms of this analytical process are understood, they are readily diffused from the prison to the factory, from the miscreant to the worker to the citizen. The diffusion of governmental technologies is not in itself surprising and is an empirical, not theoretical, question. In his most recent book, *Neuro: The New Brain Sciences and the Management of the Mind*, Nikolas Rose and his co-author, Joelle Abi-Rached, dedicate one chapter to how a new assemblage has made the brain visible in a quite different way, as 'in part, a homage to Michel Foucault and to his 1963 book, *Naissance de la Clinique*'. To make visible, then, entails the formation of an assemblage of intellectual and administrative knowledges, practices and technical spaces, equipment and labour processes. The argument is not that any particular element is necessary to the whole but rather that each is necessary for the whole to operate in the way that it does. 'To render visible', continue Rose and Abi-Rached (2013: 56), 'requires conditions of possibility within a larger, networked, distributed, assembled field of intensities and powers—connecting up . . . diverse sites. . . . Seeing, rendering visible, is thus part of epistemology, part topography, part technology, part objectification and subjectification, part network of forces, even part ethics'.

The 'London governmentalists' centred around the work of Peter Miller and Nikolas Rose search for how governmentality regimes gradually develop their knowledge base, and their practices carry a faint echo of the English Marxist historian, E. P. Thompson. Thompson sought to rescue the ways of thinking and resisting from the margins of working class history, who had suffered the condescension of historians. The 'London governmentalists', similarly, seek to rescue the ingenious authors of administrative power and knowledge from anonymity. And record the irony that passionate social reformers—despite their motives—could serve as unwitting subalterns of governmentality. Both would acknowledge—even celebrate—the demand from below, from the governed, to be governed differently. A second parallel suggests itself. Both Thompson and Foucault were hostile to the theoretical, historical and strategic sterility of Louis Althusser's structuralist Marxism, though the former was as sarcastic as the latter was respectful. There is no suggestion that either knew of the other's work, though we can be sure that Foucault would be as scathing of Thompson's humanist Marxism as the English historian would be of theorising achieved through clumsy neologisms.

Consider how British Victorian social reformers, philanthropists, eugenicists and educationalists approached notions of imbecility in the two decades before 1913. In this period, 'imbecility' moved from being a loose catch-all term to a legal category to be the object of formal, state provision. A central part of expertise is definition. One English statistician was convinced that delinquency was exacerbated precisely for want of 'proper classification' (Fletcher 1849). This will to categorise was not, however, testimony to increased professionalism and diagnostic precision. From the 1860s, idiocy was gradually broken down into discrete categories as clear systems of classification that identified different degrees of educational and social ineptitude. This prolonged knowledge work was predicated upon defining the feeble minded as a social problem, but not one that was resoluble by the existing asylum system. This anxiety about the mentally unfit assumed many forms: that they constituted a group growing faster than the population as a whole, that their education was neglected and that they may become an impossible burden on the state (Wooldridge 1994: 31).

The borderlands of imbecility were occupied by behaviours that were outside or between pathologies, somewhere between troubled, criminal and insane (Jackson 2000: 12–13). Idiots were not insane, nor were they necessarily paupers or criminals, but an alliance of reformers and eugenicists linked together imbecility and the social residuum. Eugenics explicitly regarded itself as a project to operate as a mediating instrument, providing the technical rationale and tools for social segregation, if not sterilization. Eugenics' rhetoric of commonsense morality served to diminish its claims to scientificity, without widening its appeal. The confusion of moral and scientific claims in British eugenics reduced its elite and popular traction. Equally, eugenics' gross intrusion on personal liberty, together with deep unease about massively expanding the decision-making power of experts, also limited its appeal (Larson 1991). The social history of the 1913 Idiocy Act turns on the relative influence of different groups of cranks, experts and social reformers. A governmentalist approach, however, would track the histories of technologies of definition, classification and measurement across institutions and social domains. The story of imbecility would certainly not begin or end with the 1913 Idiocy Act.

Given that the birth rate of the feeble-minded was greater than that of the population as a whole, breaking this cycle was a matter of political and social urgency. Each category was tied to different professions and institutions. Statistical precision was necessary to estimate not just the scale of the problem but to secure the necessary resources and institutions. Statistics also projected the cost of neglecting the specific requirements of imbecility in terms of degenerate families and all of their associated social evils. The claims for new techniques of categorisation and new, specific institutions was also a tacit criticism of the failures of schools, prisons and asylums to rehabilitate. For the governors of these institutions, their failings could be attributed to a failure to define imbecility as a specific category, outwith their institutional purpose. The construction of new expertise and a new object of study was to contest the technical adequacy and practical utility of established knowledge and professions. More than this, to define idiocy was to define and calibrate normalcy. This, argues Foucault, massively extended the reach of psychiatry: 'Through the practical problems raised by the idiot child you can see psychiatry becoming something infinitely more general and dangerous than the power that controls and corrects madness: it is becoming power over the abnormal, the power to define, control, and correct what is abnormal' (Foucault 2006: 221). Again, just as Weber and Foucault wrote of the logic of confession overflowing monastery walls into everyday life, so abnormal ceases to be a category reserved for monsters and madness and seeps into 'the most elementary of everyday conduct' (Foucault 2003: 132; Sandland 2013: 84–5).

Observational and statistical studies of school pupils were developed to identify the physical or psychological traits of those ill-equipped to cope with or benefit from education. Idiocy was not a form of madness but a developmental failure or lag. To define idiocy was, at least initially, an exercise with the single reference point of insanity. But, since idiocy involved some notion of process and developmental stages, to define idiocy entailed a more complex and temporal definition against some measure of normal child development (Foucault 2006: 205–6). However crude this theoretical formulation, it entailed the development of tools of measurement, appropriate medical or education expertise and appropriate forms of interventions and care. The assumption that forms of mental illness and criminality could be identified by physical stigmata remained powerful, but idiocy was especially problematic because those people often lacked such stigmata but still demonstrated troublesome behavioural traits (Stearns 1978: 388). Some of the early educational studies were on a colossal scale. By the final quarter of the nineteenth century, observation of physical stigmata had given way to scaled tests of reading and arithmetic to produce a range of scores: statistical tests of normalcy produced a scientific justification to complement and contribute to a growing moral panic and political urgency. A battery of everyday testing regimes quickly emerged, from mazes to gradated puzzles that tried to control for, say, class. Despite this burst of testing innovation, the categorisation of the mentally unfit remained 'a highly subjective and practical judgement: whether they were socially competent or not' entangled with 'judgments about individual morality or predisposition to criminality' (Thomson 1998: 244). Testing was not so much a technology of detection as a technology of defining and legitimising educational or psychological intervention. Mental deficiency becomes about redefining a population, articulating and acting upon categories in different ways; and people were left with little choice but to define themselves through, by or against a certain category.

To specify idiocy or imbecility in this way was both disruptive and productive. Producing a notion of normal child development was not the benchmark against which idiocy was defined and measured. Quite the reverse, suggest Foucault: to define idiocy conjured up a new knowledge of the normal. We can treat this example of the educational and psychological debates about child development as a way to think about the development of power/knowledge more generally. First, a specific form of knowledge becomes implicated in some form of social crisis. Second, this knowledge identifies, defines and measures the contours of the problem as an individual type and as a form of population. This allows the estimation of the scale of the current problem; some projection of the scale and severity of the problem in the future, if left untouched; and a search for lead indicators of the problem before it is fully actualised. The shifts in English asylums were quite different from the French experience that Foucault discusses. However, in both cases, idiocy becomes a category that traverses psychiatry and education, and in both, idiocy was defined, at least in part, around productivity: of either the individual child's likely capacity to earn an independent living or to compromise their household's total productive capacity.

Locating Governmentality

Social democracy and Marxism both privilege politics as the locus of, and vehicle for, freedom. Neoliberalism, conversely, regards politics as the vehicle for limiting, reducing or eliminating the state and markets as the locus of freedom. For neoliberalism, the verb 'to govern' is inherently excessive. The only wholly legitimate act of a liberal government is to dissolve itself. The neoliberal state, on the other hand, actively uses its powers to extend the reach of the market. The state is not a thing apart but rather shot through with ways of governing that cannot be defined as unique.

To say that politics happens outside government and formal politics is to state the obvious. To say that processes of governing are neither determined nor exhausted by the state is, at the least, to downgrade the state as the key actor in contemporary capitalism. This is a refusal of the distinction between 'the state' and 'the economy' or 'civil society' except insofar as such distinctions are made productive one way or another. It is one thing to *qualify* the centrality of the state as a theoretical object or as the target of a political strategy, and quite another to suggest that the state is irrelevant or loses any specificity as a more or less coherent set of institutions which are more or less bound to formal political processes. After all, to talk of politics *beyond* the state is to acknowledge its institutional presence. The novelty of 'London governmentalism' is the insistence that individuals are not simply the target of power but active in how it operates. Crucially, individual autonomy, tempered by personal responsibility, is essential to the operation of political power and not its opposite. Government, in this sense, becomes how certain problems are identified that set the agenda and obligations for governors as much as for the governed. For instance, for managers to loosen the bonds of bureaucratic management in the name of teamwork and empowerment is not to escape responsibility. Rather, it is to establish the rights of others to be managed in different ways and, moreover, to judge how well managers are sustaining or extending those rights (McKinlay & Taylor 2014). Power becomes an effect of a diverse set of languages and technologies, never simply a weapon wielded by the powerful (Rose & Miller 1992).

The 'London governmentalists' have pointed to the diversity of agencies and professions deploying specific forms of expertise to remake identities, directly or indirectly. The danger is that such accounts always read as if the subjects produced—or who produce themselves—are derived from the abstract principles of neoliberalism. All roads, it would appear, lead to— and from—Mont Pelerin. The chapter by Eric Pezet and Nelarine Cornelius offers a reading of two of the founding philosophical and fictional texts of neoliberalism by Robert Nozick and Ayn Rand. There is much more to the neoliberal imagination, they suggest, than rugged individualism. In Ayn Rand, for instance, the entrepreneur is a figure capable of collective action that is almost altruistic in its motivation: the purpose of a strike by entrepreneurs is to reveal society's dependence upon them rather than the state. The entrepreneur both operates in the market and is the bearer of the truth of capitalism obscured and effaced by the social democratic state. Ironically, governmentality does not fully acknowledge the deep paradoxes of projects that seek to individuate *and* produce social order. Every governmentalist technology is depicted as always producing a full-blown neoliberal subjectivity, irrespective of how promising the ground is. There is little sense of historical process, of pauses, reversals and resistance. Equally, despite the Foucauldian emphasis on the necessarily intertwined nature of power and knowledge, there is seldom any attempt to map what their effects actually were and how these were judged by governed and governors. Or, how did governmental technologies monitor, measure and distribute freedoms across variegated populations? How were freedom and responsibility conceptualised, for one cannot be granted without the other being accepted? Martijn Konings (2015: 27–19, 34) has extended the now wearily familiar—and justified—criticism that the Foucault of disciplinary power ignored resistance to governmentality. Despite his protestations that resistance was always immanent in power relations, Foucault conceded, stridently if somewhat reluctantly, that he had seriously under-theorised what this might mean empirically. Governmentality, particularly as voiced by the 'London governmentalists', stands accused of the same neglect of resistance. Everywhere, the decentralised, mundane nature of modern power glides uninterruptedly, making and remaking subjectivities with ease. Indeed, governmentalist subjects always seem to be remade in the same shape: as responsible, autonomous neoliberal actors. Where govermentality implies a subject at ease with their various freedoms, its endlessly individuating effects are not only at odds with the maintenance of social order but generate individuals and populations sceptical about *all* authority, not just that of the state. The engaged citizen and the avid consumer are misleading governmentalist stereotypes that ignore the proliferation of ever more diverse subjectivities and populations. Far from taming subjects, governmentalist projects are likely to produce disaffected citizenries and mainstream lifestyles infused with deviance. Only when governmentalist research accommodates the *generative* nature of power can it accommodate these much more complex, volatile outcomes.

Perhaps to see the withering away of the state is going too far in accepting the logic of one thread of neoliberalism. Now, it could be argued that this this is a legitimate reading of the unfolding of neoliberalism as the state's role has moved from direct provision of services to the brokerage of complex, often contractual, alliances across what remains understood as the public, private and voluntary sectors. That these domains are increasingly dominated by quasi-market logics is beyond doubt. Mitchell Dean and Kaspar Villadsen (2016) offer a provocative rereading of Foucault's governmentality lectures in which, they suggest, he is not advocating a theoretical dissolution of the state so much as a recognition that the role of the state in neoliberal regimes has become much more complex and varied than in the long post-war social democratic settlement. This is an altogether more modest statement that does not involve any radical theoretical gesture about the end of the state or even its theoretical decentring. There is an acknowledgement that the 'London governmentalists' fleshed out Foucault's insight that liberalism both recognises the necessity of the state at the same time as being highly suspicious of its ambitions, scope and reach into the everyday. Accordingly, liberalism uses the state to expand, consolidate and enrich the social. Neoliberalism, on the other hand, takes this liberal scepticism about the state to an entirely new level, while seeing the market as the key device for producing social order and improving individuals. For Dean and Villadsen (2016: 34–5), the 'London governmentalists' have gone much too far in their effacement of the state so that they slide from providing an acute observation of non-state powers in action to a general methodology, if not theory. By privileging populations, rationalities and identities, collective bodies such as political parties, trade unions and advocacy groups disappear from view either as bearers or as critics of specific governmentalist rationalities. More than this, to eliminate the state so completely is to ignore its continued role as a regulator of economic and social life. Perhaps the 'London governmentalists' have indeed taken their development of governmentality a step too far. That is, the power of governmentality research lies in its tracing of various forms of technologies that anticipate and construct subjectivities: citizen, consumer, worker. This historical and empirical insight need not be sacrificed even if one retains the state as a central, but not the sole or necessarily dominant, figure in social and political theory. Arguably, this theoretically untidy compromise would be consistent with Foucault's views of the active, sometimes expansive, role of the neoliberal state. Michael Behrent (2010) observes that there continue to be deep divisions amongst some of Foucault's closest colleagues and disciples about shifts in his politics in the last decade of his life. From being a post-Marxist, Foucault's politics became open to radically different interpretations. This debate centres on the governmentality lectures that moved the fate of economic management and the welfare state centre-stage. For Francois Ewald, this entailed a rethinking of political strategy that rendered notions of resistance and revolution irrelevant: for such struggles could only be waged if one accepted the very power that one resisted (Behrent 2010: 604). For Marxism to rail against the 'ruling class' was to accept the necessity of its existence and, by reinstating a form of sovereign power, entirely misunderstanding the dispersed disciplinary forms of power of modernity. Ewald's 'right Foucauldianism' was paralleled by the appropriation of Foucault's insistence that discipline was not restricted to particular spaces but general throughout society. In the hands of autonomous Marxists, this insight becomes a sense that labour is not restricted to the factory. Equally, autonomous Marxists share Foucault's sense that the fiscal crisis of the state that legitimised neoliberalism involved not so much a reduction in the state as an intensification of its role in shaping the society, the 'social factory' (Hardt & Negri 2004). Jacques Donzelot notes that Foucault recognises that it is the imaginative plasticity of liberalism that gives it such durability. Donzelot continues, with evident unease, that post-Foucault governmentality research repeatedly identifies that neoliberalism constantly seeks inventive ways to increase individual autonomy and responsibility. But, this crucial insight is somewhat devalued, even in the hands of its most skilled practitioners, by the presumption that this critique is enough in itself (Donzelot & Gordon 2008).

Governmentalist discourses are inherently performative. That is, debates about *how* to govern prisons, families or markets inevitably contain practical imperatives. The influential synthesis of Foucault and Marx offered by Pierre Dardot and Christian Laval (2013) points to the performativity of neoliberalism. Here is a version of governmentality that does not see the retreat of the state but a more complex process in which the state is a vehicle for reordering the social. This restores agency to the state which, rather than being reduced, diminishes itself as it reorders the social. This is the state exposing itself to new forms of governmentality even as it diffuses these throughout the social body. Foucault becomes a necessary, if sometimes reluctant, somewhat truculent companion to Marx. Only by drawing on Foucault can one appreciate that neoliberalism speaks to a crisis of governing that goes far beyond the economy. The very success of neoliberalism as a project for governing the social, not just the economic, has embedded its logic as the commonsense of global capitalism, making it impermeable to alternative economic agendas, however modest. The social crisis is irreducible to economics and far less to the wiles of a ruling class wedded to neoliberalism. Neoliberalism cannot be reduced to an economic logic but is a rationality that organises rulers as well as the ruled. In short, the conduct of governors is no less regulated by neoliberalism than that of the governed. In this sense, neoliberalism takes for granted its own performativity. That is, it assumes that the enterprising self and a society of competition is a natural reality that does not require to be made so much as rediscovered or made apparent. The naturalness as much as the competitive necessity of the enterprising self is a key neoliberal trope. The more enterprising one is made—or allowed—to become, the more human one is. Dardot and Laval (2013: 180) point to the performativity of contemporary forms of self-government that are not simply derived from 'a seductive managerial discourse' but contextualised by labour market uncertainty and the reach of financial and performance targets into everyday organizational life: 'The acme of self-control which is also to say the perverse mechanism that makes everyone the "instrument of themselves", occurs when wage-earners are invited not only to define the objectives they must achieve, but the criteria by which they wish to be judged'.

The measurable, calculable individual is knowable, and that individuality can be distinguished all the more sharply by comparison with others. To be measurable is, in principle, to be managed according to a new logic informed by an expertise that encompasses the particular but which is not confined by it. Measurement is, of course, necessarily partial but constitutes the organization's field of vision of the individual and the population, of whatever kind. This involves a double move. Managerial government is not addressed to an individual only rendered calculable by an accounting tool but to an individual who knows themselves in the same way. The organised subject is an embodied rationality (Townley 2005: 81). There is much more to this than the individual's assimilation of management narratives and techniques. Indeed, it is precisely the distance between discourse and lived experience that must repeatedly be bridged by the individual's use of techniques developed to deepen self-understanding. Writing of the achievement of a philosophical life, Foucault spoke of the ascetic practices used by individuals to transform themselves and so to reveal more general truths. Ascetic practices are, in effect, experiments in which the subject acts upon himself to access some truth (Foucault 2001b: 15). Such ascetic practices involve applying 'techniques of meditation, of memorisation of the past, of examination of conscience, of checking representation which appear in the mind', all techniques about understanding oneself more fully and in context (Foucault 2001c: 11, 299). Foucault concentrated upon religious and philosophical forms of self-knowledge and self-transformation. However, as Nikolas Rose (1989) points out, this far from exhausts the techniques that make—and make possible—contemporary subjectivities. How the managed individual establishes, copes with and questions this relationship with one's own subjectivity remains little explored by management and organization studies (Pezet 2006). How the practical psychology of the enterprise develops over the long-run remains, similarly, under-researched. Personal coaching and mentoring, for instance, is based on psychology, psychoanalysis or sociology but is neither an analysis nor a therapeutic conversation or even a sociological intervention (Pezet 2007). In organizational life, these commonplace ascetic practices are more or less complete and more or less explicit. The hallmark of business ascetics is that their objective is improved organizational performance and not the construction of a moral individual. Business ascetics do not lie in the moral order of good and evil: they are in the order of organization. They constitute an ascetics of performance. There is no suggestion of an equivalence between the deep meaning of religious ritual and the petty, but productive, authority invested in corporate coaching and mentoring. Nor that contemporary practices deliberately borrow from philosophical and religious pasts. Indeed, quite the reverse: the puzzle becomes how do such petty practices gain expertise, derive authority and how do they encourage individuals to know themselves differently and, perhaps, transform themselves.

Bodies and Souls

That sense of constant watchfulness that is a central feature of disciplinary power and all forms of governmentality emerges from pastoral power evident in antiquity and central to Christianity (Santner 2016: 37). In Foucault, Christian confession is a practice that entails the sublimation of the self. This practice was important in itself but, much more importantly, because it formed 'the general matrix of the hermeneutic of the self, and the source of the techniques of the self where individualisation will take the form of self-renunciation' (Macmillan 2011: 14). But, as Alistair Mutch's chapter argues, Foucault never researched the Protestant forms of confession which involved self-reflection and keeping spiritual diaries but not the subordination of the penitent to a priest. Mutch's forensic examination of the organization and accounting records kept by the Scottish Presbyterian churches has two objectives. The first is to answer a question posed by Foucault: how to consider the development of pastoral power beyond Roman Catholicism. And second, to suggest that studies of governmentality have to go beyond manuals and study actual practices: to study, in other words, deliberate codified knowledge *and* emergent practices. Foucault, as Mutch notes, had a complex, ambivalent relationship to history and to the practices of historians. The historical turn in organization studies is—or, at least, must become—a turn towards practice.

There is powerful historical evidence of the importance of confessional diaries to the self-making of Protestants. Naturally, much of the research in this area has been dominated by Max Weber's puzzle of the relationship between Protestantism and the emergence of a specifically capitalist rationality. But this classically Weberian question could be recast through Foucault. The confessional diary could usefully be regarded as a mediating instrument, a way for the individual to build an archive of the self to provide a rational, administrative order for spiritual reflection. Confessional diaries were full of worries about the tensions between worldliness and spirituality, an especially fraught issue for religions that believed in predestination and the unknowability of one's eternal fate. For Protestant entrepreneurs, this tension was especially acute. One way of resolving this tension was to maximise the accountability of the self wherever possible. Another method was to cross-fertilise business and religious forms of accountability and organization. In this volume, Alistair Mutch provides an account of how eighteenth century Scottish Presbyterian churches developed hierarchical, yet democratic, structures based around uniform record-keeping and conventions for decision making. This complex organization combined local flexibility and devolved responsibility with centralised strategy and oversight. Accountability was written into the Church's most prosaic administrative tasks just as it was inscribed into the spiritual practices of its devout members. In 1842, Robert Macfie, a devout Scottish Protestant sugar merchant, addressed a pamphlet to the organizational issues. Crucially, Macfie argued that the Church had to become a machine 'to convert sinners'. All local parishes and missions should follow the same organizational protocols and that standardised statistics should be reconciled centrally. The church's annual report should be 'in a statistical form':

> with illustrative remarks, a view of the state of the home operations; and to each yearly table should be joined an abstract of preceding ones, for the sake of comparison. This concentration of details will be useful to the Synod, and will stimulate individual congregations by showing what others are doing.
>
> (Macfie 1842: 4, 6)

To paraphrase what Foucault might have said, individuals make themselves but not in the manner of their choosing, nor by discovering some essential humanity, but always historically. This complex interaction of self-constitution through established disciplines is irreducible to external control or to the will of an autonomous individual. For the devout Calvinist, keeping a confessional diary was an essential vehicle for recording any glimpses of the sublime: any signs, however fleeting, that he was one of the elect. A religion based on predestination offered neither the absolution of Roman Catholicism nor the comfort that one was a member of the elect, irrespective of the godliness of one's conduct. On gaining his licence and his ordination to preach, the twenty-two-year-old Donald Heugh decided to keep a confessional diary. This was a solemn and demanding undertaking. The confessional diary was both a record of—and a vehicle for—deepening the individual's spiritual self-discipline: 'do keep a diary, and try thoroughly to know yourself—to watch, and, through grace, to subdue the tendencies of the heart to evil' (Heugh 1852: 27). Self-discipline required the application of reason to one's devotional duties, including solitary diary-keeping. Six days per week, Heugh's daily regime involved eight hours of solitary study: ninety minutes before breakfast, three hours in the morning; followed by ninety minutes in early afternoon; and two hours after dinner. Scripture was studied in the morning;

the afternoons devoted to history and preparing sermons; evenings were 'for devotion and reviewing my conduct through the day' (Heugh 1852: 94–5). This inwardness seldom provided solace, more often deep and sustained anxiety. In June 1812, Heugh (1852: 110–13) recorded spending two days in a 'state of terror . . . from having no evidence of true grace' and the prospect of 'eternal misery'. Melancholy could be combatted only by placing himself before 'the tribunal of his reason' (Heugh 1852: 28). The confessional diary was where one exercised judgement over one's spiritual and secular conduct. For the Calvinist, to be effective such judgment had to be rational and consistent. This was expressed in the form of the diary kept by the papermaker Thomas Cowan. Cowan's diary was printed so that the days were sub-divided into hours and activities. This permitted Cowan to record the time spent in his counting house, discharging his organizational duties for the church and his private devotions. Cowan was holding himself to account, ensuring that he struck a balance between his business and church responsibilities that allowed sufficient time to work on his soul (McKinlay & Mutch 2015). For the devout Protestant, accounting for the soul was just as serious an administrative procedure as any commercial audit.

The spiritual exercises of Saint Ignatius of Loyola were an early Christian form of a technology of the self. These are considered in the chapter by Jose Bento da Silva and Paolo Quattrone. That Ignatius' exercises had a disciplinary effect is certain, but that was neither their sole objective nor their only outcome. The Jesuits' spiritual exercises were, in a powerful sense, an accounting for the self. An archive of the development of the self was established. The spiritual exercises were mandatory for every Jesuit and proceeded through clear stages over a few days. The logic was that the individual Jesuit was gradually revealed to himself by placing himself outside of their everyday context. This highly choreographed process linked the development of the self to the organization, a self-conscious process as illustrated by Nancy Richter's account of the development of management in Siemens from the early twentieth century, which always rationalised *and* psychologised the employment relationship. There is no epochal break that separates Siemens' pioneering development of scientific management in the inter-war years and its use of 'knowledge management' in the last two decades. Early twentieth century rationalisation was—paralleled by the articulation of a notion of leadership as a necessary complement to management. Richter's examination of Siemens' management practices draws on Nietzsche's notion of three kinds of power: material, symbolic and imaginary. Through this device Foucault's concept of power/knowledge can be usefully differentiated. Accordingly, Siemens' recent adoption of knowledge management as the cornerstone of their approach to work organization need not be understood as a rupture with the corporation's deep absorption of scientific management and a rational approach to leadership development.

Contemporary capitalism no longer requires docile bodies so much as active, creative individuals. The rise of *homo sentimentalis* over the twentieth century traced the shift of psychotherapy from being an emergent, specialist discipline to 'more than a discipline': 'a new set of cultural practices which, because they were in the unique position of being located in the realm of scientific production as well as the twin realms of elite and popular cultures, reorganised conceptions of self, emotional life, and even social relations' (Illouz 2007: 6–7). Spiritual exercises of a different kind are the subject of the chapter by Alan McKinlay and Scott Taylor. They investigate the technologies of the self developed by a multinational consultancy, Psyche. While it is unlikely that Psyche will ever have the same geographical reach or historical importance of the Society of Jesus, there are three parallels between these technologies of the self. First, Psyche draws on knowledge that has deep scientific and mythological roots, although this is downplayed by their stress on the practicality of their distilled version of this archaic, yet modern, knowledge. Second, the success of Psyche's form of self-analysis depends upon the actor's willingness to suspend disbelief, at least initially, and to accept that the exercises gain practical value through repetition and use. And third, both technologies of the self share the same objective: to improve the self while enabling more effective interventions in the social world. Jung shared Weber's despair at secularisation and the disenchantment of the world. The value of religion lay, for Jung, in its psychological benefits. Religion provided access to the unconscious. For both Jung and Weber, Protestantism stripped belief of the rituals that guided and comforted Roman Catholics (Segal 2000: 65, 68). Protestants stood alone before their God. A belief in predestination deepened this loneliness: unlike Catholicism, the Protestant did not know his fate, nor so much as glimpse the sublime in his mortal life. And the Protestant did not have the possibility of confession and absolution. But there is a certain ambivalence in Weber's reading of Protestantism and Catholicism. Certainly, there was psychological and cultural damage, if not destruction, wrought by the decline of religious belief. Against this must be set the material gains of rationalised modernity. And Weber identified residual, sometimes distorted, elements of the Protestant ethic in, for instance, the ever more shallow vocation of the bureaucrat. Steven Gold's chapter offers an intensely personal and philosophical reflection on the individual and collective identity. Ironically, Gold argues, only if a condition such as chronic pain is given a clear definition can some form of collective presence or identity be constructed. For those who endure chronic pain, the absence of an authoritative set of clinical and diagnostic practices hinders their capacity to organise around this expertise. Being governed is, then, a necessary condition of being governed differently, perhaps better.

Conclusion

We end this volume with two interviews with key figures in the development of governmentality as an intellectual practice, Peter Miller and Nikolas Rose. Both shared a similar intellectual background in theoretical

Marxism and an instinct that although economics remained important, classical, cultural and Althusserian forms of Marxism were inadequate to understanding late capitalism. Equally disheartening, the dominance of structural Marxism promised to restore economic determinism, albeit in the slippery language of the 'final analysis' (McKinlay & Pezet 2010: 488). This reductive, totalising promise prompted Rose and Miller to look to more modest ways of understanding specific forms of power, knowledge and authority. Rather than provide yet another reading of the hidden ideologies behind this or that economist's or philosopher's thinking, they looked to the knowledge claims of the 'little engineers of the soul', who governed cities, factories, schools and much else besides (Miller & Rose 2008: 5). Interestingly, Miller and Rose retained the scepticism of structural Marxism around the analytical value of the term 'experience' that so energised the history 'from below' in the same period. Enter Foucault's sketch of governmentality. Rose and Miller had little interest in exegesis, critical or otherwise, of Foucault or anyone else. Nor did they feel any compulsion to extend, far less to complete, Foucault's provocative remarks on governmentality. Rather, they developed concepts around broad themes of governing different social spaces. Curiously, both authors stress that how they developed their concepts paralleled and echoed the knowledge making processes they researched. In both cases, intellectual coherence did not necessarily enjoy primacy over practical utility. The governmentalist approach is not to begin with abstract definitions and then identify those practices that conform to that definition. Rather, governmentality looks first at practices and how they seek to justify themselves abstractly. This opens up the possibility of seeing family resemblances between quite disparate forms of governmentality that would otherwise be invisible, ignored or excluded if one started with a theorised or a normative judgment. Their concepts, and those of others, as they happily admit, were judged in terms of their applied, empirical value, not how tidily they extended Foucault's intellectual project. Both suggest that they drew more inspiration from Foucault's research sensibility than from any particular concepts. The openness of Foucault, the loose relationship between key concepts was, perhaps, an antidote to the closed, over-theorised nature of Althusserian Marxism. Miller and Rose are at pains to emphasise their conceptual innovation as a form of bricolage driven entirely by the empirical and historical questions they set themselves. This was an eclectic borrowing of concepts from the philosophy of science and the contextual history of philosophy. The result was a diverse set of studies that examined how individuals came to understand themselves and be understood by others.

Both interviews suggest a certain ambivalence about the state of governmentality research today: an acknowledgement that governmentality has gained analytical traction across the human and social sciences but something of a regret that the concept is now being applied rather than reformulated according to today's needs. Perhaps the most appropriate way to close is to ask those questions anew. How are claims to govern made? How did these clams gain coherence and legitimacy? How do these claims reflect—and make—intellectual and practical authority? How are the intellectual, moral and administrative connections between abstract programmes of government and mundane life made and sustained? What are the effects of these systems of governing on our sense of ourselves and others?

References

Agamben, G. (2009), *What Is an Apparatus?*, Stanford, CA: Stanford University Press.

Behrent, M. (2010), 'Accidents Happen: Francois Ewald, the Antirevolutionary Foucault and the Intellectual Politics of the French Welfare State', *Journal of Modern History* 82/3: 585–624.

Brown, W. (2015), *Undoing the Demos: Neoliberalism's Stealth Revolution*, New York: Zone.

Dardot, P. & Laval, C. (2013), *The New Way of the World: On Neo-Liberal Society*, London: Verso.

Dean, M. & Villadsen, K. (2016), *State Phobia and Civil Society: The Political Legacy of Michel Foucault*, Stanford, CA: Stanford University Press.

Deleuze, G. & Lapoujade, D. (2007), *Two Regimes of Madness: Texts and Interviews, 1975–1995*, New York: Semiotext(e).

Donzelot, J. (1979), *The Policing of Families: Welfare versus the State*, London: Hutchinson.

Donzelot, J. & Gordon, C. (2008), 'Governing Liberal Societies—The Foucault Effect in the English-Speaking World', *Foucault Studies* 5: 48–62.

Elden, S. (2016), *Foucault's Last Decade*, Cambridge: Polity.

Fletcher, J. (1849), 'Moral and Educational Statistics of England and Wales', *Journal of the Statistical Society of London* 12/3: 189–335.

Foucault, M. (1977), 'Le Jeu de Michel Foucault', in *Ornicar?*, July 1977, reproduced in *Dits et Ecrits III: 1976–1988*, Paris: Gallimard 1994.

Foucault, M. (1980), *Power/Knowledge: Selected Interviews and Other Writings 1972–1977*, edited by C. Gordon, London: Harvester Wheatsheaf.

Foucault, M. (1983), 'The Subject and Power', in H. Dreyfus & P. Rabinow (eds), *Michel Foucault: Beyond Structuralism and the Hermeneutics*, London: Wheatsheaf.

Foucault, M. (1984), 'Le Souci de Verite', *Magazine Litteraire* 207, in D. Defert & F. Ewald (eds), *Dits et Ecrits vol. 4: 1980–1988*, Paris: Gallimard 1994.

Foucault, M. (1998), 'Nietzsche, Genealogy, History', in J. Faubion (ed.), *Michel Foucault: Aesthetics, Method and Epistemology*, New York: New Press.

Foucault, M. (2001a), 'La Philosophie Analytique de la Politique', in D. Defert & F. Ewald (eds), *Dits et Ecrits II*, Paris: Gallimard.

Foucault, M. (2001b), *The Hermeneutics of the Subject: Lectures at the College de France 1981–1982*, New York: Picador.

Foucault, M. (2001c), 'Omnes et Singulatim', in J. Faubion (ed.), *Michel Foucault Essential Work 3: Power*, London: Allen Lane.

Foucault, M. (2003), *Abnormal: Lectures at the College de France 1974–1975*, New York: Picador.

Foucault, M. (2006), *Psychiatric Power: Lectures at the College de France 1973–1974*, London: Palgrave Macmillan.

Foucault, M. (2007), *Security, Territory, Politics: Lectures at the College de France 1977–1978*, London: Palgrave Macmillan.

Foucault, M. (2008), *The Birth of Biopolitics: Lectures at the College de France 1978–1979*, Basingstoke: Palgrave Macmillan.

Gane, N. (2014), 'The Emergence of Neoliberalism: Thinking through and beyond Michel Foucault's Lecture on Biopolitics', *Theory, Culture & Society* 31/4: 1–25.

Hacking, I. (1983), *Representing and Intervening: Introductory Topics in the Philosophy of Natural Science*, Cambridge: Cambridge University Press.

Hardt, M. & Negri, A. (2004), *Multitude: War and Democracy in the Age of Empire*, New York NY: Penguin.

Heugh, D. (1852), *The Life of Hugh Heugh, D.D.*, Edinburgh: Johnstone & Hunter.

Ilouz, E. (2007), *Cold Intimacies: The Making of Emotional Capitalism*, Cambridge: Polity.

Jackson, M. (2000), *The Borderland of Imbecility: Medicine, Society and the Fabrication of the Feeble Mind in Late Victorian and Edwardian England*, Manchester: Manchester University Press.

Joyce, P. (2010), 'The State, Politics and Problematics of Government', *British Journal of Sociology* 61/1: 305–310.

Konings, M. (2015), *The Emotional Logic of Capitalism: What Progressives Have Missed*, Stanford, CA: Stanford University Press.

Larson, E. (1991), 'The Rhetoric of Eugenics: Expert Authority and the Mental Deficiency Bill', *British Journal for the History of Science* 24/1: 45–60.

Lazzarato, M. (2009), 'Neoliberalism in Action: Inequality, Insecurity and the Reconstruction of the Social', *Theory, Culture & Society* 26/6: 109–133.

Lemke, T. (2001), ' "The Birth of Bio-Politics": Michel Foucault's Lectures at the College de France on Neo-Liberal Governmentality', *Economy & Society* 30/2: 190–207.

Macfie, R. (1842), *Short Practical Hints on the Means of Inducing, Confirming, and Directing Missionary Efforts and Congregations*, Liverpool: Turner & Rose.

Macmillan, A. (2011), 'Michel Foucault's Techniques of the Self and the Christian Politics of Obedience', *Theory, Culture & Society* 28/4: 3–25.

McKinlay, A. & Mutch, A. (2015), ' "Accountable Creatures": Scottish Presbyterianism, Accountability and Managerial Capitalism', *Business History* 57/2: 241–256.

McKinlay, A. & Pezet, E. (2010), 'Accounting for Foucault', *Critical Perspective on Accounting* 21: 486–495.

McKinlay, A. & Taylor, P. (2014), *Foucault, Governmentality, Organization: Inside the 'Factory of the Future'*, London: Routledge.

McNay, L. (2009), 'Self as Enterprise: Dilemmas of Control and Resistance in Foucault's the Birth of Biopolitics', *Theory, Culture & Society* 26/6: 55–77.

Miller, P. & Rose, N. (2008), 'Introduction: Governing Economic and Social Life', in P. Miller & Rose, N. (eds), *Governing the Present: Administering Economic, Social and Personal Life*, Cambridge: Polity.

Morrison, M. & Morgan, M. (1999), 'Models as Mediating Instruments', in Morgan, M. & Morrison, M. (eds), *Models as Mediators: Perspectives on Natural and Social Science*, Cambridge: Cambridge University Press.

Pezet, E. (2006), *La Gestion des Ressources Humaines et la Fabrication de L'Individu Gouvernable. Contribution a une Theorie de l'Embodiment' de L'Entreprise,*

Dossier Soumis en Vue de L'Habilitation à Diriger des Recherches en Sciences de Gestion, Université Paris-Dauphine.

Pezet, E. (2007), *Management et Conduite de Soi: Enquête sur les Ascèses de la Performance*, Paris: Vuibert.

Raffnsoe, S., Gudmand-Hoyer, M. & Thaning, M. (2014), 'Foucault's Dispositive: The Perspicacity of Dispositive Analytics in Organisational Research', *Organization* 1–27.

Roberts, J. (1991), 'The Possibilities of Accountability', *Accounting Organizations and Society* 16/4: 355–368.

Roberts, J. (2001), 'Trust and Control in Anglo-American Systems of Corporate Governance: The Individualizing and Socializing Effects of Processes of Accountability', *Human Relations* 54/12: 1547–1572.

Rose, N. (1988), 'Calculable Minds and Manageable Individuals', *History of the Human Sciences* 1: 179–200.

Rose, N. (1989), *Governing the Soul: The Shaping of the Private Self*, London: Free Association Books.

Rose, N. & Miller, P. (1992), 'Political Power beyond the State: Problematics of Government', *British Journal of Sociology* 43/2: 173–205.

Rose, N. & Abi-Rached, J. (2013), *Neuro: The New Brain Sciences and the Management of the Mind*, Princeton NJ: Princeton University Press.

Sandland, R. (2013), 'Concubitu Prohibere Vago: Sex and the Idiot Girl, 1846–1913', *Feminist Legal Studies* 21: 81–108.

Santner, E. (2016), *The Weight of All Flesh: On the Subject Matter of Political Economy*, Oxford: Oxford University Press.

Segal, R. (2000), 'Jung's Psychologising of Religion', in S. Sutcliffe and M. Bowman (eds), *Beyond New Age: Exploring Alternative Spirituality*, Edinburgh: Edinburgh University Press.

Stearns, P. (1978), 'Explaining Social Policy: The English Mental Deficiency Act of 1913', *Journal of Social History* 11/3: 387–403.

Terranova, T. (2009), 'Another Life: The Nature of Political Economy in Foucault's Genealogy of Biopolitics', *Theory, Culture & Society* 26/6: 234–262.

Thomson, M. (1998), *Problem of Mental Deficiency: Eugenics, Democracy and Social Policy in Britain, c. 1870–1959*, Oxford: Clarendon Press.

Townley, B. (2005), 'Controlling Foucault', *Organization* 12/5: 643–648.

Wooldridge, A. (1994), *Measuring the Mind: Education and Psychology in England, c. 1860-c.1990*, Cambridge: Cambridge University Press.

Part II

Locating Governmentality

2 Getting to the Surface of Things
Foucault as Theorist and Historian of Management and Accounting

Keith Hoskin

Introduction: On the Modern Art of Governing as Product of 'Management' and 'Cost': Steps Towards Getting to the Surface of Things

'So we should not see things as the replacement of a society of sovereignty by a society of discipline, and then of a society of discipline by a society, say, of government. In fact we have a triangle: sovereignty, discipline and governmental management, [a governmental management] which has population as its main target and apparatuses of security as its essential mechanisms'.
—(Foucault 2007: 107–8: the phrase in brackets is only in the original French version)

'Getting to the surface of things' is my initial objective here, and in particular to the surface of the things that Foucault says in his analyses of modes or 'arts' of governing in his two *Collège de France* lecture series, that of 1977–78 now published as *Security, Territory, Population* (STP) (Foucault 2007) and that of 1978–79 now published *The Birth of Biopolitics* (BB) (Foucault 2008). My contention is that, if we can get to that surface—something which for various reasons is not that straightforward—and then read what then becomes visible in a 'surface reading', then we can find Foucault doing the two things I name in my title. First we can find him regularly naming 'managing' (in the French *gestion*), in different aspects, as a key means or form of governing in different eras and settings; and second, constantly naming accounting in proximity to managing, again in different aspects, many though not all associated with constructing various types or concepts of 'cost'.

Furthermore, we can even find accounting, in Foucault's analyses, acting not just as a form of *support* to managing but also as a form of *limitation* on its scope, through its *conceptual* contribution to the general emergence since the eighteenth century of the economy as what Foucault calls a 'specific domain of reality'; and stemming from this it may even help constitute the specific and consequential emergence of 'political economy simultaneously as a science and as a technique of intervention in this field of reality'

(Foucault 2007: 108). Insofar as this chapter can succeed in making these claims stand up, then there is a case for the claim made in my title, that we should perhaps see him both as a historian and a theorist of these two fields: which is not something that we have typically thought in the past.

To launch this analysis, I begin with the quotation above, which comes near the end of Lecture Four of *STP*. At first sight, it is a statement which gives a succinct summary (if in somewhat esoteric terms) of what constitutes governing in the modern era. In it, Foucault suggests that we do not live in 'a society of government'; instead what we might call the '*set-up*' for governing is a triangle made of sovereignty, discipline and 'governmental management', whose first two components, he says, carry down from earlier modes of governing. But then he names the main *form* of governing is this construct 'governmental management'—and this governs, he says, by operating on the intriguing construct 'population' via certain enigmatic 'apparatuses' (in the French *dispositifs*) of an equally enigmatic 'security'.

Yet at the same time, a reading at the surface of the *original* version of the English translation, i.e. with the bracketed phrase removed, will show that it does not make the same statement at all. Instead it now reads: 'In fact we have a triangle: sovereignty, discipline and governmental management, which has population as its main target and apparatuses of security as its essential mechanisms'. So now it is the *triangle* (in my terms the set-up) that becomes the *form*, which then works on population through the *dispositifs* of security.

This may appear over-meticulous, even fussy. But it is an example of how (in the English version at least) what appears at and as the surface of Foucault's text may not be self-evident: and in this instance it moves 'management' from centrality as a form of modern governing to a support mechanism within a completely different form—which is not what Foucault says. So, my initial interest here is in trying to read *precisely* what he says, at the surface of these texts, concerning what constitutes arts of governing in general and this contemporary art in particular: a process which, since he wrote almost exclusively in French, sometimes entails comparing the surface of translations, particularly widely circulated ones, with the original French; but which also entails a *complementary* process on the reading side of the equation, of being open to seeing what is right, so to speak, under your nose. Either way, there is a process of getting *to* the surface (through getting the surface right or getting one's focus on it right) in order to read *at* the surface.

The next two sections consider three more extracts, all from the first four lectures of *STP*, where in each case I suggest that getting to the surface of Foucault's text is not straightforward, whether for one or for both these reasons. I consider the second extract in the first of these sections, since it is directly connected to my opening quotation, both as part of the same summation on modern governing and as another instance where Foucault profiles management as a central form of governing. I shall then reflect on a first question that arises: how is it that discipline, which Foucault associates initially above with an earlier historical era, and which therefore differs in key respects from governmental management, nevertheless functions with it as part of this triangle? My answer will indicate how, in large part, it does so through enacting, in that earlier era, a specific form of accounting that enacts a powerful but *not modern* mode of 'accountability' which acts on and shapes a frequent Foucauldian concern, 'conduct'; and how, in the era of governmental management, it shifts to enacting a *second* mode of accountability for conduct which is very much still with us today.

I shall then turn to consider my other two passages, which are both instances where forms of *accounting* rather than management are the primary focus. But these are instances where, rather than enacting forms of 'accountability', the forms of accounting work at a formal and rational level to constitute types of *cost* and their associated 'cost objects'. Now Foucault's own interest in cost has of course been noted before, and in a particularly thoughtful way by Jeffrey Nealon (2008) in his *Foucault Beyond Foucault*, which although emanating from within humanities is the first work I know to recognise the regularity with which Foucault invokes the issue of 'cost' in engaging across a range of fields. His section entitled 'Foucauldian Economics: What does it Cost?' (Nealon 2008: 17–23) engages particularly with Foucault's derivation of this interest from Nietzsche, and how there is always a cost or price paid for truth-speaking in games of veridiction, particularly when engaging in *parrhesia*.

At the same time, the focus that Foucault has here on formal and accounting-derived conceptions of cost goes beyond a pure philosophical concern, as I shall seek to show. In the first passage, the type of cost constituted via accounting is what, at a level of practice and conceptually, constitutes the first *dispositif* of security that Foucault discusses in *STP*. Meanwhile, in the second passage, the type of cost constituted is what *directly* enables the establishment of a first form of a new 'economic truth' which will, as Foucault subsequently argues more fully in *BB* (2008: 30–1), set the limits within which governmental management can rationally operate. The possibility that accounting plays *these* kinds of constitutive roles in Foucault's analyses of governing (and indeed in his analyses of the construction of forms of truth) is one, I suggest, to which we have paid less attention to date.

Having then made my case for both management and accounting having a certain prominence at the surface of Foucault's narrative in these lecture series, I seek to answer the second question implicitly posed in my title. Is—and if so, how far is—Foucault a theorist and historian of management and accounting? I seek to answer this both historically, largely in the light of my earlier comments, but also theoretically, in terms of what Foucault says his theoretical approach is: not least in the very last paragraph of *STP*, where he suggests that we should approach both 'the general problems of the state' and 'the history of the state' on the basis of 'men's actual practice, on the basis of what they do and how they think . . . analyzing the state as a way of doing things [and a way of thinking]' (Foucault 2007: 358, phrase in brackets only in the French original).

Finally, I reflect on the question that then arises: if there is such an insistent engagement with management and accounting lying at the surface of these texts, then why has it seemed so difficult for us to see it? Why have even those most likely to have seen it (i.e. those working within the fields of so-called 'critical' management and accounting) been seemingly blind even to the possibility that invoking management and accounting is what, more or less in front of our noses, he was *doing*? Doubtless there is more than one reason for this. But at the same time, I would like to think that we might now overcome, in what would be a classic Foucauldian move, this blindness to the theoretical and primary significance of knowledge fields widely assumed to be 'secondary' and 'instrumental'—'academic plumbing' fields, in the phrase that Klamer and McCloskey once used to capture how economists generally perceive accounting (Klamer & McCloskey 1992: 145). If so, we might discover ourselves thinking all manner of new historical-theoretical analyses of the interplays between management and accounting.

So, I shall shortly turn to continuing to get to the surface of Foucault's texts. But, assuming I get there, what then do I mean by then undertaking a 'surface reading'? By this I mean the kind of reading that Foucault himself sets out towards the end of his analysis of the statement (or *énoncé*) in *The Archaeology of Knowledge*, as he engages with 'what the analysis of the enunciative field and of the formations that divide it up require and exclude' (Foucault 2002: 132). The reading of statements/*énoncés* that he then proposes entails three interconnected elements: 'exteriority', 'accumulation' and 'rarity'.[1]

First, as he explains it, 'exteriority' is a matter of staying at the *exterior* of texts, paying attention to the specific terms employed and deployed in describing and explaining particular issues of concern, but to only those terms (whence the significance of getting to the surface). This then enables paying attention to the specific combinations or conjunctions of terms manifesting themselves at that exterior surface and their 'specific forms of *accumulation*' (Foucault 2002: 138, emphasis added), which will include the forms of accumulation of the silences and exclusions that attend statements too.[2] Finally, this reading must pay particular attention to what Foucault describes as the 'law of rarity' which manifests itself in statements, 'based on the principle that *everything* is never said'. Instead, 'on the basis of the grammar and of the wealth of vocabulary available at a given period, relatively few things are said' (Foucault 2002: 134).

The net result should be to avoid going elsewhere to seek a solution to what the statements making up a text say, either by going first *beneath* the surface, e.g. through a hermeneutics of what was 'really' meant, or second *beyond* the surface, e.g. through commentary which, as he memorably puts it in *The Order of Discourse*, 'by a paradox which it always displaces but never escapes, . . . must say for the first time what had, nonetheless, already been said, and must tirelessly repeat what had, however, never been said' (Foucault 1981: 55–6). A surface reading becomes instead an acceptance of statements 'as being always in their own place. . . . Each statement occupies in it a place that belongs to it alone: which, as an approach, so he concludes at the end of the chapter, 'is to establish what I am quite willing to call a *positivity*' (Foucault 2002: 141, original emphasis).[3]

So I approach Foucault's statements here in this spirit—and in what may then be a newly constructive form of positivism. The main thrust of what follows will be to see what regularities of namings to be found at the surface of his text then come together to form accumulations: first around forms of managing (which call forth or implicate forms of accounting), but then around forms of accounting (which thereby give substance and effectiveness to forms of managing, but also call forth or implicate new forms of truth, and most especially economic truth). I shall return at the end to the issue of 'rarity'. But first, let me seek to 'bring to the surface' what I claim to be Foucault's insistent naming of management as a form of governing.

Management, Accounting, Discipline and the 'Governmental'

'As for discipline, this is not eliminated either. Obviously, its organization and deployment, and all the institutions within which it flourished in the seventeenth and beginning of the eighteenth century—schools, workshops, armies—are part and parcel of, and can only be understood on the basis of, the development of the great administrative monarchies. But discipline was never more important or more valued than when the attempt was made to *manage* the population: *managing* the population does not mean just *managing* the collective mass of phenomena or *managing* them simply at the level of their overall results; *managing* the population means *managing* it in its depth, [*managing it*] in all its fine points and [*managing its*] details'.
—(Foucault 2007: 107, phrases in brackets again only in the French original)[4]

Both the location and the context of this second extract from Lecture Four of *STP* are important. The location is immediately prior to my first extract, and so to the specifying of the modern governing as having this triangular set-up involving discipline. But the extract also tells us in its first two sentences that this involvement of discipline is somewhat surprising, given that it is defined in all its aspects as 'part and parcel of', and as 'what can only be understood on the basis of', the 'development of the earlier administrative state'. So there is something that needs unpacking here if we are to understand just how it could become 'never more important or more valued than when the attempt was made to *manage* the population' (in the French *gérer*), particularly through its contribution to managing at the level of the population's depth, fine points and details. I shall try to show just how this occurs, as an earlier relation between managing and accounting (specifically accounting for conduct via a first form of 'accountability') gives way to a systematically different form of both.

However, the slightly wider context of this passage is perhaps even more important. I have suggested that we have here, in my first extract, a 'summary statement', without explaining why a summary statement should appear at this particular point, just before the end of Lecture Four. Well it appears for an obvious reason—or so I shall try to show—in that Foucault has reached a point where he has set out all the major themes that will be elaborated in more detail in the rest of the two lecture series. In that respect there is a real substantive or conceptual significance to what gets said here (once it is brought to the surface).

But it also appears for a less obvious reason—or a reason that was not obvious at all at the moment of this summary's utterance to those present at the lecture series. For in the very next paragraph, Foucault will pause and announce that: 'if I had wanted to give the lectures I am giving this year a more exact title, I certainly would not have chosen "security, territory, population"' (2007: 108). At which point he introduces, for what is actually the *very first time* in the lecture series, the term which we have become used to using as the shorthand or portmanteau term covering *all* of the lectures: 'governmentality'.

So this summary passage is located in the text at what one might call a crucial 'passage point'. At this point it offers almost a paean to the importance and the reach of management, as governmental management, in modern governing, and a paean that incidentally also trumpets how essential and integral discipline is to the new set-up's success. But it is a paean whose significance has also become muted, for us who come to read it now, by the looming presence of the term which has since come to stand for what Foucault 'must' be talking about across these lecture series.

I am seeking to suspend 'knowing' what Foucault 'must' be talking about, so as to get to and stay at the surface of precisely what gets conceptually and substantively articulated across these first four lectures: and to do that, my argument now is that we not only need to have what he says in this summation precisely correct, but also to appreciate just how, and how far, what has been available to read as the English surface of his text has been wrong. Now, in saying this, it needs to be stressed that Graham Burchell, the translator of *STP*, is generally excellent in the challenging task of translating Foucault, even with other translations this is not always the case.[5] However, in this instance, in the passage immediately above, the reduction of the number of repetitions of 'managing' from eight to five has a 'muting effect' on what Foucault says; then, in the passage that follows it, the omission of the repetition of 'governmental management' reduces managing from a central to a support role in modern governing.

But at least Burchell's *STP* rendition does put 'governmental management' in play. However, there is a much more serious problem for those who have only read the 'governmentality' material in the earlier English versions, which from 1979 were 'the' point of entry into Foucault's thoughts on this topic. The versions I am referring to are the standalone versions of Lecture Four, the first the 1979 version, entitled 'On Governmentality', in the journal *I & C* (Foucault 1979), and the second a substantially identical 1991 version, re-titled as 'Governmentality', in *The Foucault Effect* (Foucault 1991).

These versions are hugely significant, firstly at a general level where they have had a longevity and reach to the worldwide Foucault readership that probably no other version has as yet matched, but I am here more concerned with the specific level of their renditions of the two extracts I have chosen (and whose significance I hope is becoming clearer). For, in both versions, the rendition of these two extracts sends the significance of management in Foucault's text into almost total concealment.

Go to *The Foucault Effect* and read the passages in their order in the text, and you will find that in the first, Foucault's insistent naming of management eight times reduces to just three, as the text reads: 'discipline was never more important . . . than . . . when it became important to manage a population; the managing of a population not only concerns the collective mass of phenomena, . . . it also implies the management of a population in its depth and details' (Foucault 1991: 102). The sense is there, certainly: but the intensity is even more muted. Turn then to the second passage, and management disappears completely. Now Foucault's triangle is made up of 'sovereignty, discipline, government': and, as with the version in *STP*, it is the *triangle* which has population as its target and *dispositifs* of security as its mechanisms. As a result, even the *possibility* that management might be integral to governing has been erased from sight.[6]

However, even if this confirms how getting to the surface of Foucault's text is, indeed, far from straightforward., it does now become possible, I suggest, so long as one operates with a *precise* translation of what Foucault says. So even though I suspect that my rendition here is the first published English translation to achieve that, it does now offer a way in for Anglophone readers of Foucault to hear precisely what he said, and to generate their own new surface readings on that basis. And I suggest that the time is opportune, on the basis that we have, I think, entered an era where those working on or with Foucault's work have never numbered so many, or across so many generations (e.g. Lawlor & Nale 2014): which is also an era when the scholarly 'discursive regularities' are shifting across many of the knowledge areas where Foucault is invoked, as the new generations question older assumptions, as is the case in management and accounting research as much as elsewhere (e.g. McKinlay & Pezet 2010; Paltrinieri 2012; Neu et al 2015; Hoskin 2015).

At the same time, older ways of thinking may still shape the new 'beneath the surface', as I suggest has been the case here. In which case, bringing his precise words to the surface more generally should arguably be thought as a necessary contribution to ongoing ways of re-thinking a whole range of old assumptions about what Foucault 'must' have been saying.[7]

So with that sentiment in mind, let me now round out this section by seeking to show more systematically how there is a case for claiming that there is an 'accumulation' of namings of management, in diverse forms, by Foucault in the first four lectures of *STP*. Of course, if one begins just with the extracts above, the namings already number ten. Read the definitive French version of Lecture Four (Foucault 2004: 91–113), and the number of namings (either in the noun-form *gestion* or the verb-form *gérer*) increases to nineteen—that is if one includes its naming in a footnote (2004: 111; cf. 2007: 108), where the reference is to the emergence under governmental management of the kind of knowledge-gathering process 'that will assure the management (*gestion*) of populations by a body of functionaries'. This constitutes, I suggest, a *prima facie* case for suggesting that there is here a Foucauldian 'accumulation'. But it is the *range* of forms of 'managing' that he names which I suggest is particularly significant. The first form is the managing of the household, which arises particularly in Lecture Four, in the context of a concern that Foucault has that, across the era of the administrative state, there is a 'blockage' and only a subsequent 'release' (e.g. 2007: 103) in both the thinking and practice of management.

This is, Foucault argues, because its major form of operation is at what, in an older spelling, we might call the '*oeconomic*' level of the family or household (the Greek *oikos*), where the head of the household must manage the proper allocation (in Greek *nomos*) of its resources. So, he argues, even well into the eighteenth century the 'idea of economy . . . only ever referred to the management (*gestion*) of a small ensemble comprising the family and the household' (2007: 103). Consequently even Rousseau can still be saying that '(t)he problem . . . is how to introduce the wise government of the family . . . within the general management (*gestion*) of the state' (2007: 95): which Foucault then argues only occurs when the family 'now appears as an element within the population and as a fundamental relay in its government' (2007: 104). So management is named in relation to the family, and with a necessary relation to accounting also understood. For within the '*oeconomic*' dynamics of the family, resource allocation required accounting, most typically in the form of tracking physical and financial inflows and outflows (i.e. of inventory and of revenues and expenses), as had been the case since the ancient world, an issue indeed that we now know Foucault had an earlier interest in.[8] That relation only intensified, however, from the 1300s, first in Italy, once households began using double-entry bookkeeping, thus also tracking asset stocks and flows in relation to liabilities, something that occurred increasingly in domestic, commercial (merchant) and merchant banking contexts (e.g. Soll 2014; Goldthwaite 2015; Sangster 2016).

But management also surfaces in one, or perhaps two, other contexts in the first four lectures of *STP*. The first is within the context of the form of governing undertaken in the administrative state. The second is within the contexts where 'discipline' was operating in that era, where the focus is on the management of 'conduct', particularly of the individual. And I say that these are 'perhaps' two contexts, since close analysis shows overlaps in the manner of management's functioning in each setting, and not least at the level of how accounting supports that functioning. Considering 'managing' at the level of the administrative state first, this has been a significant focus of analysis, not only from a Foucauldian perspective (e.g. Miller 1990) but from within mainstream historiography too (e.g. Soll 2009), in relation to the form of governing known as 'governing by inquiry'.

The argument of Soll (2009), in what is a most painstaking and extensive historical analysis of this phenomenon, is that governing by inquiry reaches an apogee in the French state, in the period (1661–83) when Colbert serves as 'Information Master' to Louis XIV, as the title of his 2009 book puts it. In his analysis, the Colbertian approach to 'inquiry' first involves the collection of every kind of legal, religious, historical, geographical, statistical and financial information, and then inquiry (derived from the Latin *inquisitio*) functions as a 'critical reading' of this information to establish the truth of a given situation. At the same time, Colbert, like Louis, operates within a structure of governing the state (and not just the French state) of a principal-agent kind. In other words, the sovereign as principal dealt with each different minister in a series of separate principal-agent relationships (dividing in order to rule); but then ministers in their turn tended to operate their own principal-agent relationships—a practice that Colbert was most adept at. So Colbert operates his own principal-agent set-up, employing an extensive network of officials or *intendants* within France and beyond who report only to him as their principal, and through him to Louis. He then has the vast flows of both primary and secondary documents which he acquires catalogued and cross-referenced in his personal library. This material he would analyse, through forensic analysis of the population of texts thus assembled, to get to the truth of a given situation and then either act himself or advise Louis to act accordingly to rectify faults or exploit opportunities.

Thus one thing that Colbert achieves is precisely what Foucault names as occurring in this period, 'knowledge of the state in its different elements, dimensions and the factors of its strength, which was called "statistics" meaning science of the state' (2007: 100–1). But he does not deploy this knowledge to manage the population; instead he deploys it within his own version of 'divide and rule', analysing it to achieve objectives such as appropriating land or financial resources for Louis from local landowners or the Church, or instructing his *intendants* to alter the conduct of specific officials, e.g. the governor of a port, or exposing and correcting the bad conduct of other officials serving the sovereign.

Accounting constitutes an integral part of his form of governing by inquiry, not least since Colbert was born into a merchant banking family where he practised double-entry bookkeeping from his youth (Soll 2009: 34–6).

But he does not implement a double-entry system to run the state. Unsurprisingly given the impossibility, when ministers operated their own discrete principal-agent set-ups, of coordinating information across the departments of state. What he does instead is use the forensic skills involved in getting double-entry books to balance in order to inquire into possible anomalies, omissions and contradictions in the mainly stewardship accounts of the state, and so establish from the accounts 'truths' which would advantage the sovereign. The major example Soll gives is where Colbert conducts extensive inquiries in the early 1660s into the Royal tax registers, where his critical reading of all the entries across several years identifies certain tax officials as committing fraud or holding back revenues due to the King (cf. Soll 2009: 58–64). This renders officials accountable and perhaps reshapes their conduct, but it does not have as its direct target the 'population'.

The same is true of the way that discipline 'manages' conduct in this era, under Foucault's analysis, which begins in Lecture One of *STP*. First the *object* of discipline's managing is not the 'population' but the 'individual'. Second the *space* within which discipline manages is not that occupied by a population, but what he describes as 'an empty, artificial space which is to be completely constructed' (2007: 19), or indeed 'architecturalised'—in the French Foucault uses the verb form *'architecturer'* (Foucault 2004: 19; cf. Elden 2007: esp 565).[9] This space therefore differs from the space of 'security' in that the latter will be a space combining both natural *and* artificial elements, so constituting the 'territory' as space within which a population may live variously. This, it should be noted, is a distinction that Foucault makes right after he has characterised discipline as operating in an 'empty, artificial space'. He goes on immediately: 'Security will rely on a number of material givens'. It then seeks to manage the natural through allowing it to take its course but shaping its ebbs and flows through artifice. So 'one will work not only on natural givens but also on quantities that can be relatively but never wholly reduced, and, since they can never be nullified, one works on probabilities' (2007: 19).

However, within the artificial space, the individual is the object of discipline. However, this individual, he says, 'is not the primary datum on which discipline is exercised'. Instead the object of discipline is the individual as located *within* the artificial space where discipline operates, and where it therefore operates not on any single individual but on a 'multiplicity'. In that respect, 'discipline only exists insofar as there is a multiplicity'; and '(t)he individual is much more a *particular way of dividing up a multiplicity* for a discipline than the raw material from which it is constructed' (2007: 12, emphasis added). Hence 'school and military discipline, as well as penal discipline, workshop discipline, worker discipline, are all particular ways of managing (*gérer*) and organizing a multiplicity, of fixing its points of implantation, its lateral or horizontal, vertical and pyramidal trajectories, its hierarchy, and so on' (2007: 12).

Within this space accounting then supports the managing of the multiplicity through enacting what Foucault will later in *STP* describe (when analysing the development of the early Christian pastorate within the monastic space) as 'an economy of merits and faults' (2007: 173). Here, within the enclosed and artificial space, rewards and punishments 'account for' the good and bad acts of each individual and so work to shape the behaviour of each and all. This is therefore a form of what Foucault had already named in *Discipline and Punish* as a 'penal accountancy' (Foucault 1977: 180), albeit in a system where 'punishment is only one element of a double system: gratification-punishment' (Foucault 1977: 180). However, the *precise* form taken by this particular 'penal accountancy' matters, i.e. as a system of *discrete* rewards and punishments. This continues across the eighteenth century, as de la Salle's *Conduct* of the Christian Brothers shows across its early editions. Good deeds are rewarded through praise or small prizes (e.g. a prayer book) and faults punished through gradated punishments, e.g. for a *pensum* (a minor infraction), a penance or imposition, such as saying graces, then up through physical chastisement and suspension to expulsion.

If we wish then to understand how discipline can function within a regime of governmental management, we need to grasp first how far both the object and the space where apparatuses of security operate change, and how far they remain the same. Space, we have already seen, becomes both natural and artificial, so 'naturalness' is new, but artificiality remains (even if its forms may change). In the case of the 'object', as it shifts from individual to population, what remains the same is its structure, as form not just of object but also as subject, and so as particular form of 'subject-object'.

In the first case, discipline cannot work on the individual as *object* of discipline unless the individual also becomes the disciplinary *subject*, carrying discipline everywhere, so that, in that famous formulation near the start of *Discipline and Punish*, 'the soul is the prison of the body' (1977: 30). In just the same way the population as collective object of management also becomes a form of 'collective subject' (2007: 42), which Foucault also therefore names more than once as 'collective subject-object' (2007: 44).[10] Indeed, the population as both object and subject is present from its first introduction, in Lecture One, when Foucault first defines the 'precise problem for this year' as 'the correlation between the technique of security and population as both object and subject of these mechanisms of security' (2007: 11). It is there still as the climax of Lecture Four nears, as it is defined as 'the subject of needs and aspirations, but also the object of government manipulation' (2007: 105).

But in that last definition of the population as 'subject of needs and aspirations', there lurks a transformation in the type of *subjectivity* that both population and individual will henceforward manifest, a transformation which follows from the change in the type of space inhabited as both natural and artificial. For within that space, the 'collective subject-object' develops its own 'naturalness' (2007: 70, in quotes in Foucault's manuscript), as a collective subject which must be diverse since 'it is dependent on a series of variables', among which Foucault names 'climate', 'material surroundings', 'intensity of commerce', 'laws', 'customs' and 'moral or religious values'.

But if the collective subject is diverse, so must the individual subjects be. As part of its varying, it 'is of course made up of individuals who are quite different from each other' (2007: 72). But in varying so systematically, Foucault says, it must not, according to eighteenth century theorists of population, vary in one respect. For them, the population has 'one and only one mainspring of action . . . desire' (2007: 72). But then this desire is in turn distributed, variously, across all its individuals.

Ultimately, then, desire transforms both the individual and the collective subject-object, and the interaction between them. On the one hand, 'desire is the pursuit of the individual's interest'; but within a regime of management concerned with promoting security, then the 'both spontaneous and *regulated* play of desire will in fact allow the production of an interest, of something favourable for the population' (2007: 73). Consequently: 'The production of the collective interest through the play of desire is what distinguishes both the naturalness of population and of the possible artificiality of the means one adopts to manage (*gérer*) it' (2007: 73). This is therefore a new situation where both population and individual become new forms of subject-object who are now *active* subjects with interests and desires, which enables them both to become objects of management and subjects who manage the self. So this is perhaps why discipline was never so important as when it was necessary to manage individuals in their fine detail; for now those individuals had interests and desires. But it was also perhaps never so effective, insofar as the form taken by the 'economy of merits and faults' also shifted towards a form of unilinear measuring of performance across the whole spectrum of good and bad acts, such that 'all behaviour falls in the field between good and bad marks', as Foucault had said in *Discipline and Punish* (1977: 180). So now each and all can have ever-shifting balance sheets of individual and population-level worth, given that 'there is this circulation of awards and debits, thanks to the continuous calculation of plus and minus points' (1977: 181).

Across the extent of the first four lectures of *STP*, we can see a significant accumulation of namings of management, in different forms in different eras, and a regular surfacing of accounting, again in different forms, to shape the actions and thoughts of different objects (who turn out to be subject-objects) in differing spaces. But at the same time, the aspects of accounting that we have identified have been for the most part those aspects that we are used to associating with both discipline and management.

Let me now turn to those aspects which I have suggested have remained more invisible to us, where accounting takes the lead, so to speak, in its interplays with managing: in the first instance as means to constituting one of the key apparatuses of security that governmental management will constantly use as means to making 'good'—in the sense of formally rational—decisions; and in the second as means to constituting that new kind of 'economic truth' which Foucault will argue in *BB* (2008: esp 31–2) will henceforward define the space within which governing can reasonably act. In each case, I shall suggest, this is the outcome of a new but account-ing-based way of approaching and comprehending 'cost objects' (whether physical or metaphysical) and then collecting all the relevant costs (but only the relevant costs) pertaining to each given such object.

Accounting, 'Cost' and the Constitution of '*Dispositifs* of Security' and 'Economic Truth'

My reading here will have as its 'hinge term' the little-big word cost (*coût*). For, in the analyses whose surface I now read, it is only, I suggest, through the presence of cost as sustained *conceptual* object of thought that both governmental management and 'the economy as specific domain of reality' come into being. But accounting, as 'academic plumbing', cannot be the means to sustained conceptual thought. So alongside cost as hinge term named by Foucault, there tend to accumulate more respectable names, such as 'the economy', 'economics', 'the economic' or 'economic truth'. I shall therefore attempt to show how accounting's apparent absence constitutes a presence. I consider two passages again, with the first coming at the very beginning of *STP*, immediately after Foucault's initial overarching theoreti-cal and methodological observations, as he turns to pose his first substantive question, which is: 'What are we to understand by "security"?' (2007: 4). To which his first answer is as follows.

'Security', he says, asks new types of questions, for instance in relation to crime. First it asks statistical ones, such as 'what is the average rate of criminality?' (2007: 4); but these are only preliminary to the central types of question, which then for half a page (2007: 5) are questions of *cost*. These include, among others: '(H)ow much does this criminality cost society, what damage does it cause . . . ? What is the cost of repressing these thefts? . . . What, therefore, is the comparative cost of the theft and of its repression, and what is more worthwhile . . . ?' (2007: 5). He then sums up the way this particular dispositif works as follows: 'the apparatus (*dispositif*) of se-curity inserts the phenomenon in question, namely theft, within a series of events . . . the reactions of power to this phenomenon are inserted in a calcu-lation of cost . . . (and) one establishes an average considered as optimal . . . and . . . a bandwidth of the acceptable' (2007: 5–6).

This is significant in two respects: first because it is the first time that he introduces that elusive term '*dispositif* of security'; but second because of how already the problem posed is one where the answer will come by look-ing at the object of concern as a *series* (here of 'criminal events'). But this object only exists as a series through undertaking the fundamental function performed by all accounting from before writing—which is not 'calcula-tion' as it is often put, but *naming* and counting (cf. Ezzamel & Hoskin

2002): every account first names the objects (physical or metaphysical) it will account for and only then counts them. So the series here comes about through the action of naming an object 'criminal events' and then counting the number of occurrences of that named object. But then the *apparatus of security* only comes about through then naming the object 'criminal events' as a 'cost object', and then assembling all the costs (but only the costs) pertaining to that object. Then it becomes possible to 'cost' each type of criminal event, and then to 'cost' the different forms of intervention or action appropriate to deal with each event type, through some form either of evaluating comparative costs, or comparative costs and benefits.

Here accounting can be quickly granted the role of performing the mundane aspects: assembling and counting the costs. But the associated thinking of a series as a cost object in the first instance is a conceptual move: and it is a conceptual move whose precondition is that a formal concern with costs to have become integral to the accounting frame of thinking: on this basis then the mundane aspects can be performed systematically. Foucault's conclusion is that there is just such a conceptual transformation or breakthrough here; it is just that he names its provenance differently, as he concludes that here: 'Basically the fundamental question is economics (*"l'économie"*), and the economic relation between the cost of repression and the cost of delinquency' (2007: 9). I stress the 'formal' nature of this concern to signify that there is a form of veridiction implicated here, in the sense that this accounting establishes what Foucault will later describe as an economic 'standard of truth', in that context in *BB*, alluded to above, where he discusses the relation of 'cost of production' to the setting of what the *économistes* will start referring to as the 'natural price' or the 'good price' (Foucault 2008: 32). But as he says there, 'this does not mean that prices are, in the strict sense, true'. Equally here following the formal process of establishing costs does not mean that the costs are in a *substantive* sense 'true', let alone the 'benefits' if the analysis also extends to costing those.

But what is also established is a form of something that he discusses briefly in his general prefatory remarks introducing *STP*, just preceding this passage (2007: 3): namely what he calls 'a field of real forces', which he then qualifies as 'a field of forces that cannot be created by a speaking subject alone and on the basis of his words'. A formal accounting-based truth about 'costs', i.e. one assembled through a rigorous and complete recording of all the costs 'relevant' to a given 'cost object', constitutes, I suggest, just such a 'field of real forces'. That is perhaps worth bearing in mind given what Foucault then goes on to say in those introductory remarks: that it is up to him, and us, 'to know on what fields of real forces we need to get our bearings in order to make a tactically effective analysis. But this is, after all, the circle of struggle and truth' (2007: 3).

Let me now turn to the second and rather different passage where accounting constitutes a form of cost. This appears in Lecture Two. But first there is an important transition passage where Foucault first moves on to suggest (2007: 11) that, having now established a first form that an apparatus of security can take, he should now identify 'some general features of these *dispositifs*'. The four features he designates are: first 'spaces of security', then 'the treatment of the uncertain, the aleatory', then 'the form of normalization specific to security', and finally 'the correlation between the technique of security and the population as both subject and object of these mechanisms of security' (2007: 11).

We have now had a first encounter with what he says about the space of security and its mix of the natural and the artificial, and how the problem of central concern that then emerges is 'the problem of the series' and particularly the 'indefinite series' (2007: 20) whose likelihood of occurrence is expressible as a probability. But now a further extension to what may constitute an apparatus of security comes with what then gets said, in Lecture Two, concerning 'the relationship of government to the event'. Here the particular event that Foucault considers is one addressed by the physiocrats, the scarcity (*la disette*) of grain; and here the new apparatus of security, he argues, inverts the way of thinking the management of scarcity found in earlier types of approach.

For instance, for the mercantilists, solutions had concentrated on the event of scarcity as such, and had sought to ensure that in scarcity grain 'be sold at the lowest possible price', thus leading to hoarding by those with surpluses, while for those who must sell, 'profit tends towards zero and peasant earnings may even fall below the cost of production' (2007: 32–3). The physiocrats in contrast began to articulate a new economic concept, whereby they think, he says, in terms 'of a fundamental theoretical principle', the 'net profit'. As they then elaborate this principle, the conclusion emerges that 'just about the only net profit (*produit net*) that can be obtained in a nation is the peasant profit (*produit*)' (2007: 33–4). And from this stems the inverted way of thinking scarcity.

Here Foucault chooses a text by Abeille to illustrate the new solution. First scarcity becomes read as one event in a series of events that fluctuate from scarcity to glut—a series which is therefore normal, but is also 'natural. . . . It is what it is' (2007: 36). But how does this lead a new form of analysis to emerge which will enable Abeille to 'manage' this series of events? Foucault says: 'Analysis will move back a notch . . . or no doubt several notches': away from an older concern over 'selling price' and 'with the phenomenon of scarcity-dearness', towards what Foucault calls '*the history of grain*, from the moment it is put in the ground, with what this implies in terms of work, time passed, and fields sown—of *cost* (*coût*) consequently' (2007: 36, emphases added). The unit of analysis is therefore 'grain with everything that may happen to it and will happen to it naturally', but in a context where artifice systematically intervenes to ensure 'the quality of the land, the care with which it is cultivated, . . . climatic conditions, . . . its marketing and so forth' (2007: 36).

Through this mix of accepting the natural and intervening with artifice, there is, Foucault says, a new 'event on which one tries to get a hold': 'the *reality* of grain' (2007: 36). This is a reality which first comprises all the relevant factors and activities across the whole 'history of grain' but then treats whatever cost summary emerges as just one event in a probabilistic distribution of cost-events. Foucault summarises what theorists like Abeille were trying to do as yet another 'apparatus (*dispositif*) for arranging things' which involves 'connecting up with the very reality of these fluctuations and . . . with other elements of reality'; and in 'working with the reality of fluctuations between abundance/scarcity, dearness/cheapness . . . an apparatus is installed . . . an apparatus of security' (2007: 37). Here there is a major economic conceptualisation, the 'net profit': but that is predicated on the equally major accounting conceptualisation of first thinking the history of grain as cost, which is a whole new level of 'metaphysical cost object' one might say. Given that, the interplay of accounting and economic conceptualisations can lead to a new level of economic discourse indeed, including the articulation of the construct which will, in *BB*, be named as putting a limit to what government-management can reasonably do: economic truth. Specifically, as Foucault then says, the physiocrats, in forming their 'fundamental theoretical principle' of the 'net profit', enact 'a new conception of the economy' and perhaps even 'the founding act of economic thought and economic analysis'. At which point the founding act of economic thought makes the prior and foundational accounting step recede into the background, as economic thought can then find it straightforwardly 'rational' to think in terms of allowing what one cannot control, in this case the 'reality' of grain, to take its 'natural' course, while at the same time deploying the apparatuses of security to 'manage' things effectively: in this case land, cultivation and climatic conditions.

And beyond this, there is the passage I have referred to in *BB* (2008: 31–2) where it is the cost of production which performs the same foundational role, and again recedes into the background. Here it is the 'natural price' of the economists that emerges to 'adequately express the . . . definite, adequate relationship between the *cost of production* and the extent of demand' (2008: 31): a relationship in which the definite and adequate dimensions for constituting the new economic reality are all on the side of the accounting that constitutes that cost. But this then 'permits the formation of . . . the true price' as 'a certain price that fluctuates around the value (*valeur*) of the product'. With that, it becomes possible for the '*économistes*' to construct 'the theory of the price-value relationship' which is the theoretical or conceptual base on which the market becomes that which 'reveals something like the truth', and also becomes that space which is no longer as earlier a 'site of distributive justice' whose function is to ensure the 'absence of fraud' (2008: 30). But once the market is the site of such a truth, that is when prices 'determined in accordance with the natural mechanisms of the market' can 'constitute a standard of truth which enables us to determine which governmental practices are correct and which erroneous' (2008: 32). This is when, Foucault then says, the market becomes not just a site of truth in itself, but 'a site of veridiction-falsification for governmental practice' and 'government has to function according to truth', which means in practice not intervening where the market and its truth hold sway.

Here, we once again very much confront a 'field of real forces' which puts limitations on governing; but it is a field that is constituted once again only once the action of accounting has constituted yet another formal kind of cost object, in this case the 'cost of production', which now constitutes a formal lower bound which the demand for sales of product or services must meet or exceed, whether over the short or longer run.

Conclusion: Getting to and Reading at the Surface of Things: Possibilities and Constraints

So here is my case, based primarily on reading the surface of the first four lectures of *STP*, for seeing Foucault as a historian and theorist of management and accounting. He is visible as naming different forms of managing insistently across these four lectures. At the same time, he is visible as naming different forms of 'cost', which I have argued are conceptually and not just practically grounded in accounting, and which he names as foundational not just to constituting specific and significant dispositifs of security but to the constitution of the first modern forms of 'economic truth'. Exteriority is joined by accumulation. But rarity? Perhaps rarity is circulating across the now visible exterior of the statements accumulated here, in the sense that Foucault can be seen, yet again, to be saying something new within the constant discursive play of the relatively few things that get said at any given time. For here there is articulated a kind of conjunction between management and accounting which may enable a new kind of understanding and analysis of their significance, past and current, so long as those who study those fields are foolhardy enough to explore that possibility further.

But can we now be so foolhardy? Let me just close with a surface reading of a text not by Foucault, but on him: but it also may suggest why it has, so far, been so difficult to think Foucault in the ways I suggest. The text in question is the volume that forms a kind of predecessor to this one, *Foucault, Management and Organization Theory* (McKinlay & Starkey 1998). Undertaking a surface reading now indicates how far away 'we' (as those active in those fields) were in general, a generation ago, from having any sense of Foucault as potential theorist of management or accounting. I say 'we' on the basis that the text was made up of contributors from across the field of more or less 'critical' management studies, all immersed in different ranges of Foucault's work. But reading through the text now, there is no hint in the presentations of his work that he might be a theorist of management or accounting, or even that he named management or accounting insistently. Instead, across the different contributions, Foucault is presented as a theorist of constructs such as 'discipline', 'conduct', 'dressage', 'pan-opticism' and of course 'governmentality'; and given that he is presented as theorist of one or more of these constructs, then 'we' had to be lead or translate him *into* the discursive fields of managing and accounting.

There is indeed just one contribution where it is even recognised that Foucault actually uses the term 'management', at least so far as I can see. This is the chapter by Norman Jackson and Pippa Carter, 'Labour as Dressage', which uses a quotation where Foucault is referring to the eighteenth century emergence of 'the great workshops employing hundreds of workers' and how in these sites there developed 'a whole technique of human dressage by location, confinement, surveillance, the perpetual supervision of behaviour and tasks, in short a whole technique of "management" of which the prison was merely one manifestation' (Jackson & Carter 1998: 54). However, the chapter's analytical focus remains principally on dressage and its relations to discipline. There is no commentary on the fact that Foucault identifies this eighteenth century workshop dressage *as* management and indeed puts it in 'scare quotes'.[11]

Perhaps most ironic of all is that there is one piece which appears to give a passage from Foucault, as an opening quotation, which begins: 'Management is possible only when the strength of a firm is known' and continues to note that for management there is needed a 'concrete, precise and measured knowledge as to the firm's strength', and knowledge 'nameable as accounting'. But the author then reveals that in the actual quote, which is a précis of what Foucault says in the Tanner Lectures at Stanford in 1979 (which are themselves a précis of the lecture series discussed here), what Foucault refers to is 'government' and 'political arithmetic' (Foucault 1988: 76–7). It is 'ironic' I say, because the author implicitly regrets that Foucault gets so close to naming management and accounting but does not: and that author, of course, was me. So I fully understand how difficult it is to get to the surface of what Foucault actually says, and how far that is because we systematically read a surface other than that which is there.

Notes

1 These three terms form the title of the ensuing chapter: 'Rarity, Exteriority, Accumulation' (2002: 133–141): hence the italicising of these terms in the main text.
2 In his chapter Foucault specifies in great detail what makes up 'exteriority' and 'accumulation'. I offer the following as summary statements. First, exteriority seeks to 'restore statements to their pure dispersion . . . without having to relate them to a more fundamental opening or difference. . . . (I)t is a question of re-discovering that outside in which, in their relative rarity, . . . enunciative events are distributed' (2002: 137). Second, analysis 'is addressed to specific forms of accumulation that can be identified neither with an interiorization in the form of memory nor with an undiscriminating totalization of documents' (2002: 138).
3 This leads Foucault to the famous conclusion: 'If, by substituting the analysis of rarity for the search for totalities, the descriptions of relations of exteriority for the theme of the transcendental foundation, the analysis of accumulations for the quest of the origin, one is a positivist, then I am quite happy to be one' (2002: 141).

4 I have added the italics not just to bring home how there are, in the original French, *eight* repetitions of 'managing' (in the verb form *gérer*) but also how, if one then listens to Foucault on tape, there is a marked vocal stress on each repetition too. Tape versions of the lectures are available on line, for instance at http://sunsite3.berkeley.edu/videodir/foucault/stp 780201.mp3.

5 On both general and specific problems posed in translating Foucault, see Vandaele (2016), who builds on earlier concerns of O'Farrell (2005: 7–8) on 'the inevitable errors and omissions' in many translations, and of Stuart Elden on his blog, *Progressive Geographies*, January 2014. In this context, Burchell is outstandingly good. In contrast, Gordon (2016: 99) refers to 'the abominable mistranslation' of 'The Order of Discourse' in the version appended to US versions of *The Archaeology of Knowledge*, 'even down to the mistranslation of the title as "The Discourse on Language"'.

6 One should add that both standalone translations of the lecture are based on just one cassette recording made by Pasquale Pasquino and published by him in Italian in the journal *Aut . . . Aut* in 1978. The English version was the outcome of a retranslation into English, not by Pasquino. A fuller provenance of this process is given in the Introduction to *The Foucault Effect* (Burchell et al 1991: p vii). As well as the omissions noted here, there is another major one at page 101 of *STP* where, as Burchell observes, twelve lines of text are 'replaced by a paragraph . . . of which there is no trace either in the recording or in the manuscript' (Foucault 2007: 101, asterisked footnote).

7 If I mention just two, it is because my personal conclusion is that these are particularly important going forward. The first is the assumption that he 'must' have shifted his mode of analysis from archaeology to genealogy—despite the fact that he says so often that his work combines both (on which see Koopman 2013; Webb 2013; cf. Davidson 1986). The second is the often connected assumption that his focus, particularly in relation to discipline or as here to governmentality, was on power-knowledge relations, when he claims—not least in these lectures as I shall seek to show—to have been constantly concerned with truth, in the sense of what he later will call 'the history of "veridictions" understood as the forms according to which discourses capable of being deemed true or false are articulated upon a domain of things' (Florence/Foucault 1994: 315).

8 See the *Lectures on the Will to Know*, his first *Collège de France* lecture series of 1970–71, which has extensive analysis of the significance of accounting in the archaic period in Ancient Greece (Foucault 2013: 103–110), with the articulation of an 'accounting memory which . . . has to preserve the identical. Writing' (2013: 108), and where 'justice takes shape in the measured system of services, debts and their repayment' (2013: 106).

9 I am indebted here to the insights on the functioning of space in relation both to discipline and security in this article of Elden's, which forms another of these significant re-thinkings of Foucault, as well as being the basis for the material on this topic in his subsequent and influential book, *The Birth of Territory* (Elden 2013). This is also an article which follows a 'close reading' strategy towards these early lectures similar to that I adopt here.

10 The term 'subject-object' is later repeated twice of the population (2007: 77).

11 At the same time, it should be noted that the paper does then discuss a subsequent emergence of 'management' in relation to labour dressage in the context of the later nineteenth century (1998: 55). Here it is noted that owners 'required agents to protect their interests and exercise control, and so a professional managerial class emerged' (shortly followed by the formalisation of management knowledge and the emergence of 'another group who could tell managers how to manage').

References

Burchell, G., Gordon, C. & Miller, P. (1991), *The Foucault Effect*, London: Harvester Wheatsheaf.

Davidson, A. (1986), 'Archaeology, Genealogy, Ethics', in D. Hoy (ed.), *Foucault: A Critical Reader*, Oxford: Blackwell.

Elden, S. (2007), 'Governmentality, Calculation, Territory', *Environment and Planning D: Society and Space* 25/3: 562–580.

Elden, S. (2013), *The Birth of Territory*, Chicago, IL: University of Chicago Press.

Ezzamel, M. & Hoskin, K. (2002), 'Retheorizing the Relationship between Accounting, Writing and Money with Evidence from Mesopotamia and Ancient Egypt', *Critical Perspectives on Accounting* 13/3: 333–367.

Foucault, M. (1977), *Discipline and Punish*, London: Allen Lane.

Foucault, M. (1979), 'On Governmentality', *I & C* 6: 5–22.

Foucault, M. (1981), 'The Order of Discourse', in R. Young (ed.), *Untying the Text: A Post-Structuralist Reader*, London: Routledge & Kegan Paul.

Foucault, M. (1988), 'Politics and Reason', in L. Kritzman (ed.), *Michel Foucault: Politics, Philosophy, Culture*, London: Routledge.

Foucault, M. (1991), 'Governmentality', in G. Burchell, C. Gordon & P. Miller (eds), *The Foucault Effect*, London: Harvester Wheatsheaf.

Foucault, M. (1994), 'Michel Foucault, 1926-', in G. Gutting (ed.), *The Cambridge Companion to Foucault*, Cambridge: Cambridge University Press.

Foucault, M. (2002), *The Archaeology of Knowledge*, London: Routledge.

Foucault, M. (2004), *Securité, Territoire, Population: Cours au Collège de France, 1977–78*, Paris: Gallimard.

Foucault, M. (2007), *Security, Territory, Population: Lectures at the Collège de France, 1977–78*, London: Palgrave Macmillan.

Foucault, M. (2008), *The Birth of Biopolitics: Lectures at the Collège de France, 1978–79*, London: Palgrave Macmillan.

Foucault, M. (2013), *Lectures on the Will to Know: Lectures at the Collège de France, 1970–71*, London: Palgrave Macmillan.

Goldthwaite, R. (2015), 'The Practice and Culture of Accounting in Renaissance Florence', *Enterprise & Society* 16/3: 611–647.

Gordon, C. (2016), 'The Cambridge Foucault Lexicon', *History of the Human Sciences* 29/3: 91–110.

Hoskin, K. (2015), ' "What about the Box?" Some Thoughts on "Corruption Prevention" and on the "Disciplined and Ethical Subject" ', *Critical Perspectives on Accounting* 28/1: 71–81.

Jackson, N. & Carter, P. (1998), 'Labour as Dressage', in A, McKinlay & K. Starkey (eds), *Foucault, Management and Organization Theory: From Panopticon to Technologies of Self*, London: Sage.

Klamer, A. & McCloskey, D. (1992), 'Acccounting as Master Metaphor of Economics', *European Accounting Review* 1/1: 145–160.

Koopman, C. (2013), *Genealogy as Critique: Foucault and the Problems of Modernity*, Bloomington, IN: Indiana University Press.

Lawlor, L. & Nale, J. (2014), *The Cambridge Foucault Lexicon*, New York: Cambridge University Press.McKinlay, A. & Pezet, E. (2010), 'Accounting for Foucault', *Critical Perspectives on Accounting* 21/6: 486–495.

McKinlay, A. & Starkey, K. (1998), *Foucault, Management and Organization Theory: From Panopticon to Technologies of Self*, London: Sage.

Miller, P. (1990), 'On the Interrelations of Accounting and the State', *Accounting, Organizations and Society* 15/4: 315–338.

Nealon, J. (2008), *Foucault beyond Foucault*, Stanford, CA: Stanford University Press.

Neu, D., Everett, J. & Rahaman, A. (2015), 'Preventing Corruption within Government Procurement: Constructing the Disciplined and Ethical Subject', *Critical Perspectives on Accounting* 28/1: 49–61.

O'Farrell, C. (2005), *Michel Foucault*, London: Sage.

Paltrinieri, L. (2012), *L'Expérience du Concept*, Paris: Publications de la Sorbonne.

Sangster, A. (2016), 'The Genesis of Double Entry Bookkeeping', *The Accounting Review* 91/ 1: 299–315.

Soll, J. (2009), *The Information Master: Jean-Baptiste Colbert's Secret State Intelligence System*, Ann Arbor, MI: University of Michigan Press.

Soll, J. (2014), *The Reckoning: Financial Accounting and the Rise and Fall of Nations*, New York: Basic.

Vandaele, J. (2016), 'What Is an Author, Indeed: Michel Foucault in Translation', *Perspectives: Studies in Translatology* 24/1: 76–92.

Webb, D. (2013), *Foucault's Archaeology: Science and Transformation*, Edinburgh: Edinburgh University Press.

3   A Dialogue with Foucault on Power

Mark Haugaard

Introduction

Michel Foucault once observed that in his work he used Nietzsche, rather than tried to be faithful to him. 'The only valid tribute to thought such as Nietzsche's is precisely to use it, to deform it, to make it groan and protest' (Foucault 1980: 54). The same follows in this essay where I use Foucault to move our understanding of power forward. Rather than being faithful *to* Foucault, this is a dialogue *with* Foucault on power.

I have always considered Foucault a highly insightful and creative thinker but also an unsystematic one who had a liking for pronouncements, which were not always integrated into a systematic social theory. I am thinking of statements such as: 'Where there is power there is resistance' (1981: 95). There is insight here and, yet, on a more specific level this assertion is clearly problematic. As Steven Lukes famously observes, the most effective form of power is created when the subaltern actor internalises the interests of the dominator, and therefore manifests no resistance (Lukes 1974: 23).

I will dialogue with what I consider to be the essence of Foucault's theory of power relative to a tighter social theory, which broadly mirrors the structure of the power debates. In creating this theoretical context, I will not give an exposition of the works of Dahl or Lukes. Rather, these will appear as a background foil, integrated within a theory, which structures the argument. The overall paradigm is socially constructivist, building upon the work of theorists who are interested in balancing agency and structure, including Austin, Giddens, Bourdieu, Searle and Alexander among others. However, I will leave it to the reader to decide what specific school the theory belongs to, if they so wish, as I agree with Foucault that these kinds of labelling are unhelpful.

The three dimensions of power, as set out by Lukes (1974), broadly correspond to three levels of theorizing in social theory. The first level consists of agency, the second of structure and the third, the local epistemic tacit knowledge that guides the agents who reproduce these structures. In addition, there is a fourth level, which concerns shaping the social ontological dispositions of social subjects. Relative to Foucault, the third dimension corresponds to his archaeological works (for instance, Foucault 1970) and power/knowledge (1980), while the genealogical analysis of the subject formation (1979, 1981 and 1982) is four-dimensional.

Agency and Structure: The First Two Levels of Power

To be an agent implies the capacity to do something. Agency entails power, which is probably what Foucault means by suggesting that power is everywhere (Foucault 1981: 93–4). In the power debates, there has been a tendency to view power as domination (see, Lukes in Hayward & Lukes 2008). This comes from the influence of Weber's famous conceptualization of power in terms of one agent overcoming the resistance of another (Weber 1991: 180), which re-emerges in Dahl's influential work in the form that A exercises power over B, to the extent to which A gets B to do something that B would not otherwise do (Dahl 1957). This form of power is power-over. However, power-over presupposes power-to, which is the capacity to act (Allen 1999). As argued by Morriss (2002) and Pansardi (2012), an agent's power-over is a subset of their power-to. Some people may use their capacity for action (power-to) for collective goals while others may wish to use it to get others to do something that they do not wish to do (power-over).

The capacity to exercise agency stems from two types of resources: from physical resources, such as strength and the natural world, or from interacting with others. Foucault observes that power and violence are different, and are in some respects opposites. 'A relationship of violence acts upon a body or upon things; it forces, it bends it breaks', while power is 'an action upon an action' (Foucault 1982: 220). This position is even more emphatically stated by Arendt in *On Violence* (1970), where she concludes that 'it is insufficient to say power and violence are not the same. Power and violence are opposites: where one rules absolutely, the other is absent' (1970: 56). Violence does not engage with the other as a social agent who structures their own action. In contrast, social power treats the other as a social agent whose social action can be structured. Of government by power, Foucault writes: '. . . it designated the way in which the conduct of individuals or of groups might be directed: the government of children, of souls, of communities, of families, of the sick' (Foucault 1982: 221). Within such a context the other is 'maintained to the very end as a person who acts' (Foucault 1982: 220). This opposition has to be qualified because it is falsifiable as an unqualified assertion. Of course, the threat of violence is frequently used by one individual to get another to do something that they would not otherwise do. So, violence can be the base for very effective power-over. Furthermore, the modern state's monopoly of physical violence gives the state highly effective power-over entire populations. These are commonplace truisms which we are all familiar with, and not what either Foucault or Arendt is attempting to refute.

Agency that derives from violence presupposes treating the other as a receptacle of pain and pleasure, which can be threatened. In combination with discipline, the threat of violence can be used to create a social order. However, a coercive order will be relatively unstable, as it is always open to opposing violence. As argued by Scott (1990), slaves (who are considered the paradigm instance of those governed through violence) often have private discourses of resistance, among themselves, which are proto-revolutionary. Thus, if given the opportunity, they will de-stabilise the order of things. The difference between power and violence can be seen using an everyday example of the power of a parent over a child. If a parent can get a child to do something without coercion, they have effective power-over the child. If, on the other hand, the parent has to coerce the child this suggests a lack of power.

In general, violence and coercion are crude forms of power, because they require the constant activation of the threat and generate resentment, thus inciting resistance—actual or potential. In contrast, the repeated exercise of effective social power tends to reinforce the power source. Social actors develop dispositions to structure in a certain way, and the more they act according to those structures the more stable the social order becomes.

A qualification: it must be acknowledged that there is a very special form of violence that, like social power, has a self-reinforcing quality, which is a regime of terror. Once the less powerful are terrorized, the more terror they experience, the more acquiescent they become. Thus terror can be used to establish a complex social order, which is relatively stable. However, when the structures destabilise, the result is prolonged anarchy and civil war. As I write, the collapse of Syria into constantly warring factions would be a case in point. Regimes of terror, although a valid subject, are not the focus of this chapter.

The ordered-ness of social life not only serves the purposes of domination, but also power-to. Non-coercive social power comes from interactive structural reproduction. The concept of structure has many meanings in social theory and, as such, like the concept of power, is a family resemblance concept that derives its specific meaning from a local language game (see Haugaard 2010). In this theoretical context, *structure* refers to the *systemic meaning* reproduced by any social action. For instance, if I tick a box next to the name of a political party or candidate at election time, the structured aspect of that action refers to the act of voting. The goal I aimed for was to elect party A, rather than party B. In normal circumstances, it is this goal-directed aspect that motivates social actors. They do not, as a general rule, reflect upon the structured aspect of their action. Exceptions to this include social critique, which involves reflexivity upon structure.

The agency of voting is based upon the existence of wider social structures of voting, which form a democratic system. It does not make sense, for instance, to have acts of voting without *standing for election*, the *counting of votes, parliament, prime minister, president* and so on. The moment that a social actor acts, by voting, or some other structured act, they are part of a process of structural reproduction, which Giddens refers to as structuration (1984). The use of the verb form of the noun (structure) indicates the performative aspects of social structures. Right now I am reproducing the structures of the English language in an attempt to explain social theory. In this case, my act of structuration is an unintended effect of my action to realise the goal of communicating a theory.

In social theory, power and constraint are sometimes opposed, which makes sense normatively, but not in terms of sociological theory (see Haugaard 2008). Following sociological theory (*is* rather than *ought*), the structural constraints of language are what give me the power to communicate my ideas. Similarly, the rules of the road constrain drivers, while at the same time those constraints enable them to negotiate a complex modern network of roads. This capacity to act (power-to) is based upon the knowledge that others will structure their actions in certain relatively predictable ways. That structuring takes place irrespective of what goals those others are pursuing. Thus, sociologically speaking, structures are both enabling and constraining (Giddens 1984).

While the enabling aspect of social structures delivers power-to, the constraining aspects reinforce the status quo, which often constitute relations of domination. The rules of the road are usually not dominating to any substantive degree but that is not the case with many of the structures that social actors internalise as part of their everyday lives. Normatively, there is a double bind here: constraints simultaneously enable power-to and facilitate forms of dominating power-over. When Bachrach and Baratz wrote their seminal article on power (1962), they had in mind precisely the fact that organizations by definition simultaneously include certain issues and exclude others—'organization is the mobilization of bias' (Bachrach & Baratz 1962: 949).

The duality of enablement and exclusion is indivisible. To make social action structured, a virtual infinity of other possible acts of structuration must be excluded. To understand why, consider the case of games, which are rigidly restricted structured systems. The rules of chess that make checkmate possible entail an inclusion of the rules of chess and an exclusion of a virtual infinity of non-chess rules. Of course, social life is not as rigid as chess, but even language only works if the structures of language are to a significant extent adhered to—social change is always possible.

That structure is both enabling and excluding means that the breakdown of social structure is not without its costs. Social actors frequently resist structural social changes because they are focussed upon the short-term gains that they make by reproducing existing social structures. A woman socialised in a patriarchal society, and who has become efficient in using those rules of that social game, may resist social change in order to protect social capital that she has built up within that system. Consequently, social change is never without its cost, which actors have to balance against the

benefits of change. This is a theoretical position that is implicitly at normative variance with Foucault's radical politics, so I will leave exploring this
point for the moment (see Haugaard 2015 and 2016).

Episteme: The Third Dimension of Power

Social structures are reproduced by interacting social actors based upon a
shared understanding of the interpretation of meaning. If I see bits of paper
with something written on them, as either a *polling card* or a *50-euro note*,
that judgement is based upon an interpretation. This is not necessarily a
discursively thought out meaning. Rather, it takes place relative to my tacit
interpretative horizon or what Foucault calls an *episteme* (Foucault 1970).

In his archaeological period, Foucault was a meaning holist. A system
of thought, or an episteme, is a relationally constituted system of meaning-
structures. The act of voting does not acquire meaning simply through the
act itself, but through its place within a political system, which is simultaneously also a linguistic system. This system is created through a series of differences and similarities which are relationally constituted. To take another
example, which is based upon Kuhn (1977: 313–19): imagine a father takes
his young daughter for a walk in a park. They come to a pond and the child
says *birds*, while pointing at some ducks. The father compliments the child
and then decides to teach her that these birds are *ducks*. They move further
along the pond, and see white geese, to which the child says *ducks*. The
father then explains that they are *geese*, along the lines that geese are a kind
of larger white duck. They come to swans, whereupon the child says *geese*,
and the father endeavours to explain the similarity and difference between
swans and geese. These three words, *ducks*, *geese* and *swans*, are relationally constituted through relational difference. We would not say that someone was a competent speaker who could not tell the difference between,
for instance, white geese and white swans. Similarly, we would not say that
someone understood what is meant by *polling card* if they failed to grasp
what it means *to vote, stand for election* or to get *elected*. Understanding
in this case means making sense within the context of a system of meaning.

Of course, the understanding of meaning is never a pure either/or phenomenon. For instance, in Ireland the democratic system includes a complex
system of single-transferable votes. Some voters do not fully understand
exactly how and when these transfers come into play. Yet, they still *vote*. In
the same way as many native speakers of English with a comparatively poor
vocabulary (say ten thousand words) are said to speak English. However,
such speakers are not as articulate, using words as accurately, as someone
who is familiar with a large vocabulary (twenty-five thousand words).

Foucault opens *The Order of Things* with a quotation from 'a certain
Chinese Encyclopaedia in which it is written that animals are divided into:
belonging to the emperor, b) embalmed, c) tame, d) suckling pigs, e) sirens, f)
fabulous . . . n) that from a long way off look like flies' (Foucault 1970: xv).

The entry makes little sense to the reader because the wider system of meaning is missing. Theoretically it is similar to aliens observing acts of *voting*, but having no idea what a democratic system is. Such aliens might conclude that this is a religious ritual or think we are doing something that is incomprehensible to us, in much the same way that Wittgenstein observed that if lions could speak, we would not be able to understand them (Wittgenstein 1967: 223).

Central to Foucault's archaeological method was the hypothesis that during the last five hundred years or so, European civilization has gone through three episteme, as follows: the Renaissance (the fifteenth to mid-seventeenth centuries), Classical (mid-seventeenth century to 1800) and Modern (from 1800 to the 1980s). He argues that there is a discontinuity between these three periods, with different relations of similarity and difference. Consequently, the same signifier, or word, shifts meaning because the system of meaning itself changes. So, to take an example, in the Renaissance period resemblance was a structuring principle of that system of thought. Therefore, Renaissance thinkers thought that walnuts were good for the brain, because of the physical similarity between brains and walnuts. Another debate concerned whether or not a flower is a right-side-up or an up-side-down human, which revolved around the equivalence of the face and the flower, or the mouth and the roots (Foucault 1970: 21). This kind of debate would make little sense in the modern system of thought, because the language games of biology do not involve resemblance.

In the modern system of thought serious scientific debate over whether or not a plant is a right-side-up or an up-side-down animal falls outside the conditions of possibility. With reference to the enabling and constraining aspects of social structures, agency within the episteme of modern science takes place at the cost of excluding resemblance as a legitimate scientific discourse. This exclusion did not take place as a consequence of some external force. Rather, it took place because of the consensus building within an epistemic community.

In Wittgenstein's private language argument (1967), social actors cannot create social meaning by themselves when they act as single individuals. Structural reproduction takes place when an orientation towards other is recognised as valid by a relevant other (see Weber 1947: 88–91). Structuration is a necessary but not sufficient condition for the reproduction of meaning. Systems of meaning involve communities of speakers who are willing to confirm-structure, or validate certain structuration practices (Haugaard 1997: 163–78).

Agents are hugely creative, and throughout their socialization make all sorts of novel structuration practices, which fail to reach the threshold of being confirm-structured by relevant others. Actors are potentially free to structure in an infinite number of novel ways but only a small number of those practices are confirm-structured. Part of socialization is learning which structuration practices will be confirm-structured. To use the analogy of evolution: genetic mutations constantly take place, but only a small number of those are actually retained in the evolution of a species. Similarly, social actors constantly make infelicitous acts of structuration, which are either ignored or penalised, and so the system remains intact. However, a small number of these are perceived of as felicitous, and confirm-structured, consequently the system changes. This characterization does not violate balanced principles of social theory by constructing social agents as cultural dupes, as in structuralism or functionalism. Yet, the workings of constraint make this perspective less agent-centred than Giddens' theory of structuration (1984).

When Foucault wrote his histories of the present, he was interested in the small petty confrontations, in which certain novel acts of structuration acts are excluded, while others are accepted. In researching *Discipline and Punish*, Foucault stumbled across the case of Pierre Riviere, who killed his family, then ran out into the street waving a blood-stained axe in the air (Foucault 1975). What fascinated Foucault about the case was the fact that an extraordinary number of documents were produced which were *un*-necessary for the conviction of Riviere, as his guilt was beyond doubt. However, the objective was different; in this case we see the early social sciences of criminology, psychology, law and medicine seizing upon a deviant individual and attempting to make him into an archetype of a pathology. By this action, these experts could make the case for the existence of categories, such as *psychopath* or *sociopath*. These new concepts were the building blocks for up-and-coming language games: the sciences of criminology or forensic psychology. This was a confrontation and change of meaning for the purposes of the creation of specific scientific discourses (see Foucault 1975: xi–xii).

We find another early nineteenth century criminal case discussed in the *History of Sexuality*, of one Lapcourt, the 'simpleton'. This refers to a young man who was in the habit of 'playing a game called "curdled milk" which was commonly played by village urchins' (Foucault 1981: 31). While this game may have been part of the fabric of village life up to this point, in this instance the young man became a medical case. The farmhand was shut up in the local hospital, to be studied as a pure object of knowledge. A new category of social subject (*paedophile*) was thus created.

While to the genealogist the social construction of meaning is self-evident, this is not apparent in everyday social life because social actors adopt what phenomenologists term the *natural attitude* (Schutz 1967). Consequently, the order of things appears as the *natural order of things*, which are considered self-evidently the way they are perceived to be. By documenting the shifts in episteme and emphasising the moments of transition, Foucault documents these moments of social construction. The Riviere and Lapcourt cases are insights into the moment of social construction. In so doing, Foucault reminds us of the social construction of our systems of thought. In essence, he is practising social critique by making us strangers to ourselves.

In emphasising the agency of actors in the creation of meaning, my emphasis differs from Foucault, who often appears more determinist. If we listen to the Chomsky-Foucault debate (Chomsky & Foucault 2011), or read his asserted death of man hypothesis (Foucault 1970: 387), Foucault appears to argue against any significant originality or freedom in meaning creation. I suspect that part of this was his desire to distance himself from the extreme voluntarism of Sartre, who describes social actors as almost deliberately creating meaning and thus being responsible for it (for instance Sartre 1969: 59). Sartre's position totally ignores the significance of constraint. In his later work, concerning care of the self (1986), Foucault suggests a level of agency consistent with what is being argued for here.

Searle argues that the social construction of institutional facts takes the form X counts as Y in circumstance C (Searle 1996). What we see in these cases of social change is an attempt by specialists to create the circumstances C, in which the behaviour of axing your family to death or playing curdled milk with little children are an X that counts as Y—*psychopath* and *paedophile*, respectively. The specialists create an epistemic community that will confirm-structure X as Y in circumstances C. As they are experts upon this type of Y, success constitutes part of creating an epistemic field in which they, as experts, have cultural capital (Bourdieu 1986 and 1990).

Foucault theorised shifts in systems of thought as discontinuities. I agree that episteme are discontinuous with each other, in the sense of having signifiers of incommensurable meaning. For instance, two persons hearing voices (identical X), one in the Middle-ages (circumstances C) and in modern times (different C) will be judged to be different and incommensurable Ys. The former may be deemed a *Saint* (Y1) or a *heretic* (Y2), while the latter may be diagnosed as a *schizophrenic* (Y3). Each makes sense within their episteme. Hence, there is discontinuity.

In his description of the three systems of thought (Foucault 1970), Foucault suggests that this discontinuity between systems of thought existed like separate archaeological layers (Foucault 1989). That is to say, in the mid-sixteenth century, and at the end of the eighteenth century, we entered new epistemic language games that covered the entire community. Given the contested nature of the change, I think the process is much more uneven than that. Such unevenness is suggested in *Discipline and Punish* (1979), where all three systems of thought are described as in competition around 1800.

When we read the Chinese Encyclopaedia entry, there is a total discontinuity of episteme between it and our interpretative horizon, as is evidenced by the fact that we do not understand the sequence. However, the Renaissance system of resemblance makes sense to us, we can understand it and, furthermore, this system of thought is still alive in certain parts of society. For instance, this kind of neo-Renaissance resemblance reasoning lives on in the pages of the tabloid press under the heading of *horoscope*. What has changed is the cultural capital associated with those kinds of statements. In the early sixteenth century, astrological resemblance was considered valid within the field of science. Now it is only considered felicitous among fringe groups.

In the late Renaissance period the Danish astronomer Tycho Brahe received a massive grant from the Danish King Frederick II to build an observatory. It is reputed that part of the argument that convinced the King to give this grant was the prospect of having at the disposal of the state the use of scientifically accurate horoscopes.

As a thought experiment, let us for a moment imagine a contemporary grant application for an observatory that was justified in terms of scientifically accurate horoscopes. The evaluation committee *would understand* the application but they would simply dismiss it. The thought experiment makes visible the double level at which meaning and truth is reproduced. In the Renaissance period discussion of astrology was part of the language game of science, while after that period it was not. Why not? It is not because astrology is no longer comprehensible—unlike the Chinese Encyclopaedia. Rather astrology is not part of the language of truth production within the language games of the natural sciences. With reference to Wittgenstein's private language argument, the scientific application that includes horoscopes has become like a private language within a specific field. However, within a different epistemic field it is still part of that local language game.

Let us now turn to episteme and performatives. Following Bourdieu and Wittgenstein, I am arguing that an *epistemic field* constitutes a language game, which has its specific rules of felicity and infelicity. These language games constitute epistemic communities within the larger episteme. Arguably, these local language games are the conceptual equivalent of what Foucault meant by *discourse formations* (Foucault 1989: 31–40). However, I am giving them a more transepistemic (transiting the Renaissance, Classical and Modern) quality than Foucault did.

What is sayable within an episteme is not driven by some kind of structural determinism that makes social actors into cultural dupes. It is perfectly possible for someone to make an application to a scientific institution based upon astrology, thus structuring a neo-Renaissance system of meaning. However, such an act of structuration will not be confirm-structured by other natural scientists. The knowledge of which acts of structuration are most likely to be confirm-structured within a field is a consequence of reflexive monitoring of action, and an understanding of the structuring principles of the field. To take a different, if anecdotal, example: recently, an environmental biologist assured me that in his academic field any reference to aesthetics, such as stating that a biological habitat was beautiful, would be considered infelicitous. An article containing such an infelicitous observation would automatically be rejected. Yet, such observations are felicitous within other fields.

These local language games are linked to truth, but enunciability is not the same as truth. Austin explained performatives (1975: 23–4) using a thought experiment in which he imagines himself walking down the docks, idly passing time, and stumbling upon a newly built vessel, which is fully prepared for the Queen of England to name her the QE 2. However, as there is no one around, Austin mischievously sneaks in ahead of the Queen and smashes the champagne bottle against the bow of the ship and declares 'I name this ship the Joseph Stalin'. He asks himself the question, has the ship been named? And the answer is no, because no one will recognise the validity of Austin's performance even though his action may be identical to the one about to be performed by the Queen. His action of naming the ship is considered infelicitous. Austin adds that this is like marriage to a monkey.

Again, what Austin did in naming the ship, or marriage to a monkey, make sense, but they are not *valid* actions. Yet, this validity is qualitatively different from the question of truth. These are acts of structuration that are not confirm-structured. They are sayable in the literal sense, yet saying them, or performing them, does not reproduce meaning. Theoretically, they are a private language act. What lies within the condition of possibility of felicitous acts is not set in stone. For thousands of years, Western civilization has refused to recognise marriage between same-sex couples. Yet, this is changing as a consequence of a long battle for equality by the gay community. That success was achieved through repeated performative acts, such as gay rights parades. These acts of structuration were a method of consensus building around a new set of social structures, which eventually were confirm-structured.

In this account of performatives, Austin suggests that performatives are specific types of ceremonial acts. I am extending this by arguing that all meaning is performative. When we speak we perform acts of structuration, which may, or which may not, receive validation or confirm-structuration from others. Not receiving validation, thus speaking a private language, is a form of exclusion of meaning. Conflict *over* the validity of meaning is qualitatively different from the conflicts that take place *within* a system of meaning, which gives us two different kinds of conflict. To see this point, compare the following three explanations of a particular storm that took place somewhere: 1) the storm was caused by an intense anti-cyclone; 2) the storm was caused by an intense cyclone; 3) the storm was caused by the wrath of the Gods. One and two are part of the language game of modern meterology, even though the second one is most likely false—storms are usually caused by anti-cyclones, although cyclones can generate high winds. So, for the sake of argument, let us say that number one is the truth. Still, number two can be engaged with, thus is considered a legitimate statement within the local language game. In contrast, number three is outside the conditions of possibility of felicitous action. Number one is both felicitous and true; two is felicitous but false. In contrast, the third is not playable within the language game, consequently not worthy of being engaged with. It is false and infelicitous.

In the transition from the Renaissance, resemblance moves into category three within the language game of the natural sciences, but still has category one and two status among astrologers. Astrologers have a serious debate about the characteristics of Gemini and so on. Similarly, a homeopathist's statement concerning the 'memory of water' will be a category one or two statement within their field but will be dismissed as infelicitous by the field of conventional science.

An episteme, or system of thought for any period, or civilization, consists of various overlapping and intersecting fields, which are local language games. Within each field certain statements qualify as felicitous while others do not. History is, in part, a struggle over the sayable. It is important to understand that social actors can be immensely creative in coming up with new meanings but such innovative structuration practices are entirely useless as levers of power and agency unless they meet with confirming structuration from others.

Social actors that refuse to collaborate with novel or inappropriate structuration do two things at once. They maintain their social capital, and simultaneously retain the systemic stability. If scientists do not recognise resemblances as a valid method, they are both keeping the scientific disciplines intact, by excluding the unthinkable, and unreasonable, and they are maintaining the value of the scientific currency in which they have invested cultural capital. To those who are excluded, this may appear an act of domination, as it reflects the interests of those with capital in that field. However, to those doing the excluding, their action represents a disinterested act of maintaining the field, which is a condition of possibility for meaningful dialogue and exchange within that field. Both interpretations are correct, and simply reflect different vantage points upon the same process.

Let us now consider episteme and reason. Foucault observes that critiquing a particular system of thought through reason is a futile exercise (Foucault 1982: 210). This is because the common language of an episteme gives actors a sense of what is considered reasonable. Reasonable in this case is not the same as rational, or true. A statement can be incorrect, and flawed in many ways, yet still be considered reasonable within the language game of a speaking community, as we saw with statement two in the weather example.

Reasonableness provides society with one of the most powerful tools of internal compulsion, which underlies the power of structural constraint. In understanding what the act of voting means, the social actor also recognises that it is only *reasonable* to concede defeat if your party has fewer votes than the other party. In US Presidential elections, custom has it that the new President is deemed to have won when his or her opponent concedes defeat. Why does the person with fewer votes concede defeat, when to do so is against their interests? Typically they do so out of an epistemic sense that not to do so would be considered entirely unreasonable.

In his discussion of liberal democratic society Rawls discusses the necessity for all conflicts within such a society to be between *reasonable*

comprehensive world-views. However, he recognises that because of pluralism of comprehensive doctrines, it 'is not surprising' that there are 'always
many unreasonable views'. This is followed by a footnote in which he as-
serts that liberal democrats have 'the practical task of constraining them—
like war and disease—so that they do not overturn political justice' (Rawls
1993: 64). Note the words *war* and *disease*: they are not something that can
be engaged with, which means they must not be confirm-structured. This
type of exclusion is of normative concern (Mouffe 2000). Yet, constraint is
a precondition of agency.

Democrats often state that they never negotiate with terrorists. What
is the harm in negotiating with terrorists? From the perspective of those
refusing to negotiate, they are refusing to engage with a certain discourse
and thus to validate it. It is not that they do not understand the terrorist,
but that they will not confirm-structure certain social structures. This is
qualitatively different from the relationship between two different political viewpoints, say extreme left and right, within the field of what is
considered *reasonable* politics. The designation of someone as a *terrorist*,
or in some way unreasonable (*fundamentalists* are another unreasonable
group) is in itself a political act (one person's terrorist is another's freedom fighter).

In the case of, so-called, terrorists, it is noteworthy that this refusal to
confirm-structure the other is often accompanied by back-channel negotia-
tions that are deemed 'secret'. This means talking to terrorists while publi-
cally pretending not to do so. This is a way of achieving shared goals with
those who are deemed excluded, without confirm-structuring infelicitous
(relative to the field of democracy) structuration practices.

The political act of exclusion, by refusal to confirm-structure, is a form
of domination (although not all domination is normatively reprehensible).
Persons who find themselves outside the realm of the reasonable are powerless, speaking what others insist is a private language. In *Madness and
Civilization*, and in *Discipline and Punish*, Foucault argues that for those
deemed *mad* or *deviant*, the only way to overcome their relative powerlessness is to affirm the discourse of reason. He (or she) 'is obliged to objectify
himself in the eyes of reason' (Foucault 1971: 249). Foucault attributes this
to the discourse of modernity. However, this is actually more fundamental
than that. If you look to the heresy trials of the Mediaeval period, you find a
boundary-setting exercise between that which can be engaged with and that
which cannot. In this regard, atheism had a special pride of place, beyond
the reasonable (Berman 1990).

Epistemic boundary maintenance between the reasonable and unreasonable takes place because social actors either cannot understand the
structuration of the other, or they can understand but consider that confirm-
structuring implies legitimation of an alternative reason. I would argue that
this is at the theoretical core of the difference between *agonism* and *antagonism* (Foucault 1982 and Mouffe 2000). *Agonism* is a conflict that includes

willingness to engage with the structuration practices of others, while *antagonism* is a deeper conflict in which confirming structuration is refused.

Social life entails two levels of conflict: those that take place within a shared set of structural constraints and those that reject those constraints. The deeper conflict, the more coercion is required. Obviously, these are ideal types and on a scale. For instance, fighting armies may conduct themselves according to shared *rules of war*, which means that there is some shared structuration and confirming structuration, within a wider context of violence and coercion.

Foucault argues that he reverses Clausewitz's assertion that war is politics continued by other means (Foucault 1980: 9). Foucault accepts that it is 'true that power puts an end to war, that it installs, or tries to install, the reign of peace in civil society' (Foucault 1980: 90). However, it does this by re-inscribing the rules of domination into a set of rules that are 'by no means designed to temper violence but rather to satisfy it' (Foucault 1977: 150). This is consistent with the idea of some structuration practices being validated and others not.

Foucault insists that we must cease to think of power in negative terms, that it represses, or that it conceals. 'In fact power produces, it produces reality: it produces domains and rituals of truth' (Foucault 1979: 194). I would argue that as all structural reproduction (re-)creates meaning, then the structuring of social life is an act of world creation, which structures the rules of the game. Specific meanings and episteme are a form of world creation, and also the creation of a set of rules of the game that make some forms of domination legitimate. Typically this constitutes a re-inscription of inequalities into an episteme (see Foucault 1980: 90). However, these processes can also have empowering and egalitarian outcomes, which is a point that is not sufficiently acknowledged by Foucault. The re-inscription of conflict into power can include egalitarian rules of the game, such as the democratic process (see Haugaard 2015).

As power and violence are opposed, this re-inscription of war, or violence, into an epistemic set of rules can have normatively desirable consequences. In order to illustrate this point, I will quote from a recent BBC commentary upon the recent Argentinian and Venezuelan Presidential elections:

> The positive aspect of the recent elections has been the willingness of the ruling parties in both Argentina and Venezuela to accept defeat.
>
> Despite Cristina Fernandez de Kirchner's obvious animosity towards Mr Macri, there was a *smooth handover of power* in December 2015, something that has been rare in Argentine politics over the past 50 years.
>
> And in Venezuela, President Maduro accepted what he termed 'adverse results' in the elections.
>
> Nicolas Maduro accepted defeat and said 'the constitution and democracy have triumphed'.
>
> (BBC 2016)

Note that de Kirchner has 'obvious animosity' towards Mr. Macri: they are engaged in conflict. And, in the history of Argentina, the outcome of such conflict is usually settled by coercion, but not in this case, as they decide to do something which is rare in Argentinian politics, which is to go for a smooth handover of power. This means non-violent power prevails, according to the rules of the democratic game. Similarly, Maduro, the defeated party, observes that democracy has triumphed. In other words, the structures of the game are more important than the conflicting goals. Antagonism is replaced by agonism.

It is important to understand that by pointing out that the democratic rules of the game are based upon consent over meaning, I am *not* going to the opposite end of the spectrum by arguing that this means that all democratic rules are necessarily just or fair, nor am I putting forward some kind of crypto-Lockean normative argument concerning consent (Locke 1924). Our meanings are *usually* not created under conditions of ideal speech (Habermas 1984). Rather, the social construction of meaning is the consequence of struggle and exclusion. Thus, it will most likely embody bias in favour of one group and against another. However, this is not intrinsically the case. Furthermore, from a normative perspective there is an inherent gain in converting conflict from violence to power, even if perfect fairness and equality are not achieved. Violence is avoided, and the less powerful are treated as social actors, not objects that are repositories of pain. Even if this is not full recognition (Honneth 1995), it is on that scale.

Finally, in this section consider the question of epistemic truth. In the pre-modern world, the greatest fear was anarchy, which was characterised as the work of the devil. Given the constructedness of social life, that is not an illogical fear. If the basic formula for social life is that X counts as Y in circumstances C: how do social actors establish that it is part of the natural order of things that an X is a Y? Foucault's practice of genealogy is a way of encouraging such questioning of perception by attempting to make people understand that 'that-which-is has not always been' and that since these things have been made, therefore they 'can be unmade' (Foucault 1988: 37). Why is it not more common for people to see that these things can be unmade? Is it simply a question of natural attitude or are there other reasons?

Foucault begins *Madness and Civilization* by juxtaposing the modern exclusion of madness with that of leprosy in the medieval world (Foucault 1971). A more appropriate juxtaposition would be between *madness* and *heresy* or *atheism*. The most effective way of establishing a link between X and Y is to claim that it is an intrinsic relationship. In other words, conventionality must be denied. Reification is the process whereby that which is *social*, thus conventional and constructed, is somehow linked to what is considered the non-social. In the pre-modern world, the most effective reification was an appeal to the divine. Durkheim (2008) suggests that when humans worship God, they are in fact worshipping society itself. The norms of society, which are conventional, are projected on to a deity and are reflected back as the will of God, who is considered a transcendental repository of infinite wisdom. Once reified through God, these norms cannot simply be undone as mere arbitrary convention. Anyone with the temerity to contest the order of things is guilty of blasphemy. This is the ultimate form of unreason, which cannot be dialogued with, and which is punishable by death. In this regard, atheism is a particularly threatening form of blasphemy as the existence of the great reifier is denied altogether.

With the advent of the Enlightenment in Western Europe, the metaphysical death of God entails that for many the reifying function of God ceases to have purchase. Even if the majority have not become atheists, the emergence of a gradual live-and-let-live relationship between Protestants and Catholics, begun by the treaty of Westphalia of 1648, means that there is no longer a single un-disputed word of God to appeal to. In that sense, Christianity loses its monotheistic unifying function. Contemporaneous with this decline, there emerges a different way of reifying social convention: scientific truth (Haugaard 2012).

In theory a scientific experiment can be replicated infinitely in different cultures and societies with the same result. Consequently, just like the word of God, it stands beyond convention. If the Y designation can be linked to science, it is considered entirely unreasonable not to confirm-structure. From our vantage point, the conventionality of some of the early supposed scientific designations are relatively obvious, for instance: 'there were Krafft-Ebing's zoophiles and zooersts, Rohleder's auto-monosexualists; and later moxiscopophiles, gynecomasts, presbyophiles, sexoesthetic inverts, and dysparcunist women' (Foucault 1981: 43). In the mid-nineteenth century these were considered facts of the natural world in the manner of a Linnaean taxonomy of plants. Once classified, or diagnosed, according to Krafft-Ebing's conceptual vocabulary, the deviant is no longer guilty of *sin*, but has a *pathology*, which requires a cure (Oosterhuis 2012). Resisting the diagnosis is symptomatic of unreason as it equates to resisting truth, while cooperation with the diagnosis and cure become equated with reasonable behaviour. Co-operation delivers social participation and membership of the system, or social integration, while refusal means unreason, non-dialogue, and a lack of access to resources. Sociologically speaking, refusal means speaking a private language, thus exclusion and powerlessness. If this is not sufficient to persuade participation, then there is always coercion—the padded cell.

The Fourth Dimension of Power

We concluded our discussion of the third dimension of power with the observation that modernity entailed a shift in reification, from deity to scientific truth. There is another aspect to this shift that Foucault picked up upon, which is a shift to the possibility of creating a new kind of social subject. Let us look at Foucault's own words on this:

This form of power applies itself to immediate everyday life which categorizes the individual, marks him by his own individuality, attaches
him to his own identity, imposes a law of truth on him which he must
recognize and which others have to recognize in him. It's a form of
power which makes individuals subjects. There are two meanings of the
word subject: subject to someone else by control and dependence, and
tied to his own identity by a conscience or self-knowledge. Both meanings suggest a form of power which subjugates and makes subject to.

(Foucault 1982: 212)

Here Foucault observes that the process of subjectification is not exceptional but mundane ('This form of power applies itself to immediate everyday life'). Foucault argues that subjectification constitutes a process that
categorises the individual ('which categorizes the individual'). The individual X becomes a Y carrier of meaning in a context C. This situates them
not just for others, but is also constitutive of their own sense of identity
('attaches him to his own identity'). This meaning marks the person's individuality, making them a particular being-in-the-world. Nor is it merely
an arbitrary social construction, but is represented as part of a regime of
truth ('imposes a law of truth'). This truth is used in this way because truth
is considered by social actors to exist beyond convention. This is not a
process of solipsistic self-discovery in which the individual 'discovers themselves' as a self-creative act. It constitutes an interactive process whereby
the individual recognises their subject position, or Yness, as perceived by
others, as context C ('which he must recognize and which others have to
recognize in him'). In this act of recognition, they become subject to someone else's normalising judgement. This constitutes a form of dependence
upon another as a validator of that subject identity and, consequently, that
other imposes upon them a form of control ('subject to someone else by
control and dependence'). Because the meaning imposed by another is not
external, but rather integral to identity, this act of knowing becomes a form
of self-knowledge which comes to define the person's perception of self
('and tied to his own identity by a conscience or self-knowledge'). These
overlapping elements constitute a form of power relationship in which the
person becomes both a subject and an object of knowledge. As an object,
they are subjected to the evaluation of others, thus constituting their subject position in society ('Both meanings suggest a form of power which
subjugates and makes subject to').

Let us return to our example of the child walking in the park, learning
the meaning of duck, geese and swan; the shaping of her episteme is not a
process that is separable from her constitution as a social subject. The child
that entered the park knowing only the word *bird* is not the same being-in-
the-world who leaves the park. Seeing the world in a certain way shapes her
social ontology. Hence, the third dimension of power feeds into the creation
of the fourth dimension.

In his critique of Foucault's model, Lukes argues that there is a tendency to equate power with socialization in general (Lukes 2005: 97). There is some truth in this, in the sense that all socialization entails subject formation. However, Foucault adds something new insofar as he alerts us to the way in which everyday socialization confers differentials of power. Furthermore, he perceived that modernity entailed a unique form of subject creation, which was part of a wider epistemic shift.

The epistemic shift that allowed for a new form of subject creation was the, so-called, discovery of 'man' (Foucault 1970), or the human social subject. According to Foucault, in the previous episteme humans could classify the world but they themselves were absent from the scheme of classification. The order of things, which in their wisdom they deciphered, was external to them and reflected a pre-ordained order. At the end of the eighteenth century a shift occurred with the discovery of the human subject as a living entity. This living subject is busy classifying the world, and is also part of their scheme of classification. Kant's discussion of a priori knowledge is paradigmatic: as humans look at the world they order it, for instance, by imposing time and space upon it (Kant 2003: 79–82). Humans are finite beings that have to limit the world by imposing categories upon it. Truth now moves from an external order, made by God, and discovered by the human subject, into an order that is the consequence of human activity and finitude. In this manner the death of God is replaced by the birth of humans as living interpretative beings.

If the human subject is the source of truth, then it matters what kind of human we are. The living, labouring and interpreting social subjects must conform to norms of truth. How do we discover these norms? We study humans to find the norms. Armed with that knowledge, we can then, in turn, normalise those subjects who fall outside established norms. Thus humans as living beings become both the subject and objects of truth. The subject-object insight required a subject-object studying and correctional device, the metaphorical representation of which is Bentham's plan for the Panopticon (Foucault 1979: 195–228). The Panopticon was conceived as a general plan that could be used as a blueprint for a number of institutions, including factories, schools and prisons. A series of cells, or work-stations, were placed around a central observation point. If possible, this was designed so that observation went one-way, from the observer to the observed. In Bentham's proposed prison this was achieved through the use of mirrors and blinds, which represented the limits of eighteenth century technology. Obviously, today CCTV achieves the same effect more efficiently. The objective of this one-way dialogue is that those in the less powerful position do not have the possibility of defining the system of meaning. In the first instance, the observer can classify the object of observation, creating a system of classification. In schools, for instance, they define what makes X (children) a good Y1 (for instance, a diligent student) and what the class of deviations (Y2) are (inattentive students) (see Foucault 1979: 178).

The Panopticon was essentially a blueprint for a classification and a socialization machine. Bentham argued that children in Panopticon schools could be used for the purposes of experimental socialization. A number of X children can be introduced into Panopticon schools to make them different Y1s and Y2s and they can be compared. For instance, in one school they teach children that two and two make four, and the geological nature of the moon, while in another they can be taught that two and two make five, and that the moon is made of green cheese. Then these two types of social subjects can be introduced so that educationalists can observe how they interact (Foucault 1979: 204–6). This entails a veritable science of human socialization.

The use of light in the Panpticon is a metaphor for the observer-observed dyad, which ensures that the observed look at themselves through the eyes of the observer. Self-observation means self-reformation. In practice, many of the prisons and reformatories failed in their task, but that failure only served to confirm-structure the signifiers of the episteme. The recalcitrant failures demonstrated the truth of the perception that there exists a whole plethora of delinquents, or sociopaths, from which society needs to protect itself.

In his theory of nationalism, Gellner (1983) observes that the modern state is not only unique for its monopoly of coercion, but also for its attempted monopoly of socialization outside the home. The nineteenth century process of industrialization required a mass of people who spoke more or less the same language, and shared a similar set of dispositions. An industrialist in Glasgow could not run their factory with a workforce some of whom spoke some variety of Gaelic, or who had not internalised clock-time punctuality. For that to happen, schools had to be set up throughout Great Britain that taught standardised English and clock-time punctuality. Foucault emphasises that both panoptical schools and prisons pay close attention to punctuality and posture. Thus we have a new social subject being created who internalises clock-time and measured space as part of their habitus and hexis. As argued by Giddens and Mumford (Giddens 1981: 133), for the purposes of industrial production the clock is as important as the steam engine. To stand before a machine, working with exact precision, while being paid so-much per hour, is possible only with social subjects who have internalised measured time and space as the natural order of things and then made this episteme integral to their bodily dispositions.

The discovery of socialization as a mass state-sponsored project took place at a time when European society was becoming characterised by increasing-self-restraint due to a number of other social forces that are not discussed by Foucault. In the *Protestant Ethic and the Spirit of Capitalism*, Weber (1976) argues that the modern social subject of capitalism is in many respects a unique creature, who is an illogical creature relative to the norms of traditional society. In traditional society people work so that they can generate enough wealth for pleasure. In contrast, the successful capitalist is someone who pursues wealth as an end in itself. This process was triggered by puritan Protestantism, in which the faithful could not achieve assurance of God's grace through either religious ritual, mediated by the magical powers of priests, or by doing good works. This helplessness created massive ontological insecurity for these social subjects. In order to avoid temptation, inner peace was found in work. The only legitimate way to spend the fruits of that work was investment in more work. The absolute and relative time spent on religious devotion and commerce was carefully recorded and analysed. The efficiency of work, whether commercial or spiritual, was a defining issue for the Protestant capitalist (McKinlay & Mutch 2015). The unintended effect of otherworldly faith was a relentless pursuit of work which, over time, became interpreted as a possible sign of God's favour. The Protestant rejection of magic created a disenchanted world. The future of the early Protestants became linear and planned. Absence of hard work became time that is *wasted*. The days, the weeks and years moved from the cyclical ritual of traditional time to a new kind of time that was linear. This led to the evolution of a social subject who was instrumentally rational and capable of massive self-restraint, which was functional to industrial society.

This increasing self-restraint is also linked to another process; the transformation of social ontology associated with an increased repression of the emotions, which Elias (1994) referred to as the *civilizing process*. To simplify a rather complex account: Elias argued that over the last five hundred years, European social ontology has been subject to increasing self-restraint. Etiquette manuals from the sixteenth century reveal an exceptionally unrestrained habitus. At that time, these books were used by aristocrats as guides to 'good behaviour' at court. By the seventeenth century, similar advice is given to the bourgeoisie. However, by the eighteenth century they, too, have internalised self-restraint as a mark of 'civilized' behaviour. Throughout the nineteenth century the manners of the bourgeoisie filtered down to the proletariat. The explanation of this downward movement of self-restraint is attributable to competition for cultural capital. In the early period the aristocracy were attempting to distinguish themselves from the rising bourgeoisie by developing more complex manners as social capital. However, the bourgeoisie soon caught up and, over time, the process moved down the class hierarchy. Elias' account of this increasing self-restraint is mirrored in Foucault's account of modern sexuality. Foucault observes that the puritan nineteenth century sexual norms were imposed by the bourgeoisie upon themselves as the equivalent of the blue blood of the aristocracy (1981: 122). In other words, sexual self-restraint became cultural capital for the bourgeoisie.

The discipline of modern education is relentless. In modern education those who study the most, and defer pleasure in the short term, gain in terms of educational qualifications. In Willis' ethnographic account of working class kids, it was their desire to enjoy themselves, and inability to sit still for hours on end, that ensured that they became the next generation of blue collar workers (Willis 1977). Current emphasis upon the autonomy of the social subject is coupled with government of self, whereby actors are negatively free, yet there is action upon the action of self (Foucault 1982; Triantafillou 2012), which is a kind of positive freedom (Berlin 2002). Contemporary neoliberalism rests upon the strange contradiction of offering more freedom, and yet insisting upon more accountability, through (so-called) *performance indicators*, *best practice* and so on (Triantafillou 2012). The new social subject is told to be free, but can only practice that freedom through constant self-surveillance according to bureaucratic criteria set out by expert committees.

In commenting upon the normative implications of this expansion of four-dimensional power, it is important to have a balanced position. With regard to subjectification, Foucault argued as follows: 'Maybe the target nowadays is not to discover what we are but to refuse what we are' (Foucault 1982: 216). This suggests that four-dimensional power is inherently normatively undesirable. By creating reliable subjects, whose predispositions are relatively predictable, four-dimensional power acts upon the actions of social subjects by making them predictable reproducers of social structure. While this undoubtedly increases negative freedom (Berlin 2002), it also increases agents' power-to by making social subjects more capable of interacting in complex organizational situations. An unpredictable social agent makes the combination of structuration and confirming structuration less likely. As Elias observes, a driver with the dispositions of a feudal knight would be incapable of negotiating contemporary city traffic (Elias 1994: 446).

With regard to normative criteria, the self-restrained subject of modernity is a condition of possibility for democratic and liberal society. Self-restraint is both constraining and enabling. In democratic elections, the loser has to have the self-restraint necessary to consent to losing, otherwise the system does not work.

Liberal principles also entail a universal way of thinking, where the position of self is viewed from the perspective of other. This is a form of panoptical self-surveillance. Our intuitive reaction to panopticism may be that it is inherently normatively reprehensible, which is the sense I get from Foucault (1979). Yet taking the position of the observing other is a predisposition that is important to modern liberal democracy. In Kantian terms, it is key to living according to general principles that can be universalised. A self-panopticising social subject internalises the self-restraint not to make an exception of self relative to the structuring principles of society. Thus universalizability becomes a principle of the actor's episteme (normatively desirable three dimensional power), and she will have the appropriate subject dispositions (four dimensional power) to live up to this. Consequently, deviation from these liberal principles becomes internalised as the height of unreasonableness. A self-panopticising social subject will have respect for the right of others to free speech even when they disagree with the use of that right because they try to imagine themselves as that other.

Yet, against that more normatively optimistic reading, there is also a pessimistic one, which Foucault had in mind when he specifically mentions the dangers of fascism and Stalinism (Foucault 1982: 209). The self-restrained modern social subject can easily be used as a bureaucratic social subject, who administers the world around them without reflection upon the consequences of their action. In a document recently made public, Adolf Eichmann appealed for clemency couched in terms of bureaucracy, authority and personal responsibility: 'There is a need to draw a line between the leaders responsible and the people like me forced to serve as mere instruments in the hands of the leaders, . . . I was not a responsible leader, and as such do not feel myself guilty' (*Guardian* 2016). While I do not consider this an entirely justified claim in the case of Eichmann, Arendt (1977) suggested a similar argument when she coined the term 'banality of evil'. She argued that once Eichmann was given the task of cleansing Germany of Jews, he undertook the task primarily in terms of bureaucratic means-ends rationality. None of this is an excuse for the horrors that Eichmann inflicted. However, once a bureaucrat is set a task, an intrinsic part of efficiency is to distance your personal and emotional habitus from the goal. You do not have to be an anti-Semite to carry out orders that contribute to the Holocaust. Following orders, and detachment, can be a sufficient condition for the creation of a bureaucratic machine that realises normatively objectionable objectives set by others. As argued by Bauman (1989), the Holocaust and modernity go together. Once the self-restrained modern social subject has been created, they can methodologically bracket their own values and emotions in order to be efficient in carrying out whatever task is set for them.

Conclusion

The evolution of the modern forms of the four dimensions of power has both normatively desirable and undesirable aspects. The change delivers the conditions of possibility for running an internally peaceful society based upon abstract principles of justice. But it also creates the conditions of possibility for a bureaucratic nightmare, which can kill, or (which may be just as normatively objectionable) has no objectives whatsoever aside from the reproduction of an organizational system as an end in itself. The latter is what Arendt aptly called 'government by nobody' (Arendt 1970: 38). This is a special kind of nightmare that haunts what Elias would term *civilized* societies.

References

Allen, A. (1999), *The Power of Feminist Theory: Domination, Resistance, Solidarity*, Boulder, CO: Westview Press.
Arendt, H. (1970), *On Violence*, London: Penguin.
Arendt, H. (1977), *Eichmann in Jerusalem: A Report on the Banality of Evil*, London: Penguin.
Austin, J. L. (1975), *How to Do Things With Words*, Oxford: Clarendon Press.
Bachrach, P. & Baratz, M. (1962), 'The Two Faces of Power', *American Political Science Review* 56/4: 947–952.

Baumann, Z. (1989), *Modernity and the Holocaust*, Cambridge: Polity.

BBC, (2016), "Latin America: The 'Pink Tide' Turns," Online: http://www.bbc.com/news/world-latin-america-35060390.

Berlin, I. (2002), 'Two Concepts of Liberty', in H. Hardy (ed.), *Liberty*, Oxford: Oxford University Press.

Berman, D. (1990), *A History of Atheism in Britain: From Hobbes to Russell*, London: Routledge.

Bourdieu, P. (1986), 'The Forms of Capital', in J. Richardson (ed.), *Handbook of Theory and Research for the Sociology of Education*, New York: Greenwood.

Bourdieu, P. (1990), *In Other Words: Essays Towards a Reflexive Sociology*, Cambridge: Polity.

Chomsky N. & Foucault, M. (2011), *Human Nature: Justice Versus Power: The Chomsky-Foucault Debate*, London: Souvenir Press.

Dahl, R. (1957), 'The Concept of Power', *Behavioural Science* 2/3: 201–215.

Durkheim, E. (2008), *The Elementary Forms of Religious Life*, Oxford: Oxford University Press.

Elias, N. (1994), *The Civilizing Process*, Oxford: Basil Blackwell.

Foucault, M. (1970), *The Order of Things*, London: Routledge.

Foucault, M. (1971), *Madness and Civilization: A History of Insanity in the Age of Reason*, London: Tavistock.

Foucault, Michel (1975) (ed.) I, Pierre Riviere, having slaughtered my mother, my sister and my brother . . . a case of parricide in the 19th century, Penguin, Harmondsworth.

Foucault, M. (1977), *Language, Counter-Memory, Practice: Selected Essays and Interviews*, edited by D. F. Bouchard, Ithaca, NY: Cornell University Press.

Foucault, Michel (1979), *Discipline and Punish: The Birth of the Prison*. Harmondsworth: Penguin.

Foucault, M. (1980), *Power Knowledge: Selected Interviews and Other Writings 1972–1977*, Brighton: Harvester Press.

Foucault, M. (1981), *The History of Sexuality Volume 1: An Introduction*, Harmondsworth: Penguin.

Foucault, M. (1982), 'The Subject and Power', in H. Dreyfus and P. Rabinow (eds), *Michel Foucault: Beyond Structuralism and Hermeneutics*, Brighton: Harvester Wheatsheaf.

Foucault Michel (1986), *The Use of Pleasure: The History of Sexuality Volume 2*, Penguin, Harmondsworth.

Foucault Michel (1988) (ed.) Lawrence D. Kritzman, *Michel Foucault: Politics, Philosophy*, Culture, Routledge, London.

Foucault, M. (1989), *The Archaeology of Knowledge*, London: Routledge.

Gellner, E. (1983), *Nations and Nationalism*, Oxford: Blackwell.

Giddens, A. (1981), *A Contemporary Critique of Historical Materialism: Vol. I, Power, Property and the State*, London: Palgrave Macmillan.

Giddens, A. (1984), *The Constitution of Society*, Cambridge: Polity.

The Guardian (2016), "Eichmann Claimed He Was 'a Mere Instrument' in Holocaust', 17 January 17, online: http://www.theguardian.com/world/2016/jan/27/eichmann-claimed-he-was-a-mere-instrument-in-holocaust-appeal-reveals.

Habermas, J. (1984), *The Theory of Communicative Action: Vol. I, Reason and the Rationalization of Society*, Cambridge: Polity.

Haugaard, Mark (1997), *The Constitution of Power*, Manchester: Manchester University Press.

Haugaard, M. (2008), 'Sociologial Lukes versus Moral Lukes: Reflections on the Second Edition of Power: A Radical View', *Journal of Power*: 99–106.

Haugaard, M. (2010), 'Power: A "Family Resemblance Concept"', *European Journal of Cultural Studies* 13/4: 419–138.

Haugaard, M. (2012), 'Power and Truth', *European Journal of Social Theory* 15/1: 73–92.

Haugaard, M. (2015), 'Concerted Power Over', *Constellations* 22/1: 147–158.

Haugaard, M. (2016), 'Two Types of Freedom and Four Dimensions of Power', *Revue Internationale de Philosophie*.

Hayward, C. & Lukes, S. (2008), 'Nobody to Shoot? Power, Structure and Agency: A Dialogue', *Journal of Power*, (now *Journal of Political Power*) 1/1: 5–20.

Honneth, A. (1995), *The Struggle for Recognition*, Cambridge: Polity.

Kant, I. (2003), *Critique of Pure Reason*, London: Palgrave Macmillan.

Kuhn, T. (1977), *The Essential Tension: Selected Studies in Scientific Thought and Change*, Chicago, IL: University of Chicago.

Locke, J. (1924), *Two Treatises of Government*, London: Everyman's Library.

Lukes, S. (1974), *Power: A Radical View*, London: Palgrave Macmillan.

Lukes, S. (2005), *Power: A Radical View*, second edition, Basingstoke: Palgrave Macmillan.

McKinlay, A. & Mutch, A. (2015), 'Accountable Creatures': Scottish Presbyterianism, Accountability and Managerial Capitalism', *Business History* 57/2: 241–256.

Morriss, P. (2002), *Power: A Philosophical Analysis*, second edition, Manchester: Manchester University Press.

Mouffe, C. (2000), *The Democratic Paradox*, London: Verso.

Oosterhuis, H. (2012), 'Sexual Modernity in the Works of Richard von Krafft-Ebing and Albert Moll', *Medical History* 56/2: 133–155.

Pensardi, P. (2012), 'Power to and Power Over: Two Distinct Concepts?' *Journal of Political Power* 5/1: 73–89.

Rawls, J. (1993), *Political Liberalism*, New York: Columbia University Press.

Sartre, J-P. (1969), *Being and Nothingness: An Essay on Phenomenological Ontology*, London: Methuen.

Schutz, A. (1967), *The Phenomenology of the Social World*, Evanston, IL: Northerwestern University Press.

Scott James C. (1990), *Domination and the Arts of Resistance: Hidden Transcripts*. New Haven: Yale University Press.

Searle, J. (1996), *The Construction of Social Reality*, London: Penguin.

Triantafillou, P. (2012), *New Forms of Governing: A Foucauldian Inspired Analysis*, London: Palgrave Macmillan.

Weber, M. (1947), *The Theory of Social and Economic Organization*, New York: Free Press.

Weber, M. (1976), *The Protestant Ethic and The Spirit of Capitalism*, London: George Allen & Unwin.

Weber, M. (1991), *From Max Weber: Essays in Sociology*, edited by H. H. Gerth and C. Wright Mills, London: Routledge.

Willis, Paul (1977), *Learning to Labour*, Farnborough: Saxon House.

Wittgenstein, L. (1967), *Philosophical Investigations*. Oxford: Blackwell.

4 Liberal Governmentalities and the Heterotopic Behaviour of the Firm

Eric Pezet and Nelarine Cornelius

Introduction

Foucault studied the history of liberalism by analysing the changing role of the state's relationship with society. The state is studied not as an institution but from the perspective of the practice of government. Governmentality is the history of governmentalization of the state, that is to say the deployment of an action on the population. Foucault's historical approach led him to study three forms of liberalism: classical liberalism from the middle of the eighteenth century, European ordo-liberalism practiced in the twentieth century and the American libertarian liberalism that distinguishes itself from European liberalism by its 'rejection' of state government.

The firm is largely absent from Foucault's research. The workshop is mentioned in passing in *Discipline and Punish* but it is discussed in a similar vein to the prison, the hospital, and military barracks. This reference might suggest that the firm is the extension of state government, but overlooks Bentham's theory of government (1983), which provides a background to these practices. However, rather than a prolongation of political government, the firm is better considered as *heterotopic*. This concept, coined by Foucault in 1967, refers to a place, a *heterotopia*, in the society which is apart from everyday life and has its own relation to time and space. A heterotopia does not fight the state and its government but has its own logic, not only the logic of government, by creating a world apart. American neoliberalism affords a significant position for the firm in society through the valorisation of the entrepreneur and development of a vision of the world where heterotopias have a major role.

Libertarian liberalism, which scholars such as Robert Nozick and Ayn Rand represent, is a survivalist liberalism. Libertarian liberalism theorises the defence of individual freedom by entrepreneurs: they view their aim as the mitigation of the actions of state and its institutions. The firm is the place of wealth creation, but it is also a place of resistance. The firm adopts heterotopic behaviour in relation to the state. It has its own relationship to space and time. The firm is involved in a power struggle with the state that the state addresses by undertaking diplomatic relations with firms. Foucault described the classic liberal government as the art of balancing forces. In practice, it signalled the break that appeared in the early eighteenth century between pastoral government and liberal government. In survivalist neoliberalism, however, fully concentrated on the containment of state, government is not a balancing of forces but the result of the encounter between managerial heterotopism and the state.

Liberalism and Heterotopias

State government, which first announced and then exemplified modernity, introduced a break with pastoral government. In the pastorate, there 'had to be a taught truth. In the system of truth of the pastorate, the pastor had to know [what was going on] in his community. Then each of the pastor's sheep had to discover a truth in himself that he brings to light and which the pastor is, if not the judge and guardian, then at least is the constant witness' (Foucault 2009: 273). When the state replaced the pastor, the rationality of following state government was no longer truth but state reasoning: *raison d'etat*. 'The state', Foucault continues, 'is organized only by reference to itself. No positive law, of course no moral or natural law, and in the end perhaps no divine law . . . no law can be imposed on the state from outside' (Foucault 2009: 290).

In the sixteenth century, merchants petitioned the state to set the objectives of accumulation of wealth and the creation of police in order to protect mercantile interests. Thus the art of government then consisted of 'manipulating, maintaining, distributing and re-establishing relations of force whithin a space of competition that entailed competitive growth. In other words, the art of government is deployed in a field of relations of forces' (Foucault 2009: 312). Crucially, from the seventeenth century, the state assumes—or develops—its role as providing security for the population as a whole, not just for the sovereign. This is delivered by the police, or, more generally, a range of institutions 'by which the state's forces can be increased while preserving the state in good order' (Foucault 2007: 313). It is through the police that the state creates order between forces that constitute society (which, of course, extends beyond the common usage of a constabulary). In France, Nicolas Delamare's text about the practice of the police notes that Foucault 'specifies thirteen domains with which they must be concerned; these are religion, morals, health and subsistence, public peace, the care of buildings, squares and highways, sciences and liberal arts, commerce, manufacture and the mechanical arts, servants and labourers, theatres, games and the care and discipline of the poor, as a "considerable part of the public good"' (Foucault 2009: 334). To be acknowledged as legitimate, the state must develop diplomacy *vis-à-vis* other states. Within the interior of the country, the state must deploy police to balance the forces at work in society. From the middle of the seventeenth century, the economy influences the *raison d'etat*. The state must govern a numerous population to be prosperous.

Liberal govermentality is a critique of the governmentality of the state of police which rules competition between strengths internal to society (Senellart 2003: 39). From the eighteenth century, 'the regulatory control of the territory and subjects that still characterise the seventeenth century police must clearly be called into question, and there will now be a sort of double system. On the one hand will be a whole series of mechanisms that fall within the province of the economy and the management of the population with the function of increasing the forces of the state. On the other hand there will be the apparatus or instruments for insuring the prevention or repression of disorder, irregularities, illegality, and delinquency' (Foucault 2009: 353). A liberal government is a government that limits state government. Economics replaces law as governemental rationality. The economic art of government presupposes a frugal state. Markets are no longer purely a place of exchange: it also becomes a place of justice and truth, a system of 'regulation, just price and sanction of fraud' (Foucault 2008: 31).

In the twentieth century, German ordoliberalism was born from the Weimar Republic, the crisis of 1929 and Nazism. The legal sovereignty of the state no longer served as the founding principle of the state: in other words, it is not law that comprises the foundations of the state but economic freedom and the market, with economic performance the sign of harmony in society. A policy is social when it allows everyone to acquire property and benefit from a state endorsed insurance system. The firm is at the centre of ordogovernmentality and the role of government is to support and encourage competition, including the fight against monopolies. Competition is not seen as a natural phenomenon, it has to be organised and is a central aim of ordoliberal governmentality. The firm is not described precisely. It is mainly a way of being present in the market. The firm is an activity which enters into competition. Foucault mentions the importance of a history of the notion of the entrepreneur and the enterprise but does not develop it (Foucault 2008: 160).

Enterprises are central in ordoliberalism: they have a function which needs to be protected through the maintenance of competition. Entrerprise is the manifestation of a personal project that finds its expression in the market. Enterprise is a space which is not analysed. Foucault does not differentiate between the individual entrepreneur and the firm, probably because his reference is Wilhelm Ropke, who refers to *non proletarian industry*, such as craft industries and small businesses (Foucault 2008: 147). Foucault focuses on the logic of government, which is the regulation of the relationship between entreprises because 'if you multiply enterprises you multiply frictions, environmental effects' (Foucault 2008: 175) and need more instances of arbitration. Enterprises have a function in society. What is important is to maintain competition more than rule their internal functioning. They are, with regard to the state, what we call heterotopic entities.

States and Heterotopias

Historically, the liberal state was not all powerful and did not govern without competition. In the nineteenth century with the rise of nation states, social entities—communities, professions, advocacy organizations—both faced and resisted the governement by the state. In his work on classical liberalism, Foucault indicates that Italy had another modality of relationship between the state and specific organizations. Foucault observes that some entities—such as the Church, the Mafia and so on—have a diplomatic relation with the state. These entities are places that *self-regulate*. For Foucault, Italy has always been a diplomatic state, 'that is to say, a set of plural forces between which an equilibrium mus be established, between political parties, trade unions, clienteles, the church, the North, the South, the mafia, and so on, which resulted in Italy beeing a state of diplomacy without being a state of police' (Foucault 2009: 317). These entities were *governmental* entities in the sense that they are collective entities, that they ruled the life of people and had their own purpose, their own relation to time and created distinct spaces, and pursued their own project and interests. They could also threaten the state. The Mafia challenges the law; the Church might contest the authority of the state; the unions contest social order. The diplomatic relations between these organizations and the state are relations of negotiation, which means that there is a relation of strengh. This relation is different to that described through the role of police in society. What is at stake for the state is not to find an equilibrium between forces. It is much more to be convincing enough and strong enough to find an agreement with an array of entities.

The very existence of these entities establish the limits—and partly define the function—of the modern state. Foucault's analysis is limited and has, perhaps, led to an underestimation of the influence of their behaviour on governmental practicies of the liberal state. Foucault developed a concept that can account for the behaviour of these organizations towards the state. This is the concept of heterotopia: we will refer to them as *heterotopic entities*. Heterotopias are other sources of normativity, places largely beyond the reach of political power. Heterotopic behaviour is when an entity has the characteristics of a heteropia. Behaviour, actions and observable feelings can be intrinsic to the entity. The Church in Italy is here to implement on earth the kingdom of God. It intrisically challenges the state. The Mafia does not accept the rule of law for its own organization: it uses the law and flouts laws when convenient. A behaviour can also be progressively acquired to face a situation, to achieve a new target. A behaviour can be called heterotopic when it is developed to create, build and protect a space. This behaviour is not rare, or even exceptional. As Foucault states: 'We live inside a set of relations that delineates sites which are irreducible to one another and absolutely not super-imposable on one another' (Foucault 1967: 3). The heterotopic entity creates 'another real space, as perfect, as meticulous, as well arranged as ours is messy, ill constructed, and jumbled' (Foucault 1967: 8). The space defined by a heterotopic organization is not a public space: you cannot freely enter into heterotopias. 'Either the entry is compulsory, as in the case of entering a barracks or a prison, or else the individual has to submit to rites and purifications' (Foucault 1967: 7). More than a decade before he wrote about the total institution of the prison he defined them as a form of heterotopia. When we consider the entities mentioned by Foucault to illustrate the diplomatic activites of the state, we observe that these entities are not *of* the state, but have to protect their space, define their knowledge base and assert their autonomy. Heterotopias co-operate with, fight and resist the state. The existence of heterotopias compels the state to adopt and develop diplomatic behaviour with all sorts of institutions that are irreducible to the state.

Heterotopic behaviour also creates a specific relation to time. Heterotopic entities are heterochronic, they tend to have their own time frames, different from the one occurring within social or political society: further, they redefine space as well as time. Heterotopic entities conduct people to 'arrive at a sort of absolute break with their traditional time' (Foucault 1967: 6). For the Church the focus is eternity; for politicians, the five-year election cycle; for the firm, the annual return on capital, and so on.

Diplomatic relations are reinforced as heterotopic behaviour is more sustainable, as it has a function in society. This function may change over time: 'Each heterotopia has a precise and determined function within a society and at the same time heterotopias can, according to the synchrony of the culture in which it occurs, have one function or another' (Foucault 1967: 5). This function can be created through permanent violence and threat (recall the Mafia), but it can disappear if the state challenges them, and triumphs. Italy is an example of the power of the Mafia against the state but also of the fight of the state against it. Thus, heterotopic behaviour comprises the maintenance of relationships with the state while maintaning distance from the influence of its police and rules. Heterotopic behaviour is perceived by the state as denoting the relative strength of social bodies, part of its diplomatic calculus. Furthermore, heterotopic behaviour involves the development of strategies to preserve independence from the state, especially regarding the organization of space and the structuration of time. For firms, we observe that the juridical framing of work-time length is central to social history and remains a source of contemporary conflict. In ordoliberalism, the heterotopic behaviour of the firm was nurtured by the state. The relation is not diplomatic in the same sense as it was for the Italian state of the ninettenth century: rather, the relationship is functional. In contrast, neoliberalism creates diplomatic relations between the state and the firm.

Libertarianism and the Heterotopic Behaviour of the Firm

Consistent with his historical methodology, Foucault describes libertarianism, focusing on the role of the state in this economic doctrine. Even if liberalism is 'the art of the least possible government', in European liberalism, the state governs (Foucault 2008: 28). In American liberalism, the state does not govern: libertarianism institutes a process of degovernmentalisation of the state. To degovernmentalise is to remove from the state its own logic of government. The logic of goverment comes from human rights or economic logic. This process of degovernmentalisation is reinforced as libertarians invite citizens to constantly resist the state when it encroaches on what are argued to be the perogatives of the society. It is an approach by which firm defends itself from the state.

Freedom in relation to the state is freedom to work and benefit from the revenue of that work, and a revenue is 'a product or return on a capital' (Foucault 2008: 224). Foucault observes that the economist Gary Becker notes that human capital produces satisfaction (Foucault 2008: 226). All together, human capital constitutes an 'abilites machine', a telling phrase that suggests cold calculation and therefore individuals become something less than fully human. The self, in this view, the object of an individual strategy: this includes good genetics, educational investment, time and care given by parents and the educational system, professionnal training (Foucault 2008: 229). An important issue in American neoliberal governementality is the nature of stimulations that increase the qualities of human capital. In libertarian capitalism, communities and associations are the places which are most effective for this. Foucault suggests that for libertarians, the economy influences the state by making politicians and national administration contain the actions of the state. By this reasoning, if the state is contained it affords more freedom for society: however, society is not only composed of individuals. It is composed of entities that have their own projects. Governing is the aim of the state; governing is a means to an end for the firm. The examples given by Foucault (Church, Mafia) are still present. Although business is missing from his list of examples it should not be overlooked.

Communities: The Social Substance of Libertarianism

Friedrich Hayek calls for the development of liberal utopias that can counter socialist utopias (Foucault 2008: 219). Nozick responds to Hayek's call for a liberal utopia by suggesting an ideal which could 'thrill the heart or inspire people to sacrifice or to struggle' (Nozick 1975: 297). Freedom is collectively exercised through communities where people share norms of living. Writing about libertarian society, Nozick describes an impossible world of innumerable utopias. These utopias are 'communities which people can enter if they are admitted, leave if they which to, shape according to their wishes. A society where utopian experimentation can be tried, different style of life can be lived and alternative visions of the good can be individually or jointly pursued'. We contend that utopia is based on a project of alternative society while libertarianism is based on projects that include a resistance dimension to the state. It is unlike socialist utopias that strive to develop a prototype of a new society. However, libertarianism is not strictly based on utopias but on heterotopias. The aim is to develop associative projects on a platform of constant vigilance towards the state. This constant vigilance and this readiness to resist the expansion of state administration affords American liberalism a survivalist dimension.

Nozick argues that in the real world utopias have difficulties to become real for several reasons: 'In the actual world communities impinge upon one another, creating problems of realtions and self defence, necessitating modes of adjudicating and dispute resolution between communities', and further, that 'there are information costs in finding out what other communities there are, and what they are like, and moving and travel costs in going from one community to another', as 'some communities may try to keep some of their members ignorant of the nature of alternative communities they might join to try to prevent them from leaving their communitu to join another. This raises the problem of how freedom of movement is to be intitutionalized and enforces whent there are some who will wish to restrict it' (Nozick 1975: 307–8). The experiments of living represented by these manifold utopian projects are provided by the environment. For Nozick, the liberal utopia is a meta-utopia, a general social environment: 'utopia is meta utopia: the environment in which utopian experiments may be tried out' (Nozick 1975: 312). Thus, communities have to protect themselves from the dominant agency which is represented as the state. The difficult existence of experimental communities makes this libertarianism survivalist, where resitance to a hostile environment is an essential part of everyday life, perhaps a necessary part of the utopian project itself.

Nozick cannot completely avoid consideration of the firm but—curiously—he does not present it as a utopia. He gives a rather negative appreciation saying that it a place where individuals can lose their self-esteem and that they endure 'a long period of being frequently ordered about and under the authorithy of others, unselected by you, lowers your self-esteem and makes you feel inferior' (Nozick 1975: 246). Furthermore, work is not necessarily constructive: that is to say meaningful and satisfying. Meaningful and satisfying work is associated with self-esteem. And provides 'opportunity to exercise one's talents and capacities, to face challenges, and situations that require independent initiative and self direction (and which therfore is not boring and repetitive work), in an activity thought to be of worth by the individuals involved, in which he understands the role his activity plays in the achievement of some overall goal and such that sometimes in deciding upon his activity he has to take into account something about the larger process in which he acts' (Nozick 1975: 247). Nozick underlines the contradictions of the firm with respect to freedom. It is a place where democracy can be experienced but also a place where self-esteem can be lost. Therefore, competition between firms is not organised by the state, it is implemented by individuals themselves who will search for democratic structure, which provides them with self-esteem and satisfaction. A solution is to provide internally democratic structures (Nozick 1975: 250). People will choose firms where they are offered constructive work.

To illustrate how communities resist the state and its intitutions, Nozick refers to Ayn Rand's novel *Atlas Shrugged* (Rand 2007). According to Nozick, Rand's novel illustrates a stable organization where 'a diversity of persons with a diversity of excellences and talents, each benefiting from living with the others, each being of great use and delight to the others, complementing them' (Nozick 1975: 306). Rand's novel describes the heterotopic behaviour of the firm in a neoliberal environment and how entrepreneurs can resist the state.

Rand's novel is saturated with cold war tropes and in which any collective action was equated with socialism and so to be combatted. Nozick's reference gives it a new perspective: the entrepreneur not only mans the ramparts against socialism but, above all, is the vigilant hero who fights against any trace of collectivism in the state's behaviour. This world is defended from the state by heroes who do not make any concessions to the altruistic world. They can do this because entrepreneurs are protected from any temptation of collectivism by their egoistic state of mind. Indeed, in her novel Rand is less concerned with the heterotopic functioning of the firm than the heterotopic behaviour of business people. This is captured also in the title of the novel that refers to the ancient Greek myth of Atlas. Rand highlights the resistance of business men and women, through the device of industrial action, the strike, as the main vehicle for the narrative. Indeed, strike—La Greve—was retained as the title for the Francophone edition of the book. The business people use the workers' strategy of the strike to pressurise the state. This is how the entrepreneurs confront and constrain the state.

The novel is set during a deep economic depression that strikes the United States. Colorado, which is still an industrial centre, needs a train service. Dagny Taggart (female) is one of the main characters, and President of Taggart Transcontinental. Dagny wants to build a railway line, the Rio Norte line, using an innovative metal created and produced by Hank Rearden. She also tries to deliver a new technology for the motor. However, the American government wants to force business people to sell their inventions through the State Science Institute, and establishes legislation which limits the development of companies in specific sectors: and so effectively nationalises the railroad industry. Many industialists retire or simply mysteriously disappear. Dagny finds the Hidden Valley where many industrialists had taken refuge. The leader of *Atlantis*—the hidden valley—John Galt, is an engineer, and the inventor of the innovative technology that Dagny wants to use for her engines. Not all business people are resisters. James Taggart, for example, Dagny's brother, uses the advantages that give him proximity to government to weaken his competitors. Some of the industrialists in Atlantis challenge the government by becoming activists: they organise workers to defend the mills, they speak on the radio and call for resistance. John Galt's speech so alarmed the government that it tries to forge an alliance with him. When diplomacy fails, however, the state captures and tortures Galt. John Galt is freed by his companions and they defeat the government. Anarchy is not what they want, however. Their objective it to force the state to consider their fate and to engage in diplomatic behaviour with them, in constrast to the state's previously domineering posture.

Rand shows that liberalism calls for heroes and, as Minsaas (2007) underlines, she describes them by referring to three myths where individuals face the gods. The first myth is that of the Titan Atlas, who is condemned to carry the world on his shoulders. Another myth is that of Prometheus, who defies divine authority but also possesses forethought (Minsaas 2007: 133). The third is that of Phaëthon, the son of Helios, through the frequent reference to Richard Halley's *Concerto of Deliverance*, or Fifth Concerto. In that concerto, contrary to Greek mythology, Phaëthon succeeds in driving his father's chariot (Minsaas 2007: 133). Dagny Taggart is inspired by this concerto, which gives her courage and serenity during difficult times. The concerto, where the myth itself is distorted, appears to be the mood music of this *liberal survivalist* revolution. A myth can transmit an eternal truth. In Rand's novel, through their courage, entrepreneurs make the world work. The hero is somebody who is admired for her courage but she is also somebody who knows the truth, who know how success and happiness can be obtained. The relationship between reader and the hero is intended to be a very emotional one: exemplified by the love that develops between John Galt and Dagny Taggart. They are viewed as visionaries who have to face the hypocrisy of civil servants. By ceasing to support the world, business people hinder the world. The world is impossible without entreprenerus, for only they know the truth about how to achieve prosperity and happiness. Like Nozick, Rand refers to a utopia, the city of Atlantis, that Plato describes in *Timaeus*. Rand presents Atlantis as a real, tangible place of resistance. John Galt builds a city, independent from state, protected from government: an alternative world to the state. Separation can only be overcome through diplomacy. By referring to Greek myths, Rand underlines the uchronic dimension of the firm: it is a place where eternal truths can be seen. Thus, the firm is not not a utopia, it is a heterotopia. It is the place where resistance is possible and may be successful. It is a place where self-esteem can be developed. It is also a place governed by heroes who face adversity with courage. Only selfless self-interest can shape how we govern and how we are governed. Only entrepreneurs know how to proceed in times of uncertainty and only they can inspire admiration and devotion.

Libertarian Governmentality

The liberal behaviour of citizens and organizations is heterotopic behaviour towards the state. In other words, citizens develop their own projects towards space and time. The behaviour of liberal entities is heterotopic in that it aims to develop a programme, or spaces—such as Atlantis—with a temporality of their own, quite distinct from that of the state. For Foucault, heterotopias are linked to 'slices in times' and they 'begin to function at full capacity when men arrive at a sort of absolute break with their traditional time' (Foucault 1967: 6). Heterotopias can have their own time, different from that of the social or the polity. This is the idea of a place of all times that is itself outside of all times. The heterotopic time of the firm is that of innovation, organization and production.

The state is viewed as an agency which threatens the others agencies. The libertarian position towards the state is bellicose. The state is seen as so strong a threat that firms need to engage in survivalist behaviour. This analysis of liberalism can be enriched by studying the relationship between the state and the company because the company is one of the means by which citizens exercise their freedom and from which they defend themselves from the state. Robert Nozick's philosophy and Ayn Rand's novels are particularly interesting to study the entrepreneurial behaviour as heterotopic and survivalist. In American liberalism the purpose is to make people obtain the most they can from themselves (body, mind, social networks and so on): this capital is evaluated through work (acquisition of salaries, etc.), forms of capital which can be valued and realised through work. This individual work on the self is not necessarily undertaken through the channels offered by the state (e.g. through education). The investment in education for example can be made through communities: alternatives would include home schooling or private education, internships. Foucault distinguishes between 'private space and public space, between family space and social space, between cultural space and useful space, between the space of leisure and that of work' (Foucault 1967: 2). The firm is dedicated to deliver products and services to the market. The firm is a place where we work, quite different from places of leisure or culture. The firm is a space where the most productive possible organization of work, space and time is sought. Foucault's work on enterprise highlights its heterochronous nature. For those on the shopfloor, work is a division of time in sequences depending on the length of shifts, eight or twelve hours and so on. This division of time has effects on the social life of employees. The firm is a place that has an influence on those who labour there, that extends beyond their earnings.

There is a paradox in American liberalism. On the one hand, neoliberal economists promote a biopolitics which should make the individual self-improving. On the other hand, the institutionnal and political reality of the development of institutions make the entrepreneurial hero a central character. Liberalism is about individual freedom, but the hero is a central character of libertarianism. The association she commands should be ideally a democratic association but directed by somebody who is admired for his knowledge of the truth and capacity to protect communities from state aggression. In this survivalist liberalism, the paradox is that where degovernmentalisation of the state is a central consideration, people are governed in an archaic *pastoral* manner by heroes who understand, embody and embed the truth.

The Firm: The Generative Heterotopias of Liberalisms

A heterotopia always presupposes systems of opening and closing but maintains a contolled relationship with its environment. Heterotopias differ from public spaces: you cannot freely enter into heterotopias. There is a system of entering and closing between the firm and the state but there is also a reciprocal relationship. The relation between the firm and the state is about the way firms influence public policies. We focus here on the relations of the firm with the state and polical government from a governmentality perspective. We contend that ordoliberalism is primarily concerned with the implementation of law and regulation. In neoliberalism, the primary concern is the preservation of freedom from state interference and erosion of freedom.

Firms are an integral part of the social processes already in motion, and their relation to time defines them as a site of otherness to both real and utopian spaces. Firms exist outside the chronologies that dominate human life in real social space. Or, more precisely, the structure of disciplinary power implies an alternative relation to time, marked by the perpetual and indefinite accumulation of time, constituting a place of all time that is outside the realm of normal chronology. Firms can have their own time zone or even none at all. They can mark absolute breaks with traditional time, where time stands still. They can create spaces with their own rules, their own norms, their own spatialization and time. Yet, 'heterotopias are not random space, but is in a sense a great time machine, a contraption that is part vacuum and bellows, simultaneously gobbling and abolishing as it preserves and hoards cultural concepts of time and identity, all the while accumulating, suspending, converging, and compressing space and time in its vortex' (LaFever 2013: 60). They can organise several spaces that seem heterogeneous and incompatible into one other space. In addition to neoliberal heroism that makes manifest the heterotopic dimensions of the enterprise through the character of the hero, history also shows that even European, ordoliberalism faced the heterotopia. This encounter was not so much a confrontation, as in survivalist neoliberalism confronting the state, but rather a strategic game in which the state seeks to influence the firm and guide the heterotopia. What is striking is that firm has always adopted heterotopic behaviour.

Accounting History and the Heterotopic Behaviour of the Firm

Accounting history is one of the main disciplines that allows us to understand better liberalism in action. Accounting studies a key site of liberal capitalism, is where political knowledge and power is weak and where the liberal individual is formed, acted upon and in turn, acts. Accounting history has uncovered much about how people are governed in the firm (Hopwood 1987; Hopper & Macintosh 1998; Jackson & Carter 1998; McKinlay & Starkey 1998). The aspects of this kind of government are so numerous that their studies can be construed as a *complete* anthropological approach to liberalism.

Many public policies are oriented towards the control of economic life. Political government influences managerial government and tries to govern at a distance by influencing decisions. In turn, public policy uses programmes that orient managerial strategies. These programmes influence, for example, choices of investment. Central planning is *one* possible programme to structure economic policy, but only one. Public policies are more likely to seek to influence firms by encouraging the circulation of knowledge about markets and improved management techniques. In particular, they use the educational system to promote a certain way of managing people in the firm, for instance. To carry out their policies, political government influences management practices (Knights & Morgan 1991; Knights 1992). Many researchers in organization studies demonstrate how social science research is used in management and, in fact, is essentially managerialist (Jackson & Carter 1998). They also show that managerial discourse creates new norms of behaviour and that firms develop particular techniques in order to govern (Alvesson & Deetz 1999). For example, managers create new structures; they create the possibilities of a career and systems to manage long-run careers which also allow individuals to chart their relative progress (McKinlay 2002). On the other hand, employees resist managerial power (Bhimani 1994; Bain & Taylor 2000). These studies also highlight how expectations, vocational training and committees of worker representatives are important actors in managerial government. They underline the central importance of the action and behaviour of agents inscribed by and inside systems of governmentality.

The relation between the state and the firm must not be seen as unilateral. Heterotopia influences but also is influenced in return. Research on collective bargaining in France during the 1970s focuses on how a government aimed to better integrate workers into consumer society, a programme called *mensualisation* (Pezet 2012). Put simply, every worker should be paid monthly, instead of hourly. This involved changing the regularity of pay as well as offering several social advantages. The implementation of this programme was made in cooperation with firms that had developed their own programmes. In the steel industry, employee unions and employers developed an agreement to classify jobs, which, for the first time, allowed workers to envisage a long-term career in the firm. From this point on, employment stability could be imagined, made possible by mensualisation. The most influential model for the steel industry agreement had been elaborated and negotiated by the truck-maker, Berliet, after the liberation.

This relation between state and enterprise shows that the firm is a place from which the government may revisit and recover new possibilities for governing society. Through the development of a new system of careers it was possible to create life-long careers for workers, making it easier for the government to integrate them into consumer society. So, the firm can be viewed also as a space of recovery affording new forms of governmentaltity. The French experience, like German ordoliberalism, places the firm at the centre of liberal govermentality. However, in constrast to the ordoliberal doctrine, French social history illustrates a case where the relationship between the firm and the state can be seen as a diplomatic relation, a relation where an agreement can be found in the context of adversity. The pressures of the first and second World Wars provide many examples of the re-organization of production, including the role of women, productive organizations and society. Diplomatic relations are a property of classical liberalism where the equilibrium of forces is also a property of the governmentality.

The Firm and the Generation of Neoliberal Governmentalities

As Michael Senellart (2003: 41) observes, liberalism is 'the original solution to a problem historically situated. Therefore it can not remain perpetually identical to itself'. There is also no absolute separation between different types of liberalism. In American neoliberalism also, diplomatic relations exist where each party acknowledges the other and the relation is based on a balance of power. What is at stake here is the possibility of thinking the unthinkable of Foucault's theory: specifically, that firms are an element of understanding liberalism.

We considered heterotopia also in the context of Italian liberalism where the heterotopic behaviour of organizations, such as the Church and the Mafia, which force the state into diplomatic behaviour with places which did not necessarily want to contribute to the functioning of the state. With German ordoliberalism and American neoliberalism, we found different contexts: where the firm is central to neoliberal governmentality but adopts opposite perspectives when considering the state. In ordoliberalism, the firm is the target of the state. In American neoliberalism, which is a survivalist neoliberalism, the firm is not only the guardian of the state but also the guardian of communities against the state's inherent excesses. In both cases, the firm appears to be a specific space that has to be investigated or protected. So, applying the concept of heterotopias, and especially that of heterotopic behaviour, to firms leads us to redefine the way we consider firms as a source of normative power and the constructed relations of power therein, as well as the site they occupy within the spatialization of liberal society. The concept of *counter space* is constitutive of liberalism. For neoliberalism, especially as described by Nozick, counter spaces are defined as associations, but these counter spaces are actually imaginary. Firms do exist *and* yet appear to be heterotopias which are generative of liberalism and of liberal governmentality. Therefore, liberal governmentality may be thought of in terms of the relationship between state and this specific counter space that is the firm. For ordoliberalism, the firm is a place to regulate and to control. For neoliberalism, the firm is the place from which the state can be contained in order to allow the emergence of free associations.

In ordoliberalism the state maintains competition between firms. The state was present through laws concerning the market and the internal operations of the firm to ensure that people gain insurance (protections) and property from their labour. European ordoliberalism combines two conceptions of law, one where 'freedom is based on the rights of man and the other starting from that of the governed' (Foucault 2008: 42). The American approach defines freedom as the independence of the governed with respect to the state. The foundational text of American neoliberalism, written by Henry Simons in 1934, is entitled *A Positive Programme for Laissez Faire* (Foucault 2008: 216). From the 1940s, American neoliberalism has constructed its adversary and target: Keynesian policy and the growth of federal administration (Foucault 2008: 217).

Foucault describes heterotopia in terms of their function, which 'unfolds between two extreme poles. Either their role is to create a space of illusion that exposes every real space, all the sites inside of which human life is partitioned, as still more illusory (perhaps that is the role that was played by those famous brothels of which we are now deprived). Or else, on the contrary, their role is to create a space that is other, another real space, as perfect, as meticulous, as well arranged as ours is messy, ill constructed, and jumbled. This latter type would be the heterotopia, not of illusion, but of compensation, and I wonder if certain colonies have not functioned somewhat in this manner' (Foucault 1967: 8). And, just as surely as all utopias are unrealisable, so every governmentalist project entails hubris to a greater or lesser extent. The function of heterotopias may change over time. If 'each heterotopias has a precise and determined function within a society and the same heterotopias can, according to the synchrony of the culture in which it occurs, have one function or another' (Foucault 1967: 2). If we think in terms of function, there is a continuum. We contend that the relationship between firms and political space may range from state influence and control of firms in ordoliberal governmentality to the watchman role of the firm in American liberal governmentality. In ordoliberalism a place is created through regulation and competition. In neoliberalism a place for the market is created through the multiplication and growth of communities. The law regulates the market in the neoliberal approach by legally empowering the individual. This empowerment is with regards to individual human rights which would be more a protection and acknowledgment of fundamental rights. For neoliberalism, empowerment is the possibility for individuals to act with ever less interference from the state. For both ordoliberalism and suvivalist neoliberalism, the firms appear to be counter spaces, that is to say a space where the everyday nature of life is different from the dominant one. The everyday nature of liberalism is to think in tems of market. Rationality and decisions are important concepts for the individual. Irrationality is damage that has to be corrected through economic policies. The relation to time is related to the collection and the treatment of information. This can be instantaneous, for example algorithmic, or high speed, high frequency stock market trading. The heterotopic relation to time reinforces the possibility for the firm to remain a counter space.

The two liberal governmentalities share one important point in terms of the role of the firm. The firm is basis for the regeneration of liberal government when political insitutions challenge—or have utterly failed—society. German ordoliberalism was developed after 1945. In France, when the state feared a leftist grip on society at the end of the 1960s, it was through managerial government that the French citizen-worker was established. In the US, managerial government inspires and influences politicians. This is made possible by the heterotopic position of the firm in society. The everyday life of a firm is a constant preoccupation of the ordoliberal state which develops policies to influence it. The firm is a counter space but also a space to be controlled through labour law and fiscal controls. In survivalist neoliberalism, the firm is a space constructed and governed by heroes who preserve it from the influence of the state. It is a counter space for the state, not a space to be controlled but a space from which to exercise vigilance against the state. In both cases, the counter space is central to understanding the functioning of liberal governmentality. It is a space which makes liberalism thinkable and changeable. A space from which neoliberalism is conceived and can be though differently. Firms and the state are both the condition and the threat to liberal freedoms. Ordoliberalism controls the firm through market regulation. It constrains the state by focusing it on the defense of human rights and social wellfare. Libertarianism fights 'heroically' against the state and counts on the muliplicity of competitive heterotopias to limit its power. It would seem that the function of the firm considered as heterotopic entity is not a function of compensation, but to generate liberalism.

Conclusion

Neoliberalism deals with the question of sovereignty of the state through the degovernmentalisation of the state. In American survivalist liberalism, the law becomes a technology for the implementation of economic individualism. Law is not used to structure society but to guide individual behaviour. Behavioural sciences become important as they help to make the individual behave more rationally. The consequence is that the main interest of neoliberalism is first individuality within the market in order to benefit public policies such as health or security policy. In all cases, individual choices—and perhaps identities—are nudged by incentives and sanctions. In the association to which he/she belongs, he/she is pastoraly governed refering to the truth. Within these associations there is a consciousness of his/ her interest and how it evolves: an association is based on a consciousness of interest. The interest in which public policies and market are based change through the action of associations and individuals. These evolutions make liberal governmentality change their politics based on interests and these interests can be very different.

Firms plays a central role in the generation of neoliberalism. Two explanations can be proposed for the generative impact of firms on neoliberal governmentalities. The first one is that for neoliberalism, the government has to be productive. Managerial government is the one whose productivity is the more visible and firms are places where power is productive. The second explanation could be that the central importance of the firm is the generation of neoliberalism, as system producer of rights, or as a purveyor of liberal heroes, and may be sustained by the fact that it supports the idea that there is an invisible hand. It is this that produces the goods and services proving that pastoral government is well associated with the truth of the market.

References

Alvesson, M. & Deetz, S. (1999), 'Critical Theory and Postmodernism: Approaches to Organizational Studies', in S. Clegg & C. Hardy(eds), *Studying Organization: Theory and Method*, London: Sage.

Bain, P. & Taylor, P. (2000), 'Entrapped by the "Electronic Panopticon"? Worker Resistance in the Call Centre', *New Technology, Work and Employment* 15/1: 2–18.

Bentham, J. (1983), *Constitutional Code: Volume I*, Oxford: Clarendon Press.

Bhimani, A. (1994), 'Accounting and the Emergence of "Economic Man"', *Accounting, Organization and Society* 19/8: 637–674.

Foucault, M. (1967), 'Of Other Spaces', *Diacritics* 16/1: 22–27.

Foucault, M. (2007), *Security, Territory, Population: Lectures at the College De France, 1977–1978*, New York: Picador.

Foucault, M. (2008), *The Birth of Biopolitics: Lectures at the Collège de France, 1978–1979*, New York: Palgrave MacMillan.

Hopper, T. & MacIntosh, N. (1998), 'Management Accounting Numbers: Freedom or Prison: Geneen versus Foucault', in A. McKinlay & K. Starkey (eds), *Foucault, Management and Organization Theory: From Panopticon to Technologies of Self*, London: Sage.

Hopwood, A. (1987), 'The Archaeology of Accounting Systems', *Accounting, Organization and Society* 12/3: 207–234.

Jackson, N. & Carter, P. (1998), 'Labour as Dressage', in A. McKinlay & A. Starkey (eds), *Foucault, Management and Organization Theory: From Panopticon to Technologies of Self*, London: Sage.

Knights, D. (1992), 'Changing Spaces: The Disruptive Impact of a New Epistemological Location for the Study of Management', *Academy of Management Review* 17: 514–536.

Knights, D. & Morgan, G. (1991), 'Corporate Strategy, Organizations and Subjectivity: A Critique', *Organization Studies* 12/2: 251–273.

La Fever, K. (2013), 'Foucault's Heterotopia and Pedagogical Space', *Didactiques* 15: 55–65.

McKinlay, A. (2002), ' "Dead Selves": The Birth of the Modern Career', *Organization* 9/4: 595–614.

McKinlay, A. & Starkey, K. (eds) (1998), *Foucault, Management and Organization Theory: From Panopticon to Technologies of Self*, London: Sage.

Minsaas, K. (2007), 'Ayn Rand's Recasting of Ancient Myths in Atlas Shrugged', in E. W. Younkins (ed.), *Ayn Rand's Atlas Shrugged. A Philosophical and Literary Companion*, London: Ashgate.

Nozick, R. (1975), *Anarchy, State and Utopia*, London: Blackwell.

Pezet, E. (2012), 'Pacifying the Social: Creating the French Citizen Worker, 1968–1975', *Management & Organizational History* 7/1: 61–71.

Rand, A. (2007), *Atlas Shrugged*, London: Penguin.

Senellart, M. (2003), 'Michel Foucault: La Critique de la Gesellschaftspolitik Ordolibérale', in P. Commun (ed.), *L'Ordolibéralisme Allemand: Aux Sources de L'économie Sociale de Marché*, CIRAC/CICC, Université de Cergy-Pontoise.

Part III

Bodies and Souls

5 Governmentality and the Historian

Scotland and the History of Protestant Pastoral Power

Alistair Mutch

Governmentality as developed in the work of Miller and Rose (2008) and others such as Power (1997) has been criticised for its failure to pay attention to history (Maltby 2008). A return to Foucault's formulation of governmentality suggests the importance of history. Specifically, he argues that governmentality is shaped by the history of pastoral power. This pastoral power was developed from a review of the history of the confessional in Roman Catholicism (see McKinlay & Taylor 2014: 103–11). In this discussion, promises were made to develop a history of Protestant pastoral power, but this was never delivered. Rather, Foucault turned back to classical antiquity. Work in the history of religion would suggest that there are significant differences that need to be explored in Protestant pastoral power. As Mac-Culloch observes, the concern within Reformed churches was 'with sins that could be defined as public rather than private: matters which affected the community as a whole, rather than the inner thoughts of the heart' (Mac-Culloch 2004: 597). Scotland provides a good site for the exploration of the development of this pastoral power over time, given its status as the most thorough-going instantiation of Reformed religion in Europe (Marshall 1980). It is possible to trace the development of systems of discipline at national and local level which suggest a form of systemic discipline involving an entire system of practices, outlined in textual form, embodied in formal organizational units and recorded in a variety of forms (Mutch 2015). I use this context to address the question of how to apply historical methods to the study of governmentality, suggesting that Foucault prompts us to look at taken for granted practices. The focus is therefore on the relationship of Foucault to history. The chapter looks at different phases of Foucault's approach, with a particular focus on his later work as developed in his focus on pastoral power. This suggests that the focus on genealogy is a misleading one and that there is more in 'conventional' history than is often allowed. This is because the image of history against which Foucault is contrasted is one which fails to take account of the heterogeneity and innovativeness of history.

Megill (1987: 117) records Foucault's sardonic observation, 'I am not a professional historian; nobody is perfect'. It may be interesting to reflect on what Foucault might have been comparing himself to, what his image of the 'professional historian' was. In a roundtable discussion with historians in 1980 he observed:

> The way they [historians] work is by ascribing the object they analyze to the most unitary, necessary, inevitable and (ultimately) extra-historical mechanism or structure available. An economic mechanism, an anthropological structure or a demographic process which figures the climatic stage in the investigation—these are the goals of de-eventalized history. (Of course, these remarks are only intended as a crude specification of a certain broad tendency.)
>
> (Foucault 1991a: 77)

What was this broad tendency? The evidence would seem to suggest that it was the Annales school associated in particular with Braudel, concerned with the *longue durée* and the examination of mentalities (Megill 1987). This then has to be seen in the broader context of French intellectual life and the prestige of the structuralist approaches against which Foucault revolted. The problem here is that there were debates within history. Within the parallel British tradition, for example, there had been E. P. Thompson's (1978) broadside against Althusserianism in *The Poverty of Theory* and a flourishing of new approaches to history as typified in the journal *History Workshop*. For example, there was the work on sexuality by Jeffrey Weeks which paralleled Foucault's concerns about the role of theory and methodology (Weeks 1982). In other words, we have to be careful not to reduce the variety of history to a caricature which is then rejected in favour of genealogy. There is much more in the historical repertoire that is available to us.

The objections of historians to Foucault's work are ably summarised by Rowlinson and Carter (2002): obscure style, avoidance of narrative, ambivalence to truth, getting historical facts wrong, neglect of relevant historiography and questionable explanations. They use these objections to critique the failings of some of those deploying Foucault and claiming to use historical evidence. This, however, does not give us any practical guidance on what the appropriate approach to history might be. In order to do this, we need to explore Foucault's practice in a little more detail. We are helped here by the publication of transcripts of Foucault's lectures, which perhaps require us to reassess our views (Foucault 1999, 2009). This is because Foucault's ideas and practice changed together with his overall project. The genealogical research that we most associate with his name might therefore be misleading. Examination of his later work on pastoral power suggests a greater degree of attention to what we might term more traditional forms of historical inquiry.

Foucault argued in 1980 that 'my books aren't treatises in philosophy or studies of history: at most, they are philosophical fragments put to work in a historical field of problems' (Foucault 1991a: 74). He is often seen as using these fragments to disturb our understanding of the present, to problematise contemporary situations, rather than exploring the deep roots of such situations as they might have unfolded over time. Indeed, in his early work the focus was seen to be on radical discontinuities, although Foucault came to eschew such a characterisation. The early work was also concerned more with intellectual, rather than social history, although it is with the latter, most notably with the publication of *Discipline and Punish*, that Megill (1987) argues Foucault comes to have broader influence. In 1968 he outlined his project as:

> To determine, in its diverse dimensions, what the mode of existence of discourses and particularly of scientific discourses (their rules of formation, with their conditions, their dependencies, their transformations) must have been in Europe, since the seventeenth century, in order that the knowledge which is ours today could come to exist, and, more particularly, that knowledge which has taken as its domain this curious object which is man.
>
> (Foucault 1991: 70)

Thus we have the distinctive focus in genealogy not on what is done and said but on what allows some things to be done and said. However, Foucault's overall project was a fluid, changing one. In a 1981 interview he confessed:

> When I was studying asylums, prisons, and so on, I perhaps insisted too much on the techniques of domination. . . . Having studied the field of power relations taking techniques of domination as a point of departure, I would like, in the years to come, to study power relations starting from the techniques of the self.
>
> (Foucault 1997: 177)

With this shift came a change in emphasis. In his roundtable with historians Foucault argued that historians (and we have seen by this that he seemed to have in mind the *Annales* school in particular) has neglected the 'event'. By an event he meant 'making visible a singularity at places where there is a temptation to invoke a historical constant, an immediate anthropological trait, or an obviousness which imposes itself uniformly on all' (Foucault 1991: 76). From the event one could trace a complex network of elements brought into relation, of relations and of domains of reference. However, one might argue that this was just what Le Roy Ladurie (1978) was doing in his famous examination of Cathar heretics in *Montaillou*, first published in 1975. (Le Roy Ladurie drew on Foucault in his earlier work). So it would be wrong to take Foucault at face value in his criticism of historians. This is both that historians are more flexible than the caricature suggests and that Foucault was shifting his ground. We can see this shift further if we examine the development of the notion of 'governmentality'.

For Foucault, governmentality was a way of moving from the 'microphysics' of power that constituted his earlier studies to a macrophysics (Gordon 1987). Governmentality was to do with the 'conduct of conduct' in the context of the shift to examining techniques of the self. It was seen as the extension of forms of governing conduct from the individual to whole populations, arising from the combination of pastoral power as developed within Christianity and the emergence of 'police' in the eighteenth century. The focus in this discussion is on the notion of pastoral power. Foucault's focus here is on religion as social practice. He argues that:

> It seems to me that the history of the pastorate has never really been undertaken. The history of ecclesiastical institutions has been written. The history of religious doctrines, beliefs, and representations has been written. There have also been attempts to produce the history of real religious practices, namely, when people confessed, took communion, and so on. But it seems to me that the history of the techniques employed, of the reflections on these pastoral techniques, of their development, application, and successive refinements, the history of the different types of analysis and knowledge linked to the exercise of pastoral power, has never really been undertaken.
>
> (Foucault 2009: 150)

In his 1982 roundtable, he defines practices 'as places where what is said and what is done, rules imposed and reasons given, the planned and the taken for granted meet and interconnect' (Foucault 1991: 75). The specific practice for his focus in his initial discussion of pastoral power is the confessional within the Roman Catholic Church (Foucault 2009: 171–95). This focus reveals some problems, for it was heavily dependent on the work of Lea, an American historian who produced a multi-volume treatment in 1896 (Foucault 2009: 195). Lea was not a dispassionate observer of his topic, although his treatment appears to have been thorough. His reason for exploring the confessional, he tells us in his introduction, was that 'the history of mankind may be vainly searched for another institution which has established a spiritual autocracy such as that of the Latin Church' (Lea 1896: v). His exploration of the confessional was to seek the roots of a core mechanism which supported such control. Now, whether the mechanism operated in the totalizing form which such statements imply is open to doubt. Other investigations suggest the difficulties that the church had in implementing high level prescriptions (Taylor 2009: 49) Here we see an example of the criticisms of Foucault that he ignored developments in historiography, as well as using sources which led him into errors of interpretation. In this case Payer (1985) demonstrated that sexual matters tended to diminish as part of the repertoire of sins covered by confessional practice, rather than increasing as Foucault had argued. But Payer also acknowledged that while his grasp of history was shaky, Foucault was right to argue for the socially constructed nature of sex and sexuality. From this we can suggest that Foucault's problematics might well provide the spur to further investigations, although his practice is no reliable guide to how to conduct such inquiries.

In fact, Foucault realised the problems with his account of pastoral power (Elden 2002). It was one which was profoundly shaped, as Carette (2000) has argued, by his upbringing in a Catholic milieu, in which the practices associated with Catholicism were those 'to hand' for analysis. Abandoning his ambitions to develop a history of Protestant pastoral power to complement that which he acknowledged was profoundly shaped by Catholicism, he turned back to classical antiquity to look for the roots of rules for the conduct of conduct. It is interesting to note, as Philip Gorski does, that:

> One would expect a brief overview of the various disciplinary mechanisms invented by Protestant and Catholic religious reformers and of the ways in which territorial rulers utilized them as part of their strategies of domination. But, instead, Foucault launches into a lengthy discussion of Machiavelli's Prince and the various treatises written in reaction to it from the late sixteenth century onwards. . . . On the concrete social mechanisms through which this power operated, the central concern of so much of his work, Foucault is strangely silent.
>
> (Gorski 2003: 24)

Gorski goes on to suggest that such an overview would locate the origins of the disciplinary revolution not in Catholicism and eighteenth century France, but in Reformed Protestantism and seventeenth century Netherlands. This is a line of inquiry that parallels my own work on Scotland and here I seek to problematise the focus that we find in Foucault on programmatic works and their relationship to practice. This is not only to be found in this work, but is still more problematic in works such as *Discipline and Punish*. Foucault insisted that his attention to programmatic works was not because of what they told us about the 'real' but for their effects in the world (Foucault 1991: 81). In his work on the confessional manuals, for example, he acknowledged that 'they were effectively put to work in the formation of confessors themselves, rather than in the average faithful among the people' (Foucault 1999: 191). This suggested a need to examine the sites of such formation, notably the seminaries. This raises questions about how to explore such relations, questions which send us back to primary sources in a way not pursued by Foucault. Once again, Foucault provides us with some suggestions about how to proceed, but little concrete guidance about how to do so. In the balance of the chapter, I explore how to take these hints and apply them to a project of delivering on Foucault's promissory note to examine the history of Protestant pastoral power. In doing this, there are some broader questions about how to actually practice history in management and organization studies.

Protestantism as it emerged in the Reformation is a broad tradition, so it is necessary to focus the discussion. MacCulloch (2004) distinguishes three broad traditions with significant influence: the Lutheranism of Germany and Scandinavia; the Anglicanism of England, important because of the later spread of empire; and the Reformed tradition, characterised in particular by the influence of Calvin in Geneva. This latter tradition, in the form of Presbyterianism, found its fullest instantiation in Scotland, and this is the site for much of the discussion which follows. The focus here is on religion as a social practice, as opposed to theological distinctions (although it is accepted that these are profoundly important for the shaping of such practices). In these terms, two aspects of Presbyterianism stand out: its particular form of organization and its focus on discipline (Mutch 2015). Presbyterian is conciliar in its organization, with what have been described as a concentric set of courts or governing bodies, each enabling a degree of 'lay' participation. What stands out in the popular memory is the imposition by these courts of church discipline. This is particularly the case at the local level, where the 'kirk session', a body of about four to six ordained men (and they were always men) chaired by the minister (the clerical incumbent) as 'moderator' inquired into the conduct of parishioners and handed out punishments. The focus of these investigations were on 'crimes' of a sexual nature, particularly adultery, sex before marriage and children born out of wedlock, and the punishments often seemed to fall disproportionately on women. These punishments would generally involve public display, with the sinner being forced to occupy the 'place of repentance' in full view of the congregation and to hear their crimes recited. This was undoubtedly a harsh system, although, arguably one accepted grudgingly by the majority of parishioners because it formed a means of dealing with matters that concerned the whole community (in particular because unmarried mothers and their children, if abandoned by the father, would become a burden on the parish). It was also a system which had means of dealing with the poverty and distress arising from scarcity, age and infirmity. The system was never generous, relying as it did on the contributions of the faithful, but it was a function of the session to administer it (McPherson 1945). These functions, the enforcement of discipline and the relief of distress, as well as the support of the rituals of the church led to certain taken for granted practices, and it is these that are the focus of this investigation. This is because a larger question, in the context of governmentality, is how such practices might have become available, as Foucault argued, for the wider management of conduct. The challenge is how to investigate such practices which, in large part because of their mundane nature, can be obscured from view.

Paul Veyne (1984) has suggested that one crucial technique is that of comparison. He observes that 'if in order to study a civilization, we limit ourselves to reading what it says itself—that is, to reading sources relating to this one civilization—we will make it more difficult to wonder at what, in this civilization, was taken for granted' (Veyne 1984: 7). Accordingly, although my prime focus is on Scotland, I will use the Anglicanism of the Church of England as a counterpoint. If we examine the central sacrament of communion in each church, we get a sense of not only the difference in the taken for granted practices but also of the ways in which liturgical rituals also in their turn occasion certain practices, call them governance practices, which are necessary to put the rituals into motion. In common with many churches in the European Reformed tradition, the new Church of Scotland rejected many of the sacraments associated with Roman Catholicism as unwarranted by scripture, finding place for only two: baptism and communion (MacCulloch 2004). Because of these beliefs, communion was taken to be a central ritual to be available to only those who based the test of adequate belief. It was also to be taken infrequently, to mark its special symbolic standing. In the period under consideration, the eighteenth century, this meant that communion was taken only once a year. Preparation for communion became a central part of the rhythm of the year and required particular spatial arrangements (Yates 2009). Communion, or the Lord's Supper, was taken seated round large tables. Access to these was controlled by officials of the church, so that only the faithful might approach. These arrangements required governance practices, which took material form. The need to restrict the taking of communion to those considered worthy required meetings to determine on status and forms of recording which eventually led to communion rolls, records of those considered worthy. Restricting access to the tables meant that some badge of suitability was required and this took the form of the communion token, a small lead token often inscribed with the church name and year, which was distributed immediately before communion and surrendered on the day of taking communion. In this way a liturgical practice was shaped by theological commitments and generated specific practices of organizing which placed a premium on accurate records.

By contrast the Church of England, emerging as a reformed church as much from considerations of state as from theological concerns, adopted a broad church approach in which several theological currents coexisted with different degrees of unease (Gregory & Chamberlain 2003). This gave a different flavour to communion, as the church aspired to be the national church open to all believers (and indeed, adherence to the forms of the church was to different degrees required by law). At times certain currents within the church attempted to close communion to those considered unworthy and similar systems of tokens were employed in isolated parishes (Boulton 1984; Haigh 2000). But these organizational innovations never took hold. Other sacraments remained important and the impulse in the eighteenth century was to more frequent celebration of communion (Gregory & Chamberlain 2003). This was taken from the hands of the clergyman at the communion rail that demarcated the sacred area of the altar from the body of the church. Lay involvement was needed to organise the bread and wine which were the symbolic resources of the ceremony, but there was no place for, or the need for, the degree of record keeping that we find in Scotland. The comparison of the two systems, that is, has given us a clue as to the nature of mundane practices that can stand further examination.

As we know, Foucault's method was to draw upon a range of sources in order to glean examples to sustain his arguments. Such sources were often of dubious reliability, as with his reliance on Lea's work on the confessional. One challenge for the organizational scholar is determining the amount of weight that can be placed on secondary sources. In too many cases, assertions are made on the basis of a slim corpus, particularly on more popular works. If we relate this to the question of the mundane practices that are our area of interest then the problem is compounded, because these practices have only been mentioned in passing, if at all. The focus of most works is on the exercise of discipline or the conduct of worship, rather than on the practices that made these possible. This is because the focus of most historians has been on the result of such practices, which form an unexplored part of the context. Historians tend to rather take organizational matters for granted, but this is where organizational theorists can make a contribution, by bringing such practices out of the shadows. In order to do so, however, we need to go past the secondary works and examine more contemporaneous material. Here it is that we confront the procedure manuals that form such a large part of Foucault's evidence base.

As we have seen, the lectures on governmentality and pastoral power have a more nuanced view of the role of such advice works than earlier works such as *Discipline and Punish*. In that work the discussion of, for example, the emergence of school discipline, is heavily dependent on a single source, a source moreover that is concerned to lay out an ideal blueprint. This might be to stand for the construction of a particular discourse, although we might want to know how typical such blueprints were and how they stand in relation to other examples. But if we set that to one side, there are two concerns, concerns that contemporary organization theory is much concerned with. An examination of contemporary management practices would urge caution about a simple reading off of organization practices from handbooks of procedure or even declarations of adoption. We know from this work that what is adopted in practice often varies considerably in practice from the laid down blueprint. And we also know that blueprints cannot contain all the answers that routines have to be and are adapted to meet new circumstances. If we turn these insights onto the 'procedure manuals' of the Scottish church then we can see the gaps, gaps which become visible when we turn to primary sources.

What is particularly interesting about the Scottish example is that such blueprints exist in considerable detail, for this was a church (unlike the Church of England) which had explicit debates about and formulations of the nature of its organization. As Kirk (1989: xv) argues, 'the new kirk was accorded that rare and exhilarating experience, denied to most churches, of determining its own programme and constitution'. Because of the growing importance and availability of print, this meant that the church produced a series of programmatic statements, starting with John Knox's (1905) *Book of Discipline* in 1560. This laid down the broad parameters of church organization, which were refined over the following years. These were years of considerable contention and bloodshed, as the leaders of the Scottish church resisted attempts to insert bishops on the Anglican model into the Scottish system. This resistance was finally successful with the coming to the English and Scottish thrones of William of Orange in 1688. The confirmation by a grudging monarch of the Presbyterian form of the Church of Scotland saw the publication in 1696 of the *Overtures concerning the discipline and method of proceeding in the ecclesiastick judicatories in the Church of Scotland: humbly tendered to the consideration of the several Presbytries, and to be by them prepared for the next, or some ensueing General Assembly* (Anon 1696). This laid down in considerable detail the procedures to be followed by church bodies. Its contents were debated by successive General Assemblies, and some of its contents were adopted as church practice. Other elements were carried forward into Walter Steuart's *Collections and Observations Methodised, concerning the Worship, Discipline and Government of the Church of Scotland*, first published in 1709 and frequently reprinted thereafter (Steuart 1802). This influential work, which is still cited in much more recent work on the laws of the church, contained much of the material found in the earlier *Overtures* and seems to have become the de facto procedure manual of the church.

Examination of these printed sources enables us to draw some preliminary conclusions about the governance practices. One feature is the emphasis on the recording of church decisions, with detailed advice on the format and content of records. There is even consideration of an archiving process for such records. We will examine these strictures against practice shortly. But what is also important is the way that the procedural guidance gives us a broader perspective on the disciplinary system. For this was not only to be deployed against sinners at the local level, but was also to monitor the conduct of church officers, especially its clerical members. It was a key concern of the founders of the church to avoid the emergence of a 'priestly caste' that they saw as a disfiguring element of Catholicism. Here we have a manifest difference between the notion of pastoral power in Roman Catholicism and that in Reformed Protestantism. While Foucault's focus is on the emergence of priestly power, especially as manifested in the practices of the confessional, an examination of the Presbyterian literature indicates an impulse to restrain such power. Here the power is to reside at the level of an integrated system, in which the totalising claims of the church are enforced against all its members. One index of this is the provision for 'privy censure'. In all kirk sessions, the 1696 *Overtures* proposed that, twice a year:

> The Moderator of the Session is to cause the Clerk read the Roll of the Members; and beginning at the beginning of the Roll, they are one by

one, after another to be removed, and then the rest of the Members are, by the Moderator to be enquired concerning the Walk and Conversation of the Member removed, concerning his Diligence, and Prudence in his Station; and whatever any have observed, and informed worthy the Noticing; is freely and with Love, and Tenderness to be communicated.

(Anon 1696: 24)

This process was to apply to elders, but the same process was to be engaged in at the meetings of the presbytery. This body consisted of all the ministers from a group of parishes (typically between fifteen and twenty) and some representative elders. As well as this examination by peers of the conduct of ministers, they were also subject to the presbyterial visitation of their parish on a regular cycle. The *Overtures* envisaged this to happen every year and laid down a detailed process of questioning, which began with the inspection of the written records of the session. This was then followed by the questioning, in turn, of the principal inhabitants about the conduct of their minister and session, of the elders about the conduct of their minister and of the minister about the conduct of his elders and flock. It is interesting to note that the *Collections and Observations* of Walter Steuart, a leading 'lay' elder, place much greater stress on the form and nature of the questions to be put to the minister. These are presented in extraordinary detail, of which the following is just an excerpt:

Hath your minister a gospel walk and conversation before the people? And doth he keep family worship? And is he onewho rules well his own house? Is he a haunter of ale-houses and taverns? Is he a dancer, carder or dicer? Is he proud or vain-glorious? Is he greedy, or wordly, or an ursurer? Is he contentious, a brawler, fighter or striker? Is he a swearer of small or minced oaths? Useth he to say, Before God it is so; or in his common conference, I protest, or, I protest before God. Or says he, lord, what is that? All of which are more than yea or nay? Is he a filthy speaker or jester? Bears he familiar company with disaffected, profane or scandalous persons? Is he dissolute, prodigal, light or loose in his carriage, apparel, or words? How spends he the Sabbath after sermon? Saw ye him ever drink healths?

(Steuart 1802: 48)

To get a sense of this, the eight suggested questions that Steuart outlines take over 1,000 words to propound; by contrast, his questions to the session, also eight in number, extend to only 372 words. Of course, this gives us a good sense of what debates were like at a national level, but not whether these debates had any impact at local level.

It is here that examination of the archives is essential, sensitised by the concerns outlined in the procedure manuals. In particular, the archives can help us with two questions: were the procedures promulgated at national level put into practice in the localities and were there practices engaged in that were not laid down by the national guidance? Here we are looking at two aspects of the records: their content and their form. It is their content which has been most used by historians exploring questions such as the nature of church discipline and the operation of poor relief. If this is our focus then we can indeed see that systems of visitation were in operation, particularly in parishes in the southern Lowlands and in the earlier years of the eighteenth century. For example, on 10 April 1706, the registers of the Presbytery of Edinburgh record a visitation of the parish of Kirk Newton. Their report extends to over 2,000 words and follows the format laid down in the national guidance. Part of the reason for this extent was some disputes amongst members of the Session, but the register records:

> The Minister and Elders being removed, the Heritors and heads of families were Enquired anent the life and Conversation of the Minister and Elders and concerning the Discharge of their respective duties. Answered unanimously they had no Complaints against their Minister or Members of Session, but were well satisfied with them as to the discharge of their respective duties.
>
> (Presbytery of Edinburgh 1706)

What we can see in the registers, therefore, is not only the putting into practice of processes for the monitoring of conduct but also the deployment of a particular genre. However, this is simply to give an illuminating example. If we are to generalise about practice, then we need to consider the question of sampling.

Sampling is a problem for historians, given the often fragmentary state of archives. This is not to say that historians do not engage in such practices when the traces of practice allow them. In particular, the capabilities of information and communication technologies to capture, store and analyse large bodies of data and so to seek patterns. In an interesting example, Keith Snell (2006) has carried out two such investigations to test perceptions of place in England in the nineteenth and early twentieth centuries. One project involved the examination of 18,000 marriages to test for marriage within parish boundaries. Of his sampling strategy he notes, 'I have picked clusters of parishes in disparate English regions, to check for national homogeneity, or to allow any possible regional patterns to emerge. Rural parishes rather than larger market towns were chosen so as to replicate earlier historiographical findings, and to give this study a rural coherence which it would lack if a fuller range of parishes across the whole rural-urban spectrum was used' (Snell 2006: 168). Another piece of research seeking to establish the importance of place looks at mentions of place on gravestones, using records of over 16,000 gravestones in 87 burial grounds. These examples point to the ways in which historians can use systematic gathering of evidence, although the state of records does not always allow this. This is particularly true of the eighteenth century and earlier, which is the focus of my research. Here, there is a dramatic difference in the survival of records between England and Scotland, a difference which can be related to the overall nature of the two systems. In this research, two administrative units of the two churches were selected for examination. They were designed to be broadly comparable, both being predominantly rural areas defined by their place in the respective authority systems. The Deanery of Bingham in Nottinghamshire contained 50 parishes amounting to some 90,000 acres with a population of nearly 16,000. The Presbytery of Garioch in Aberdeenshire, by contrast was larger in area, at 112,000 acres but only contained fifteen parishes with a population of 11,909 (on the two areas in more detail, see Mutch 2013). These two broadly equivalent areas varied not only in ecclesiastical structure but dramatically in terms of record survival. In Scotland, eighteenth century records for thirteen parishes running to over 8,000 pages have been lodged in the National Records of Scotland. By contrast, only twenty sets of church warden records, many of them fragmentary in character, have survived in the Nottinghamshire Record Office. This pattern of record retention tells us something by itself about the nature of the two systems, but it does mean that systematic sampling and analysis are much easier to perform in the Scottish context.

However, the performance of such analysis, despite the limitations, reveals some interesting contrasts between practice in the two countries. So, for example, examination of the financial records indicates that of 347 annual balances examined in the Garioch, only 3% were negative. By contrast, of 672 balances examined in Bingham, 53.27% were negative. This illustrates substantial differences between the two areas, but these differences can be extended to the *form* of the records. It is clear from examination of the records that the form and detail with which financial transactions were recorded varied considerably both between the parishes and, more importantly, between the two countries. Thus, many of the records in England would not allow for the reconstruction of expenditure by date and type of spending until late in the eighteenth century; by contrast, in the Scottish parishes one often came across detailed accounting formats showing full details of spending and the construction of running balances from early in the eighteenth century. The challenge is then how to represent such differences? A coding scheme was drawn up, running from one for bare summaries in word form, to twelve for separate, detailed accounting records (the latter being only found in Scotland). A summary of this exercise is given in Table 5.1, which is a broad pointer to the key differences between the two countries.

This exercise suggests the importance in Scotland of practices of detailed record-keeping that emerge from ultimate theological concerns. The Scottish context enables this to be extended because of both the comprehensive nature of the collection and the existence of an electronic catalogue covering those records. This can be used to, for example, explore the emergence of

Table 5.1 Accounting Formats

England		Scotland
Average transaction code	Quarter century	Average transaction code
4.22	1700–1724	6.71
5.52	1725–1749	6.97
6.45	1750–1774	8.50
7.61	1775–1799	8.86

separate books of account, linked to the broader system of accountability and record-keeping. Using spreadsheets to capture and then analyse the catalogue entries of separate accounts indicates that the practice began in the early seventeenth century in Edinburgh and was adopted in the southern and eastern units of the church (Mutch 2012b). From here it spread across the rest of the lowland areas during the eighteenth century, such that about a quarter of all the church's parishes were maintaining separate books of account by the end of the eighteenth century. This exploration not only confirms the picture of detailed record-keeping obtained from the examination of local records, but it also can be related to the Scottish dominance of the writing of accounting text books by the second quarter of the eighteenth century.

What does this brief examination of practice (which is explored in much more detail elsewhere, see Mutch 2011, 2012a) tell us about the advice books that we explored earlier? It suggests that the exhortation to record matters of church discipline, both as they applied to individual wrongdoings and to poor relief, were widely followed across the country. A culture of systemic accountability, based on detailed record-keeping, is outlined by the advice books and is exhibited in local practice. However, facets of that practice not only play variations on a central theme but also innovate practices which are not laid down in the central procedures. This is particularly the case with practices of accountability for poor relief. The central guidance stresses responsibility in this regard, but is largely mute about how such responsibility is to be exercised. The 1696 *Overtures* laid down that at visitation 'the Church Bible, Confession of Faith, Acts of the General Assembly, Session Registers, and Poors Box; are all to be produced and laid before the Presbyterie', but this is to assume a good deal (Anon 1696: 37). In particular, the complex processes that sessions engaged in and which are clearly laid out in the registers of reconciling the cash held in the 'box' with the accounting records and the decisions noted in the register of discipline are nowhere laid down. This may have been because, often hailing from the parishes where detailed accounting was already in place, the framers of guidance took this for granted. This is the tentative conclusion that the analysis of the electronic catalogue suggests. However, what the detailed examination of the primary sources indicates is the danger of resting just at the level of printed sources.

Of course a genealogical account which rests on such sources may be able to tell us a good deal about the construction of particular forms of discourse. For example, it is possible to read the *Overtures* and other guidance material against other printed works such as Stair's *Institutions of the Laws of Scotland* (Walker 1981). Such an exercise suggests a common focus on systematic exposition from first principles based on the influence of Roman Law as mediated through experiences of exile and education in the Netherlands. This is a valuable exercise in its own right, but it can only go so far. For the techniques that constituted governmentality were not just a deliberate construction but also emerged from practice. Such practices may have been shaped by the guidance literature that in its turn was animated by theological concerns, but they were also innovative in their own right. This is because guidance has to be put into practice. The liturgical rituals of Presbyterianism, for example, required specific administrative practices which were mundane and taken for granted, but nonetheless influential for all that.

Snell (2006: 14) argues that his project is one of 'trying to infuse cultural meaning into administrative history, to extend such history to show how it has many cultural and social causes and ramifications, and to demonstrate how those interacted with administrative reforms'. This is a useful example of the ways in which debates in organizational theory can operate with a caricature of the historical enterprise. Based often, it would seem, on particular examples, often drawn from business history, it underestimates both the methodological and theoretical sophistication that characterises much historical work. Snell's work is instructive here. He notes:

> I have deliberately not engaged very openly with sociological and cultural theory in this book, even though there is some theoretical literature on the theme of belonging, and far more on communities, identities, globalisation, and secularisation, from across the social sciences and humanities.
>
> (Snell 2006: 23)

In part this is because such discussion would occupy too much valuable space, but also because Snell, like other historians, prefers to integrate such discussion into the discussion. In addition, 'Some of the theoretical literature contains many historical mistakes, and it is probably best to use it as a jumping-off point, inspiring new questions, rather than regard it with too much respect' (Snell 2006: 23). Thus, we have to be careful of reading a particular form of presentation of theory with an absence of theory altogether. That said, there are historians who recognise that more explicit attention to theorising would be of considerable value. For example, Chris Wickham, the eminent medievalist, has observed that:

Historians tend to avoid theorising; it is one of the most characteristic cultural features of the discipline, in fact. But if is also one of its major weak points, for the attachment of historians to the empiricist-expository mode only-too-often hides their theoretical presuppositions, not only from others, but from the writers themselves. As a result, historians can fall into contradictory arguments, and risk overall incoherence; entire historical debates have, on occasion, depended on theoretical presuppositions which were indefensible, and which would have been immediately seen as such had they been articulated.

(Wickham 2001: 221)

It follows also that historians might also not be as clear as one would like about methods. Indeed, the primacy of the archives is often taken for granted. Veyne (1984: 23) puts this in extreme fashion when he argues that '[h]istorical experience is acquired by working; it is not the fruit of study, but of an apprenticeship. History has no method, since it cannot formulate its experience in definitions, laws, and rules'. But this has to be seen in the context of a particular target. Just as his friend Foucault took aim at what he saw as the pretensions of the Annales school and generalised his critique to cover all historians, so Veyne takes aim at what he considers the 'pseudo science' of sociology (Veyne 2010a). 'For lack of having recognised that it is history without the name', he argues, 'it believes itself obliged to do science; the same can be said of ethnology. Sociology is a pseudoscience, born of the academic conventions that limit the freedom of history' (Veyne 1984: 264). But his own work, not only in its discussion of historiography but in its concrete account of religious practices in history does in fact contain some guidance as to how we might approach practice (Veyne 2010b). As we have seen, comparison is a key element. Then he suggests that there are some difficulties in examining practice, difficulties which suggest an indication of where we might look.

First, the event is difference; but history is written from sources whose editors find their own society so natural that they do not divide it into themes. Second, 'values' are not found in what people say but in what they do, and the official headings are often deceptive; mentalities are not mental. Third, concepts are a perpetual source of misinterpretations because they vulgarize and they cannot go without caution from one period to another. Fourth, the historian has a tendency to stop the clarification of the causes at the first freedom, the first material cause, and the first chance that came along. Fifth, the real offers a certain resistance to innovation; whether it be a political enterprise or the composition of a poem, a work is done more quickly if it follows in the old ruts of a tradition that seems so natural that it is not conscious. Sixth, the historical explanation is a regression to infinity; when we reach tradition, routine, inertia, it is difficult to say whether it is a reality or an appearance the truth of which is more deeply hidden in the shadow of the non-eventworthy. Finally, historical facts are often social, collective, statistical; demography, economics, customs. They are to be seen only at the foot of a column of figures; otherwise they are not seen or the strangest errors are made about them.

(Veyne 1984: 217)

This suggests the need to examine practice from a range of perspectives and not to rest at the level of the manuals which purport to suggest how that practice ought to be carried out.

Conclusion

The aim of fostering a historical turn in organizational analysis is a laudable one, but the suggestion that this be done by a turn to genealogy in the Foucauldian sense is only a partial solution. As we have seen, Foucault's relation to history is a more complex one. Once we get beyond the caricatures, then we see that as Foucault developed his engagement with history, he increasingly developed a focus on everyday practices. Genealogy provided the tools for examining the broader discourses which shaped such practices and made them possible, but his later focus on governmentality suggested that this was not enough. His own investigations here, which are understandable given the nature of his project, tended to stop at the level of the printed sources, especially the advice manuals which purported to set out blueprints for practice. Here, Foucault gives us some hints about the form of analysis we should undertake. He notes that we need to look at who used the advice manuals and how, and he specifically addresses the material dimensions of practice in his brief notes on the confessional box. What this suggests is the need to search for the traces that practice has left behind. Historical work will always be a matter of working with partial sources and survivals, but the discussion above has suggested a number of ways of dealing with these traces which perhaps go some way to giving a little more detail about methods.

One is the initial need to make practice visible. We might almost say that we need to make the taken for granted strange, and Veyne suggests that this is best done by comparison. Our comparisons should seek to establish how what is taken for granted differs between different contexts, with the precise aim of making it visible. Once this has been done, then the traces of that practice might be found as much in the *form* of the surviving evidence as in the *content*. Indeed, as we have seen in the comparison between England and Scotland, the mere fact of differential survival can itself tell us much about the underlying practices. Having established such patterns, then the systematic comparison of the traces left by practice can build on practices of sampling and coding that are familiar from much work in the institutionalist tradition. The patterns that are established then need to be placed in the broader social, political, economic and cultural context, often by a return to the secondary literature with renewed and fresh questions.

What this necessarily brief account suggests is that the confessional is not the only social practice that shaped the formation of subjectivities in modernity. If the confessional gives us therapy, then, arguably, the Reformed Protestant tradition gives us the self-help manual. The relentless focus on self-examination in order to ascertain the marks of grace would give some assurance about salvation manifested itself in practices of diary-keeping which then became secularised.

References

Anon (1696), *Overtures Concerning the Discipline and Method of Proceeding in the Ecclesiastick Judicatories in the Church of Scotland*, Edinburgh: George Mossman.

Boulton, J. (1984), 'The Limits of Formal Religion: The Administration of Holy Communion in late Elizabethan and early Stuart London', *London Journal* 10: 134–154.

Carrette, J. (2000), *Foucault and Religion: Spiritual Corporality and Political Spirituality*, London: Routledge.

Elden, S. (2002). 'The Problem of Confession: The Productive Failure of Foucault's History of Sexuality', *Journal for Cultural Research* 9/1: 23–41.

Foucault, M. (1991), 'Questions of Method', in G. Burchell, C. Gordon, and P. Miller (eds), *The Foucault Effect: Studies in Governmental Rationality: With Two Lectures by and an Interview with Michel Foucault*, Chicago: University of Chicago Press.

Foucault, M. (1997), *Ethics, Subjectivity and Truth*, New York: The New Press.

Foucault, M. (1999), *Abnormal: Lectures at the Collège de France 1974–1975*, New York: Picador.

Foucault, M. (2009), *Security, Territory, Population: Lectures at the Collège de France 1977–1978*, Basingstoke: Palgrave Macmillan.

Gordon, C. (1987), 'The Soul of the Citizen: Max Weber and Michel Foucault on Rationality and Government', in S. Whimster and S. Lash (eds), *Max Weber, Rationality and Modernity*, London: Routledge.

Gorski, P. (2003), *The Disciplinary Revolution: Calvinism and the Rise of the State in Early Modern Europe*, Chicago: University of Chicago Press.

Gregory, J. & Chamberlain, J. (eds) (2003), *The National Church in Local Perspective: The Church of England and the Regions 1660–1800*, Woodbridge: Boydell.

Haigh, C. (2000), 'Communion and Community: Exclusion from Communion in Post-Reformation England', *Journal of Ecclesiastical History* 51: 721–740.

Kirk, J. (1989), *Patterns of Reform: Continuity and Change in the Reformation Kirk*, Edinburgh: T and T Clark.

Knox, J. (1905), *The History of the Reformation of Religion in Scotland: With Which Are Included Knox's Confession and the Book of Discipline*, London: Melrose.

Le Roy Ladurie, E. (1978), *Montaillou*, London: Penguin.

Lea, H. (1896), *A History of Auricular Confession and Indulgences in the Latin Church*, Philadelphia: Lea Brothers & Co.

MacCulloch, D. (2004), *Reformation: Europe's House Divided 1490–1700*, London: Penguin.

Maltby, J. (2008), 'There Is No Such Thing as Audit Society', *Ephemera* 8/4: 388–398.

Marshall, G. (1980), *Presbyteries and Profits: Calvinism and the Development of Capitalism in Scotland, 1560–1707*, Oxford: Clarendon Press.

McKinlay, A. & Taylor, P. (2014), *Foucault, Governmentality, Organization: Inside the 'Factory of the Future'*, London: Routledge.

McPherson, J. M. (1945), *The Kirk's Care of the Poor, with Special Reference to the North-East of Scotland*, Aberdeen: John Avery.

Megill, A. (1987), 'The Reception of Foucault by Historians', *Journal of the History of Ideas* 48/1: 117–141.

Miller, P. & Rose, N. (2008), *Governing the Present*, Cambridge: Polity.

Mutch, A. (2011), 'Custom and Personal Accountability in Eighteenth Century South Nottinghamshire Church Governance', *Midland History* 36/1: 69–88.

Mutch, A. (2012a), 'Systemic Accountability and the Governance of the Kirk: The Presbytery of Garioch in the Eighteenth Century', *Northern Scotland* 3/1: 45–65.

Mutch, A. (2012b), 'Data Mining the Archives: The Emergence of Separate Books of Account in the Church of Scotland 1608–1800', *Scottish Archives* 18: 78–94.

Mutch, A. (2013), 'Shared Protestantism' and British Identity: Contrasting Church Governance Practices in Eighteenth Century Scotland and England', *Social History* 38/4: 456–476.

Mutch, A. (2015), *Religion and National Identity: Governing Scottish Presbyterianism in the Eighteenth Century*, Edinburgh: Edinburgh University Press.

Payer, P. (1985), 'Foucault on Penance and the Shaping of Sexuality', *Studies in Religion* 14/3: 313–320.

Power, M. (1997), *The Audit Society: Rituals of Verification*, Oxford: Oxford University Press.

Presbytery of Edinburgh (1706), Minutes 1705–1708, National Records of Scotland (NRS), Edinburgh, CH2/121/6.

Rowlinson, M. & Carter, C. (2002), 'Foucault and History in Organization Studies', *Organization* 9/4: 527–547.

Snell K. (2006), *Parish and Belonging: Community, Identity and Welfare in England and Wales, 1700–1950*, Cambridge: Cambridge University Press.

Steuart, W. (1802), *Collections and Observations Methodised, Concerning the Worship, Discipline and Government of the Church of Scotland*, Arbroath: T. Oliver.

Taylor, C. (2009), *The Culture of Confession from Augustine to Foucault: A Genealogy of the 'Confessing Animal*, New York: Routledge.

Thompson, E. P. (1978), *The Poverty of Theory and Other Essays*, London: Merlin Press.

Veyne, P. (1984), *Writing History: An Essay on Epistemology*, Manchester: Manchester University Press.

Veyne, P. (2010a), *Foucault: His Thought, His Character*, Cambridge: Polity.

Veyne, P. (2010b), *When Our World became Christian*, Cambridge: Polity.

Walker, D (1981), *James, Viscount of Stair, The Institutions of the laws of Scotland. Deduced from its Originals and Collated with the Civil, Canon and Feudal Laws, and with the Customs of Neighbouring Nations*, Edinburgh and Glasgow: Universities of Edinburgh and Glasgow Presses.

Weeks, J. (1982), 'Foucault for Historians', *History Workshop* 14: 106–119.

Wickham, Christopher (2011), '*The problems of comparison*', Historical Materialism, 19: 221–231.

Yates, N. (2009), *Preaching, Word and Sacrament: Scottish Church Interiors 1560–1860*, London: T & T Clark.

6 Government at a Distance

The Spiritual Exercises of Saint Ignatius of Loyola

Jose Bento da Silva and Paolo Quattrone

Introduction

Until the eighteenth century, 'government' referred to self-control, guidance of the family, management of the household and the direction of the soul (Foucault 2009). It is only after the eighteenth century that government begins to refer mainly to the State. Foucault's later work addressed this shift and the attempt to relate 'subjectivation' (Foucault 1982) with the emergence of the modern State using a single analytical perspective: governmentality. Foucault's approach to governmentality draws on the hypothesis that the modern State is a combination of political power (rooted in Greek political thought) with pastoral power (rooted in Christianity and its practices to direct individual conduct). Christianity developed a group of practices that facilitated the analysis of an individual, using individual reflection upon one's actions and desires and the spiritual director's supervision as the founding mechanisms of government over individuals. Furthermore, a different type of knowledge is associated with pastoral power: the knowledge of the inner truth (Foucault 2009). Pastoral power, having spread in the sixteenth century to other institutions (Foucault 2009), is related to the government of the modern State insofar as the latter relies on the knowledge it has of each individual and of the population as a whole (Foucault 2009). Although the State aims neither at the salvation of individuals, nor at the guiding of individuals to a better life in the afterworld, it does rely on the need to improve the welfare of the population as a whole. It is the principle of the welfare of the population that allows the creation of several apparatuses of security, underpinned by political economy as the preferred form of knowledge of the modern State (Dean 2010).

However, Foucault never detailed how the Pastorate might have transformed itself into a governmental form of power. This shift identified by Foucault was also never fully historicised, since most of the work done after the introduction of governmentality into organization studies looks at either how discourses translated into practices (notably by the 'London Governmentalists'), or into 'forms of knowledge and techniques that most intimately target the individual while also constructing particular populations'

(McKinlay et al 2012: 9). Although the work of the 'London Governmentalists' mostly kept the Foucauldian emphasis on the State, liberal societies and political economy (Miller & Rose 1990), governmentality studies did make its way into subject areas within organization studies (see *inter alia* Clegg et al. 2002; McKinlay & Pezet 2010). Furthermore, governmentality studies, and Foucauldian approaches for that matter, cannot ignore 'historical research that remains largely uncharted territory' (McKinlay et al 2012: 10). Governmentality studies have therefore clearly emphasised historical research. Some of the London governmentalists' most famous studies are historical in their nature (see *inter alia* Rose 1999; Miller & Rose 2008); and within critical accounting scholarship, one can hardly separate Foucauldian studies from historical research (see McKinlay & Starkey 1998; McKinlay & Taylor 2014). However, extant scholarship has rarely looked beyond the nineteenth century and seldom tried to historicise how governmental forms of power might have emerged from the Pastorate.

In this chapter we will reply to a call for more historical research on practices of governmentality, understood as the 'conduct of conduct' (Foucault 2009), through the analysis of one sixteenth century 'practice on the ground' (McKinlay et al 2012: 10), the *Spiritual Exercises* of Ignatius of Loyola.1 The *Spiritual Exercises*, we will argue, allow us to better understand how the Pastorate's practices, namely the direction of conscience and the confession, were put together so as to order the individual and the population.

Ignatius of Loyola was the founder of the Society of Jesus (Jesuits) and the *Spiritual Exercises* was the only book he ever wrote. It is in the *Spiritual Exercises* that one finds the roots for what is known within the Society of Jesus as the 'way of proceeding', which should characterise each individual Jesuit's behaviour and inform the way the Jesuit *corpus* (the organization) should also behave. The *Spiritual Exercises* are ultimately this 'way of proceeding' (Certeau 1973). They are not, in this sense, a book to be read, but a 'book to be practiced' (Quattrone 2009) following a predetermined set of exercises to guide action upon the self, organised around key moments, and which guide the exercitant's discovery of an inner truth. The discovery and verbalisation of an inner truth was part of the Pastorate's confession and direction of conscience (Foucault 2009). The *Spiritual Exercises* move beyond these techniques for the production of truth and allow us to revisit governmentality studies and their search for rationalities, their mediating technologies and the calculable and 'governable person' (Miller & O'Leary 1987).

In the *Spiritual Exercises* the manifestation of truth is subsidiary to the (or even replaced by, we argue) search of a place (*topoi*—Certeau 1973), which is closer to the truth. The *Spiritual Exercises* are in this sense about the unfolding of truth (Quattrone 2015) and not about verbalising and manifesting it (Foucault 2009). Order at the individual and the population levels unfolds via the procedural logics of the *Spiritual Exercises* (Quattrone 2015) and not through adherence to a specified substance.

This chapter is organised as follows. The first part will briefly describe governmentality, framing it within a search for 'technologies of the self'—technologies which constitute and shape a 'desiring subject'. The second part will analyse the *Spiritual Exercises* as a technology for the government of 'desiring subjects'. The third part will discuss how the Society of Jesus transformed a 'technology of the self' like the *Spiritual Exercises*, apparently used only for the shaping of individual behaviour, into a technology for the government of the '*corpus*'.

Governmentality

The type of power associated with governmentality is related to ethics, in the sense that governmental forms of power aim at conducting the individual, delimiting fields of action, rather than aiming at the individual's consent or at the deployment of mechanisms of domination. The governmental form of power is therefore beyond the 'juridico-discursive' and the strategic forms (Foucault 1997). Following these assumptions regarding the nature of governmental power, an analytics of government should entail an analytics of truth (Thompson 2003) which is underpinned by rational forms of knowledge, which, together with techniques for the direction and the regulation of behaviour, allow the deployment of practices of government that will be capable of delimiting the way individuals govern their conduct.

An analytics of government should therefore try to assess what is the specific reasoning behind the deployment of a group of practices that foster the shaping of individual behaviour. This means that governmentality and its analytics go far beyond the search for mechanisms of hierarchical observation and domination. Mechanisms of observation and domination, while related to another type of power, call for the assessment of practices for disciplining the subjects. However, as far as 'governmentality studies' are concerned, an analytics of government is more focused on the assessment of technologies of the self that allow individuals to freely conduct themselves through the application of practices that are aimed at the body, the soul and thought. Technologies of the self, although deployed at the governmental level, are put into action at the individual level: it is the individual who believes that she can modify her behaviour in a way that leads her to what she believes to be a better state of being, a better self.

Notwithstanding, 'governmentality studies' go beyond the capabilities of the individual and look for the mechanisms that shape autonomous individual conduct in a heteronymous way (Lemke 2010). 'Governmentality studies' critically analyse how a type of subjectivity can be constituted that leads to a determined form of agency. In the context of Foucault's work, this refers to an aesthetics of existence, whose practices shape the self according to a desired end-self. It is the autonomous self who looks forward to conducting an existence which is meaningful, *id est*, aesthetically relevant. However, the autonomous self is shaped through heteronymous practices which call for a rationality. Given that this rationality is not transcendental in character, it is through history that one can assess the way different sets of heteronymous practices have shaped different autonomous selves.

The rationality that sustains the shaping of an autonomous self is historically contingent, but even so pointing towards predetermined ends deemed capable of bettering the subject. In that sense, the governmental form of power can be at odds with the subject's individual will. In *Dits et Écrits*, when Foucault refers to the 'conduct of conduct', he precedes it by the expression '*action sur des actions*' (Foucault 1994: 237). A governmental form of power presupposes action over how the individual acts—it entails the possibility of delimiting individual action according to an overarching rationality of betterment, be it of the individual or of the population. And the desired end of betterment, which guides the governmental form of power, is informed by specific forms of knowledge and technologies. A genealogy of governmentality, its underpinning forms of knowledge and technologies, cannot therefore be detached from a genealogy of the autonomous self. That is what Foucault does when he analyses the shift from the Pastorate's 'rationality' of betterment towards the modern State's predicament of welfare. In his genealogical work, Foucault (1981) ascertains that one major shift occurred with the emergence of monastic life: the technologies of the Self came to be defined in accordance with the search for inner truth. In the Classical and Imperial periods, technologies of the self were primarily related to self-mastery, harmony and moderation. These were the principles that ruled the relation one had with one's master/philosopher. However, following the emergence of Christianity, the relation with the Pastor, the new master, was defined according to the desire for a life in the afterworld and with the revealing of one's inner truth. The knowledge of one's inner truth is what permits, in the context of Pastoral power, the rule over the individual's conduct and, *a fortiori*, the emergence in the modern world of practices of administration, control and normalisation (Foucault 1993). However, the relationship of the master to disciple, in the monastic context, is still asymmetrical: the master has direct power over the disciple. The difference between this asymmetrical form of power relation and other forms of power, also asymmetrical in their nature, is that Pastoral power relies on a relation of truth and not on a relation of either consent or domination. The fact that the power relation is a relation of truth, Foucault (2009) argues, will pave the way to the emergence of other forms of power also made visible as a relation of truth—governmental power.

However, in governmental practices there is still the need to resolve the antinomy between the individual and the power instance: 'Regimes of governmental practices constitute, for Foucault, specific types of governable subjects; they do so by shaping the individual's conduct from within: the individual acts in accordance with the conceptions of self-identity implicit within these practices' (Thompson 2003: 130). The latter are heteronymous practices, which are the crucible of an autonomous behaviour insofar as the rationalities behind those practices constitutes the rationality that shapes individual behaviour. In his *History of Sexuality*, Foucault (1981, 1990, 1992) traces the emergence of processes of stylisation of the self, which, through the emergence of Christianity and its focus on the knowledge of the individual's inner truth, led to a shift in the practices of examination and confession. These practices would subsequently form the basis of the emergence of modern practices of government, which call for the need to know populations, shape governable typologies and deploy welfare practices for the government of the population (Foucault 2009; Dean 2010).

In this sense, the critical assessment of a governmental mode of power can only operate, on the one hand, through the uncovering of the forms of truth that shape individual identity. On the other hand, the practices of government deployed at the entity/State level should be contrasted with the rationality of government that directs individual conduct. A critical engagement with such forms of government will therefore look for the ends of both types of practices, insofar as power relations' shifts should be sought for in the ends, and not in the means. This form of 'analytics of government' (Dean 2010), as a methodology, has resulted in several contributions to the field of governmentality studies, mainly following the template of the London Governmentalists' work (McKinlay et al 2012). However, among some of the criticisms that can be made to such an 'analytics of government', two are relevant for us. First, the various studies that follow an analytics of government have been framed within a specific historical period, the twentieth century, and looked for how a neoliberal rationality (Rose 1999) has been first problematised (Dean 2010), and then 'solved' via the construction of governable individuals who form populations 'perfectly' manageable and calculable. Second, as Bevir (2010: 430) puts it, 'work on governmentality can lose sight of the fact that people create meanings and practices'. Put simply, governmentality studies end up looking for how it is that individuals create one and only form of meaning and generate the same type of practices. This has lead to contributions on governmentality studies that most often seem to take for granted the success of every governmentality project, seldom taking into account issues such as resistance. Furthermore, 'governmentalists have shown little concern about tracking ideas over time and between quite different forms of institutions' (McKinlay & Taylor 2014: 21).

It is in this respect that we think the *Spiritual Exercises* might be of relevance for our understanding of the interplay between the Pastorate and governmental forms of power that emerged in the sixteenth century. The *Spiritual Exercises*' relevance is twofold. First, an analysis of the *Spiritual Exercises* from a governmental point of view moves governmentality studies back to the sixteenth century: 'government as a general problem seems to me to explode in the sixteenth century' (Foucault 1991: 87). Second, the *Spiritual Exercises*, as a practice, challenge governmentality studies' assumptions regarding how specific problematisations (Dean 2010) underpin forms of rationality, constraining individual action through mediating technologies. Even though the Jesuits problematised geographical distance, no specific rationality informed neither the *Spiritual Exercises*, nor their main practices for managing the Jesuit *corpus*. The apparatus of practices deployed by the Jesuits, and identified by Quattrone (2004, 2009, 2015), were to be performed locally and locally adapted. Furthermore, the local performance of the various practices generated local and geographically dispersed meanings, allowing the *corpus* to engage in multiple and apparently disconnected activities. In this chapter we will look at how multiple and local meanings might have been generated through the analysis of one practice, the *Spiritual Exercises*. The latter, we will argue, furthers the call for more studies adopting a governmental framework within organization studies, namely looking into how governmentality has been conceptualised rather than at its 'practices in action' level (McKinlay et al 2012: 9). Even though we will analyse the *Spiritual Exercises* as a practice (which they are), our main concern in this chapter will be to show how they point towards a specific conceptualisation of the autonomous, yet governable, self.

The Spiritual Exercises

The *Spiritual Exercises* are not a book as we would normally understand it. First, the *Spiritual Exercises* cannot be even considered to have been written by Ignatius. The text is the result of a writing process in which Ignatius spent around twenty-six years of his life (Bertrand 1974). The *Spiritual Exercises* started being written in Manresa, near Barcelona, Spain, sometime between March 1522 and mid-February 1523 (Arzubialde 2009), and the final Latin version was published in 1548. Along this process other 'authors' contributed to the final version of the text, namely Paschase Broet, Alfonso Salmerón, Pedro Faber and Juan de Polanco, all members of the early Society of Jesus. The participation of these Jesuits in the process of writing and translating the *Spiritual Exercises* signals the relevance of this 'book to be practiced' for the setting up of the order.

It is important also to understand that since they were first 'practiced', the *Spiritual Exercises* were destined to anyone who wished to take a decision in accordance with God's will (Rahner 1971) or change her life. In their original form, the *Spiritual Exercises* were to be practiced in retreats for the duration of one month, with four different phases, called 'weeks', even though the duration of each 'week' is not necessarily seven days. The process entailed by the *Spiritual Exercises*' four 'weeks' is that it will lead to a change of the practicing self. However, what is to be changed and how the self is supposed to achieve such change is not determined in the *Spiritual Exercises*. The *Spiritual Exercises* are no more than a group of rules and experiences which, through different ways of composing images, allow the 'ordered self' to unfold (Quattrone 2015). Therefore, what constitutes the ordering of the self is not predetermined. Moreover, the *Spiritual Exercises*' text has no external referent (Certeau 1973). What the *Spiritual Exercises* do is to direct the self towards a 'way of proceeding' ('modo de proceder' or 'orden de proceder'), which is a trajectory that starts with the 'current self' and ends in a 'place of greater truth' (Certeau 1973). The latter reinforces the fact that the *Spiritual Exercises* are a process with no predetermined way of being, no established end, and in which truth is neither confessed nor verbalised. Instead, truth is never achieved, but always searched for.

The Structure of the Spiritual Exercises

The first 'week' of the *Spiritual Exercises* is entitled 'Spiritual Exercises to overcome oneself and to order one's life, without reaching a decision through some disordered affection' (Loyola 1992: 21) and begins with a meditation on the 'Principle and Foundation' of life:

> Human beings are created to praise, revere, and serve God our Lord, and by means of doing this to save their souls. The other things on the face of the earth are created for the human beings, to help them in the pursuit of the end for which they are created. From this it follows that we ought to use these things to the extent that they help us toward our end, and free ourselves from them to the extent that they hinder us from it. To attain this it is necessary to make ourselves indifferent to all created things, in regard to everything which is left to our free will and is not forbidden. Consequently, on our own part we ought not to seek health rather than sickness, wealth rather than poverty, honour rather than dishonour, a long life rather than a short one, and so on in all other matters. Rather, we ought to desire and choose only that which is more conducive to the end for which we are created.
>
> (Loyola 1992: 23)

This meditation specifies the main objective of the *Exercises*: to decide in such a way that all possible outcomes are truly indifferent. The indifference looked for in the *Spiritual Exercises* is a design principle. In reality, no one is ever perfectly indifferent, and indifference manifests itself, at the individual level, in many ways. This multiplicity is made visible in the *Spiritual Exercises* by the fact that they enact actions, but not necessarily the same action for every individual Jesuit. The Jesuit who therefore results from this practice *cannot* be made visible, calculable and governable via mediating technologies like accounting (Miller & O'Leary 1987).

The four parts that constitute the *Exercises* are organised around this principle of indifference, which makes any decision existential in its nature (Rahner 1971). However, the indifferent individual is not fully indifferent insofar as he stops being indifferent after the moment he chooses the 'correct' option. Furthermore, indifference is not a relativist stance, but a call for more, or 'magis'. The self, driven by the '*magis*', the indifferent subject, is not the self-mastered subject of stoicism or asceticism (Foucault 1981,

1990, 1992), but a truly autonomous self. The indifferent subject is not nullified by ascetic practices, self-mastery or external forms of rationality, but is active in his search for continuous improvement. The 'magis' together with indifference constitute the *Spiritual Exercises'* autonomous self. However, the autonomous self is also a self-accountable one.

Unfolding Order—A Jesuit Way of Governing the Individual Subject

The *Spiritual Exercises* drew upon an analytical method to build a system of imagery construction that informed Jesuit rationality underpinned by practices of spiritual self-accountability (Quattrone 2015). This created and sustained a structure that supported a belief in the possibility of improving morals, the 'magis', and defining legitimate social behaviours and order, a 'way of proceeding', without fully defining this order. The *Spiritual Exercises* are a method of continuous ordering, for which no final desired status is provided. They start by providing a method of examination of conscience and to 'train' the Jesuits in preparing and disposing their soul to identify and remove the 'disordered affections' that prevented 'seeking God's will' (Loyola 1992: 1). The book also contained a series of analytically detailed guidelines for the Director of the Exercises, who gave them, and for the exercitant, who received them. It prescribed, for instance, the place where to perform the *Spiritual Exercises* (which was to be isolated and silent) and also the exercitant's body position (e.g. kneeling, standing, sitting, gazing upward depending on the kind of meditation to be performed). The *Spiritual Exercises* were organised analytically in a hierarchical tree where each exercise was divided into prayers, preludes, points and colloquy, and these in turn, were subdivided further into other analytical categories (see Barthes 1971: 57). The first week continued with 'a moral inventory of life' (O'Malley 1994) through a particular and a general examination of conscience intended to prepare the soul for confession. In the daily examination of conscience, the exercitant was asked to interrogate himself on his daily sins twice a day: The first after the noon meal and the second after supper at night. For the noon examination, for example, he was asked to provide 'an account of oneself with regard to the particular matter one has decided to take for correction and improvement. One should run through the time, hour by hour of period by period, from the moment of rising until the present examination' (Loyola 1992: 25).

Nowhere in the Exercises was the exercitant provided with a definition of God: he was simply given guidelines on how to praise God's glory. The contents of the Exercises were thus primarily methodological and illustrated procedural (the means, how) rather than substantial knowledge (the end, why). The *Spiritual Exercises* relied rather on the composition of imageries. A specific visual inscription was prescribed for this examination of conscience. For each sin committed from the moment of rising until the first examination, he was required to enter a dot (a punctus) on the upper line of the first series of lines (Quattrone 2004). This step was followed by 'one's resolution to do better during the time until the second examination' (Loyola 1992: 25) at night after supper. At that time, other dots were placed on the lower line of the series for that day, and the exercitant was asked to see if his behaviour had improved or worsened over the course of the day. The same process was repeated for virtuous behaviour. This examination was to be repeated each day of the week (from Sunday to Saturday, as indicated by each letter next to each set of lines), with the space available for inscribing sins on the lines reduced in length each day, signalling to the exercitant the need to improve his behaviour and establishing what Barthes (1971: 70) described as a system of 'accounting for sins'. This reflexive moral inventory of the self constitutes only the beginning of an imaginary journey that is obsessively punctuated by visualisations that will eventually lead to a choice (the election) that can prompt action. In that first week of the Exercises, the journey continues with the exercitant being urged to meditate about the seven deadly sins. He was asked first to compose the place where the action took place, in this case the sins committed, and remember how they brought himself 'to greater shame and confusion' (Loyola 1992: 50), to almost feel the pain inflicted by these sins to the body and soul.

Similarly, through the meditation on hell, one has to compose the space of hell by thinking of its 'length, breadth, and depth' (Loyola 1992: 65) and then 'see with the eyes of the imagination the huge fires and . . . the souls within the bodies full of fire' (Loyola 1992: 66). The exercitant, thanks to this imagery, 'will hear the wailing, the shrieking, the cries, and the blasphemies against [the] Lord and all of his saints' (Loyola 1992: 67); by his 'sense of smell (one) will perceive the sulphur, the filth, and the rotting things' (Loyola 1992: 68); by the 'sense of taste, . . . experience the bitter flavours of hell' (Loyola 1992: 69) and by the sense of touch 'feel how the flames touch the souls and burn them' (Loyola 1992: 70). The construction of these disturbing feelings is sometimes accompanied also by physical flagellation so as to reinforce imagination and mark the experience. These visualisations were intended to construct a completely immersive bodily and material experience. They were, as much in the art of memory, 'imagines agentes', i.e. images generative of effects rather than simply representations of mental and moral statuses (Carruthers 1990, 1998).

The practice of the second week of the *Spiritual Exercises* was in stark contrast with the first, and constituted a further step in the exercitant's journey. Here he was asked to perform a series of positive contemplations such as on 'The life of eternal King' (Loyola 1992: 91–8) or on the 'Nativity' (Loyola 1992: 110–17). He was to imagine the 'smell the fragrance and taste, the infinite sweetness and charm of the Divinity, of the soul, of its virtues, and of everything there' (SE, [124]). After having constructed these positive images, the exercitant was ready to meditate on the 'two standards, the one of Christ . . ., the other of Lucifer' (Loyola 1992: 136) and to finally make an election, i.e. a choice. Here, once again, the exercitant was asked to imagine a scene, almost a scenography, for the meditation to take place. He was asked to visualise two opposite camps, one close to Jerusalem for Christ and the other to Babylon for Lucifer, to imagine Lucifer seated on a 'throne of fire and smoke, in aspect horrible and horrifying' (Loyola 1992: 138), whereas God resides in 'an area which is lowly, beautiful and attractive' (Loyola 1992: 155). This is the prelude, or the condition for an election: The exercitant finally chooses God, and through this choice he finds himself.

The mirroring and imagery processes prompted by practicing the Exercises are always incomplete, where human incompleteness and fallibility are the pre-condition for further examinations (Knorr Cetina 1997). Meyer (1986) reminds us that the accounting for sins through the *Exercises* is useful to make sense of the invisible and opaque, rather than to represent what was factually visible (Quattrone 2004). What constituted the glory of God (*Ad Maiorem Dei Gloriam*, the Jesuit motto) was left undefined, and for the exercitant to discover through rhetorical practices of praising it, that is, by performing the *Spiritual Exercises* and its visual inscriptions in a search for God that unfolded indefinitely. But how can incomplete visualizations, which always show the fallacy of the self, sustain an accountability process without causing frustration and despair in the exercitant? The *Spiritual Exercises* supplemented the incompleteness of visual representations by asking the exercitant to perform a ritual that motivated him along a path which began with the self-recognition of being a sinner and ended with the possibility of the joy of salvation. The exercitant's work of analytic composition *in puncti* (points) reproduces the rhetorical rhythm which engages users in methods of meditation (O'Rourke Boyle 1997: 10). Thanks to this punctuation, which marks a rhythmical progression (Barthes 1971: 68) where the exercitant is explicitly requested to pray 'according to rhythmic measures' (Loyola 1992: 258), the *Spiritual Exercises* define a sensible and convincing route in that journey that the Jesuit member is asked to undertake. The *Exercises* offered what Carruthers (1998: 266ff) defined as a liturgical ductus, i.e. a way, a flow and a movement, an orthopraxis, analogous to an aqueduct, that begins with the realisation of being in perdition and eventually ends with the possibility of making the right choice, of finding salvation and realising a vision of truth, as was also the case with liturgy. They help the exercitant to construct and reinforce a belief in the possibility of moral improvement and salvation. This path, the 'ductus', was the classical rhetorical structure of 'medieval and renaissance masters of choice (where) a character (in this case the exercitant's self) was plotted as a traveller on the path of life, confronted at crossroads with moral decisions' (O'Rourke Boyle 1997: 10), such as the election of the standard of God versus that of Lucifer. Yet, this journey was punctuated by invocations to look to the future, for instance, before going to bed the exercitant was exhorted to think about the meditations and exercises of the following day. As much as in Ignatius's autobiography, the intent of the *Spiritual Exercises* was then not on the 'conveyance of information, but on the persuasion of judgement' (O'Rourke Boyle 1997: 3). The text of the *Spiritual Exercises* is not aimed at representing the self, but to engage (O'Malley 1993: 42) and train the self for it to become a means of judgment to praise God, where this God is inextricably linked to the self.

As noted by Barthes (1971: 45), the Exercises prompted 'a language of interrogation', in which the exercitant interrogated himself on his own nature in order to construct his self through the search for an absent God to be made present in the liturgy of the *Spiritual Exercises'* orthopraxis. And yet, being on a road to salvation is not enough for a good and wise election. The *Spiritual Exercises* state that in a good election: 'I ought to find myself indifferent . . . to such an extent that I am not more inclined or emotionally disposed toward taking the matter proposed rather than letting go of it. . . . I should find myself in the middle, like the pointer of a balance, in order to be ready to follow that which I perceive to be more the glory and praise of God our Lord and the salvation of my soul' (Loyola 1992: 179–80). The exercitant was asked to mediate in the double sense of being 'in the middle' (from medium, 'mid', 'middle of'), but also to be a medium to translate the glory of God into practical actions. He was asked to construct and inhabit a space in between two opposites, such as God and Lucifer. This being in-different (in the middle of difference) could eventually lead to a choice, not imposed by an overarching logic found in the orthodoxy of some sacred texts, but created and re-invented purposefully through ritual enactment of a series of methodological guidelines (Carruthers 1998), and the use of material artefacts such as the technology of accountability contained in the graphical 'accounting for sins' (Quattrone 2004). Definitions of God and of 'good' behaviour changed each time the ritual was enacted: definition of ends and means unfolded. The *Spiritual Exercises* then are a book 'not to be read, but to be practiced' (de Guibert 1964: 111). This indifference between the choice of two opposites, as Barthes notes (1971: 73), defines the 'virtuality of the possible' that was channelled only when the construction of individual morality encountered the always changing pragmatic purposes that the Jesuits had to satisfy when pursuing missionary, pedagogical and economic activities. It is praising God that generates the idea of God. Thus, the significance of the *Exercises* is 'moral not empirical' (O'Rourke Boyle 1997: 3): they prompt reflection (as in a mirror) but not representation (as in the modern sense of accuracy and isomorphic identity of an image to reality). In other words, the *Exercises* produce images that interrogate, and not merely represent, the morality of the self, and prepared it for being part of a collective enterprise. They are concerned with the production of knowledge and religious truths, and supplement the incompleteness of representations with a meditative structure that reinforces a belief in improvement, where this improvement takes place thanks to a movement along a path (again, the ductus) constructed through rhetorical practices. Going through this ductus is the means through which the ends are constructed, made practical, and recursively questioned.

Knowing the Soul?

The *Spiritual Exercises* lead to a specific kind of knowledge, existential knowledge (Rahner 1964), which as such is always subject to a continuous re-definition and which presupposes a mystical 'vision'. It is precisely the possibility of each individual's mystical approach to God's will, manifested individually, that is to be ordered at the population level. The ordering of Jesuit individuals was a problem Ignatius of Loyola faced even before he officially founded the Jesuits. First, of the first group of followers he gathered, in Barcelona and Alcalá de Henares, Spain, none persisted in their willingness to follow Ignatius. Second, the group that with Ignatius founded the Jesuits in Vicenza and Rome, Italy, was soon geographically dispersed. Lastly, after its foundation the Jesuits experienced exponential growth and an unusual geographical dispersion of its members and operations. This rate of expansion engendered management problems (Anselmi 1981). The Order faced the problem of co-ordinating its pedagogical and missionary activities with the more mundane but equally pressing economic aspects of its work (see Martin 1974, for France). Ignatius of Loyola addressed these problems effectively by combining harsh discipline with a profound spirituality (Evennett 1970), enabling the Order to adapt itself to cultural differences and historical changes while maintaining its principal object. The core of the 'methodological apparatus' (Barthes 1971: 45) devised to achieve this success was designed by Ignatius of Loyola himself in the *Spiritual Exercises*.

In the specific practice of the examination of conscience (Loyola 1992: 24–31), the exercitant was asked to interrogate himself on his daily sins, establishing what Barthes (1971: 71) described as a system of 'accounting for sins': 'Dealing with sins . . . helps to create between the sinner and the countless number of his sins a narcissistic bond of property: lapse is a means of acceding to individual's identity' (Barthes 1971: 70). This system closely resembles what has been written about the role played by accounting and accountability (Hoskin & Macve 1986; Roberts 1991, 1996; Hoskin, 1996; Willmott 1996; Watson 1997; Alvesson & Wilmott 2002) in the constitution of the self, and how this was even more crucial within Christian practices (Walker 1998). Willmott (1996) draws upon the ideas developed in Herbert Mead's theory of the formation of the self in childhood: 'In short, accountability is possible because human beings are endowed with a capacity to identify themselves as centres of consciousness that can engage in (seemingly) self-determined activity. Through processes of social interaction, human infants are expected, and are induced by others, to develop a sense of subject-object separation in which there is both an 'I' (e.g. a putative centre of consciousness) and a 'Me' (what others identify as the 'I')' (Piaget 1977; Willmott 1996: 34). This 'relationship between the self and accountability can be seen as an interior one, since the self is discovered only in the process of being called to account by others' (Roberts 1996: 44). It is, first and foremost, a dialectic established at an individual level, in which the 'Other', to whom our self ('Me') becomes accountable and visible, is represented by our own 'I'. However, in practising this examination, the Jesuit exercitant was not merely mirroring his own self by accounting for sins, but interrogating himself on his own nature, constructing it and discovering it through the search for God. As soon 'as a response is given, then [he] is positioned in some historical social space' (Wilmott 1996: 24), which, in the case of the *Spiritual Exercises*, takes the connotations of the space and time of the Jesuit *corpus*.

If it is true that 'the only way to God for a Roman Catholic was through the Church' (Searle 1974: 83), then the daily exercises devised by Ignatius for the 'salvation of souls' played a crucial, although not causal and linear, role in this ascension. These practices acted not as if they were superimposed upon the Jesuit member, but as thanks to his effort. As Alvesson and Wilmott (2002) observe, the development of 'mechanisms and practices of control . . . , do not work "outside" the individual's quest(s) for self-definition(s), coherence(s) and meaning(s). Instead they interact, and indeed are fused' with the work of identity construction which the exercitant is doing. Thus, before being accountable to God, one needs to enact (Weick 1979) the abstract idea of what God is, and the search for God to secure the salvation of one's soul is nothing but the fusion of one's self with this idea. Accounting for sins is, thus, first and foremost, accounting for God. In interrogating one's self, the exercitant was constructing the idea of God. This questioning and subsequent process of fabrication is inextricably intertwined with a broader network of political, religious, social and practical issues, practical being the nature of the *Exercises*. The exercitant is then a 'self' (a human being), for he becomes a member of a broader '*corpus*'. He, in turn, is recognised as a member of this '*corpus*', for he acquires the status of an individual being (Wilmott 1996).

This process of identity definition became even clearer when the exercitant was asked to make a choice in the second week of the exercises. Having prepared the soul of the exercitant, the second stage made it ready for making a choice on the 'state of life', under which 'his Divine Majesty wishes to serve him' (Loyola 1992: 135). This stage was conducted through a series of meditations and through 'a meditation on the two standards, the one of Christ, our supreme commander and Lord, the other of Lucifer, the mortal enemy of our human nature' (Loyola 1992: 136). It entailed a choice between two opposite states: one positive (God) and one negative (Lucifer), with no possibility residing between the two. A standard (the choice of the banner) is therefore a choice to pursue an unambiguous objective. In commenting on Ignatius' crucial call for a clear choice, Barthes observed: 'The language of interrogation developed by Ignatius is aimed [. . .] at the dramatic alternative by which finally every practice is prepared and determined:

To do this or to do that? [. . .] the duality of every practical situation corresponds to the duality of a language articulated in demand and response' (Barthes 1971: 48). Thus, within the articulation of the structure of the Ignatian language, which is common to virtually all western societies, one finds the basic condition to discern between 'good' and 'evil' and 'positive' and 'negative'—a system that, as argued by Hoskin and Macve (1986), places the 'zero' as a watershed between the two opposites, defining the longitude and the latitude of the accountability space. The accountability system developed by Ignatius in the *Exercises* seems to go beyond this vertical and horizontal demarcation, that would create a unique space and time. Surely, the 'accounting for sins' does create a horizontal dichotomy between 'I' and 'Me', as much as its 'bottom line' deepens this dichotomy vertically, digging into the self of the exercitant to find God and to make the self accountable to this super-ordered entity. The existence of an unambiguous number—be it the number of sins committed, the balance of a T account, the Profit or Loss of the Income statement or the Net Capital of the Balance Sheet—makes this accountability possible (Dent 1991; Roberts 1996). Analogously, the choice between the Standard of God and that of Lucifer is unequivocal: one must choose one or the other. However, despite the crucial importance of this dichotomy in the ordering project of the Jesuits, it is not sufficient to explain the complex nature of Jesuit accountability.

In this respect, what seems to be a horizontal dichotomy (e.g. I/Me) is simultaneously vertical—as it was for Nietzsche or Foucault (Macintosh 2002)—but also multiple, embedding as it does the enacted idea of God by each individual exercitant. The accountability system developed by Ignatius is powerful, not only because it constrains but also because it makes the individual free to find within himself what he believes God to be. The vertical and horizontal axes typical of a system of accounting and accountability take the shape, in the Jesuit case, of an accountability crux which works regardless of the position it assumes, and which constitutes the basic unity of the Jesuit hierarchical system. The *Exercises* presented the fusion between Ignatius' directives to define the 'good' Jesuit, a system of identity regulation (Alvesson & Wilmott 2002) and the construction of the identity of the exercitant. This was a fusion, however, the result of which was precarious. As Ignatius stated: 'It is necessary to keep as my objective the end for which I am created, to praise God our Lord and save my soul. Furthermore, I ought to find myself indifferent, that is, without any disordered affection, to such an extent that I am not more inclined or emotionally disposed toward taking the matter proposed rather than letting go of it, nor more toward letting it go rather than taking it. I should find myself in the middle, like the pointer of a balance, in order to be ready to follow that which I perceive to be more the glory and praise of God our Lord and the salvation of my soul' (Loyola 1992: 179–80).

This is the 'Ignatian balance sheet', as Barthes referred to (1971: 73), in which the choice, the mark between the two standards, should be of 'divine origin'. Barthes continued: '. . . one of Ignatius' disciples, Jerome Nadal, when asked what he had decided, replied that he was inclined toward nothing save to be inclined toward nothing. This indifference is a virtuality of possibles which one works to make equal in weight' (Barthes 1971: 73). The 'two standards' and their divine origin bring us again to the problem of the need for an outside rationality. However, not only is God never defined, but in the *Spiritual Exercises* the *procedure* matters more than the substance, not the least because the substance is never determined by any source external to the individual. For the Jesuit practising the *Exercises* enacted Ignatius' abstract directives, making them his own, and saw in them what he wanted to be, thereby granting a meaning to the choice of a state of life in doubt between the two standards of God and Lucifer. He finally chose God, and in this choice he found himself. Nothing seems more compelling and powerful—and indeed, it was extremely successful—than this system of individual accountability that was the base of a broader organizational accountability, where the absolutism of God is fused with the individualism of the self.

This sophisticated 'methodological apparatus' (Barthes 1971) constituted a fractal of three principles which were then recursively applied to the Order as a whole. First was a holistic individualism, the methodological principle of constructing the whole Order from its fundamental constituent, i.e. the Jesuit member as individual. However it was a construction that was not descendent and imposed from the top as in a disciplinary regime (Foucault 1977), although it was compatible with a disciplinary gaze. Rather this was a construction which was ascendant from the individual to God, through the enacting of the abstract Latin motto which guided the Jesuits (*Ad Maiorem dei Gloriam*, in the greater glory of God), experienced by each Jesuit by practising the *Exercises*. Second was a process of analytical (de-)differentiation: the fanatical obsession for division, of space, time and entities, which accompanied the search for the unity of God and the self. As with anatomy, in which the fragmentation of the body and the differentiation of its parts enables a new understanding of a body, including a body of knowledge (Sawday 1995), analogously the analytical reflection of the exercitant on himself through the particular examination facilitated the emergence of a new self. Third, was a double reductionism from God to the individual and vice versa. As Latour (1999: 70–5) stated, an ordering project assumes a correspondence between reality and its representation—a 'meeting point between things and the forms of the human mind' (Latour 1999:71). A precarious correspondence between the Jesuit member—the periphery of the order—and the glory of God—its centre—which needed to be analysed and monitored to ensure that: 'Each sequence (of orders) flows "upstream" and "downstream", and in this way the double direction of the movement of reference is amplified. To know is not to simply explore, but rather is to be able to make your way back over your own footsteps, following the path that you have just marked out' (Latour 1999: 74). These three principles embody a dual and apparently irreconcilable trend: one towards individuals and their heterogeneity and the other towards the unity and homogeneity of the whole. All three present a reflective embodiment in which each element presents the character of the others, which combines to produce a powerful methodological unity.

The Ordering of the *Corpus*

Governmentality as the 'conduct of conduct' emerged around the sixteenth century as a development of a previous form of power, which Foucault (2009) termed Pastoral power. Pastoral power is a form of power exercised by Christian Pastors throughout the mediaeval period over individuals and groups of individuals (the 'flock'). Foucault's analysis of the Pastorate was framed within a particular period, mediaeval Christendom. Foucault also treated Pastoral power as concerning all forms of relations between a Pastor and an individual or a group of individuals. This means that Pastoral power was addressed as a concept capable of describing a particular form of power unknown until Foucault's (2009) analysis, as well all the social settings that emerged in the Roman Catholic Church, namely its Religious Orders. Although Foucault defined the concept of Pastoral power as characteristic of all Christendom, he did mention the relevance of Religious Orders to an understanding of how the Catholic Church deployed such a unique form of power (Foucault 2009). Religious Orders give social reality to the type of social body that Pastoral power assumes, inserted in a specific space and time (Carrette 2000), and deploying the practices of Confession and Direction of Conscience, in which knowledge of the inner truth of the individual was to be verbalised. The *Spiritual Exercises* are not related to the practices of confession and the direction of conscience, and the result of this practice is not the verbalisation of the individual's inner truth. The *Spiritual Exercises* are not, therefore, a process of "analytical identification, subjection and 'subjectivation' proper of the 'procedures of individualisation'" the Pastorate entailed (Foucault 2009: 184) and which informed the analytics of a central concern of the 'London governmentalists'. In this chapter we point towards a different possibility. The Jesuit *Spiritual Exercises*, and the specific way of accounting they entail, start from a rationality that does not presuppose an external ordering principle. Instead, 'Jesuit rationality' unfolds (Quattrone 2015) through the procedure. Furthermore, the apparently 'individualising' practice of the *Spiritual Exercises* enabled the Jesuits to build a dispersed and ordered *corpus*, or social body, of individuals. The *Spiritual Exercises* do not turn individuals into 'subjectivised' selfs, capable of being measured, made calculable or differentiated via centralised administrative apparatuses. However, even without the putting of numbers into individuals, the Jesuit *corpus* does achieve order beyond the geographical limits imposed by territory. The Jesuit *corpus* was, therefore, a distinct, if early version, of what later emerged as modern organization. Following Foucault's analysis of 'governmentality', the way the Jesuits structured themselves is aligned, on the one hand, with a bottom-up analysis, which begins from how men think and act. On the other hand, the Jesuits also did use accounting both for economic matters and for the care of self and the examination of conscience, integral to the processing, though without the imposing of numbers on human performance, as in the late eighteenth century way (see Quattrone 2004, 2009, 2015). The Jesuits' governmental form of power entailed practices along the entity and the subject levels, and centred on the 'problematisation' of how to govern geographically dispersed members without losing uniformity of behaviour and doctrine. Accounting and performance review practices were all aligned with the need to overcome distance and allow the centre in Rome to know each individual member, even when situated at a significant geographical distance. All these practices assume the possibility of knowing the individual. However, they are not informed by any form of substantive rationality, the population of individual Jesuits has no fixed territory and they do not aim at the security of the population but rather at individual salvation. The management of individuals and of the Jesuit *corpus* is not based on heteronomous practices that coercively constrain behaviour, but on the assumption of the possibility of autonomous behaviour based on the deployment of practices that build a 'space of desire' (Certeau 1973) limiting the individual's set of possible actions: the *Spiritual Exercises*.

Note

1 All citations of the *Spiritual Exercises* are taken from Loyola, Ignatius (1992). *The Spiritual Exercises*. Translated by George E. Ganss. Saint Louis: The Institute of Jesuit Sources.

References

Alvesson, M. & Willmott, H. (2002), 'Identity Regulation as Organisational Control: Producing the Appropriate Individual', *Journal of Management Studies* 39/5: 619–644.

Anselmi, G. M. (1981), 'Per Un'Archeologia della Ratio: Dalla "Pedagogia" al "Governo"', in G. Brizzi (ed.), *La 'Ratio Studiorum': Modelli Culturali e Pratiche Educative dei Gesuiti in Italia tra Cinque e Seicento*, Rome: Bulzoni.

Arzubialde, S. (2009), *Ejercicios Expirituales de S. Ignacio—Historia y Análisis*, Bilbao/ Santander: Mensajero/Sal Terrae.

Barthes, R. (1971), *Sade, Fourier, Loyola*, Paris: Editions de Seuil.

Bertrand, D. (1974), *Un Corps pour l'Esprit*, Paris: Desclee de Brouwer.

Bevir, M. (2010), 'Rethinking Governmentality: Towards Genealogies of Governance', *European Journal of Social Theory* 13: 423–441.

Carrette, J. (2000), *Foucault and Religion: Spiritual Corporality and Political Spirituality*, London: Routledge.

Carruthers, M. (1990), *The Book of Memory: A Study of Memory in Medieval Culture*, Cambridge: Cambridge University Press.

Carruthers, M. (1998), *The Craft of Thought: Meditation, Rhetoric and the Making of Images (400–1200)*, Cambridge: Cambridge University Press.

Certeau, M. (1973), 'L'Espace du Désir', *Christus* 20: 118–128.

Clegg, S., Pitsis, T., Rura-Polley, T. & Marosszeky, M. (2002), 'Governmentality Matters: Designing an Alliance Culture of Inter-Organizational Collaboration for Managing Projects', *Organization Studies* 23/3: 317–337.

Dean, M. (2010), *Governmentality: Power and Rule in Modern Society*, London: Sage.

de Guibert, J. (1964), *The Jesuits, Their Spiritual Doctrine and Practice: A Historical Study*, St. Louis, MO: The Institute of Jesuit Sources.

Dent, J. (1991), 'Accounting and Organizational Cultures: A Field Study of the Emergence of a New Organizational Reality', *Accounting, Organizations and Society* 16/8: 705–732.

Evennett, O. (1970), 'Counter-Reformation', in J. Bossy (ed.), *The Spirit of the Counter-Reformation*, London: Blackwell.

Foucault, M. (1977), *Discipline and Punish*, New York: Pantheon Books.

Foucault, M. (1981), *The History of Sexuality: The Will to Knowledge*, Volume 1, London: Penguin.

Foucault, M. (1982), 'The Subject and Power', *Critical Inquiry* 8/4: 777–795.

Foucault, M. (1990), *The History of Sexuality: The Care of the Self*, Volume 3, London: Penguin.

Foucault, M. (1991), 'Governmentality', in G. Burchell, C. Gordon & P. Miller (eds), *The Foucault Effect: Studies in Governmentality*, Chicago: University of Chicago Press.

Foucault, M. (1992), *The History of Sexuality: The Use of Pleasure*, Volume 2, London: Penguin.

Foucault, M. (1993), 'About the Beginning of the Hermeneutics of the Self: Two Lectures at Dartmouth', *Political Theory* 21/2: 198–227.

Foucault, M. (1994), *Dits et Ecrits (1954–1988)*. Tome IV, Paris: Gallimard.

Foucault, M. (1997), *The Essential Works of Michel Foucault*, New York: The New Press.

Foucault, M. (2009), *Security, Territory, Population: Lectures at the Collège de France (1977–1978)*, New York: Palgrave Macmillan.

Hoskin, K. (1996), 'The 'Awful Idea of Accountability': Inscribing People into the Measurement of Objects', in R. Munro & J. Mouritsen (eds), *Power, Ethos and the Technologies of Managing*, London: International Thompson Business Press.

Hoskin, K. & Macve, R. (1986), 'Accounting and the Examination: A Genealogy of Disciplinary Power', *Accounting, Organizations and Society* 11/2: 105–136.

Knorr Cetina, K. (1997), 'Sociality with Objects', *Theory, Culture and Society* 14/4: 1–30.

Latour, B. (1999), *Pandora's Hope. Essays on the Reality of Science Studies*, Cambridge, MA: Harvard University Press.

Lemke, T. (2010), 'Foucault's Hypothesis: From the Critique of the Juridico-Discursive Concept of Power to an Analytics of Government', *Parrhesia* 9: 31–43.

Loyola, Ignatius (1992), *The Spiritual Exercises*, Saint Louis, MO: The Institute of Jesuit Sources.

Macintosh, N. (2002), *Accounting, Accountants and Accountability. Poststructuralist Positions*, London: Routledge.

Martin, D. (1974), *The Jesuit Mind*, Ithaca NY: Cornell University Press.

McKinlay, A., Carter, C. & Pezet, E. (2012), 'Governmentality, Power and Organization', *Management and Organizational History* 7/1: 3–15.

McKinlay, A. & Pezet, E. (2010), 'Accounting for Foucault', *Critical Perspectives on Accounting* 21/6: 484–493.

McKinlay, A. & Starkey, K. (1998), *Foucault, Management and Organization Theory*, London: Sage.

McKinlay, A. and Taylor, P. (2014), *Foucault, Governmentality, and Organization—Inside 'The Factory of the Future*, London: Routledge.

Meyer, J. (1986), 'Social Environments and Organizational Accounting', *Accounting, Organizations, and Society* 11/4&5: 345–356.

Miller, P. & O'Leary, T. (1987), 'Accounting and the Construction of the Governable Person', *Accounting, Organizations and Society* 12/3: 235–267.

Miller, P. & Rose, N. (1990), 'Governing Economic Life', *Economy and Society* 19/1: 1–31.

Miller, P. & Rose, N. (2008), *Governing the Present*, Cambridge: Polity.

O'Malley, J. W. (1993), *The First Jesuits*, Cambridge, MA: Harvard University Press.

O'Malley, J. W. (1994), 'The Society of Jesus', in R. de Molen (ed.), *Religious Orders of the Catholic Reformation*, New York: Fordham University.

O'Rourke Boyle, M. O. (1997), *Loyola's Acts: The Rhetoric of the Self*, Berkeley, CA: University of California Press.

Piaget, J. (1977), *The Development of Thought: Equilibration of Cognitive Structures*, Oxford: Basil Blackwell.

Quattrone, P. (2004), 'Accounting for God: Accounting and Accountability Practices in the Society of Jesus (Italy, XVI–XVII centuries)', *Accounting Organizations and Society* 29/7: 647–683.

Quattrone, P. (2009), 'Books to be Practiced: Memory, the Power of the Visual, and the Success of Accounting', *Accounting Organizations and Society* 34/1: 85–118.

Quattrone, P. (2015), 'Governing Social Orders, Unfolding Rationality, and Jesuit Accounting Practices: A Procedural Approach to Institutional Logics', *Administrative Science Quarterly* 60/3: 411–445.

Rahner, K. (1964), *The Dynamic Element in the Church*, London: Burns & Oats.

Rahner, K. (1971), *Meditaciones Sobre los Ejercicios de San Ignacio*, Barcelona: Editorial Herder.

Roberts, J. (1991), 'The Possibilities of Accountability', *Accounting, Organizations and Society* 16/4: 355–368.

Roberts, J. (1996), 'From Discipline to Dialogue: Individualising and Socialising Forms of Accountability', in R. Munro and J. Mouritsen (eds), *Power, Ethos and the Technologies of Managing*, London: International Thompson Business Press.

Rose, N. (1999), *Governing the Soul: The Shaping of the Private Self*, London: Free Association Books.

Sawday, J. (1995), *The Body Emblazoned*, London: Routledge.

Searle, G. W. (1974), *The Counter-Reformation*, London: London University Press.

Thompson, K. (2003). 'Forms of Resistance: Foucault on Tactical Reversal and Self-Formation', *Continental Philosophy Review* 36: 113–138.

Walker, S. P. (1998), 'How to Secure your Husband's Esteem: Accounting and Private Patriarchy in the British Middle Class Household during the Nineteenth Century', *Accounting, Organizations and Society* 23/5&6: 485–514.

Watson, T. J. (1997), 'The Manager as "Self" and "Other"', in R. Munro & K. Hetherington (eds), *Ideas of Difference*, Oxford: Blackwell.

Weick, K. E. (1979), *The Social Psychology of Organizing*, Reading, MA: Addison-Wesley.

Willmott, H. (1996), 'Thinking Accountability: Accounting for the Disciplined Production of the Self', in R. Munro & J. Mouritsen (eds), *Power, Ethos and the Technologies of Managing*, London: International Thompson Business Press.

7 Birth of the Pain Clinic
Governmentality, Identity and Chronic Pain

Steven J. Gold

Pain—pain of the crippling sort that never departs. Severe Life-Long Chronic Pain (LLCP) has existed as long as sentient creatures have walked the Earth. The challenge those of us with LLCP face navigating the modern workplace begins with the clinical intent to control the pain adequately and allow the LLCP individual to manage chronic and breakout pain attacks such that a day's work is possible. In the United States, the past few decades have seen an extraordinary shift in the treatment for those with LLCP. Institutionally, a single point of control emerged at the end of the twentieth century herding those with LLCP into a discrete, and entirely new, corner of the governmental-medical-pharmaceutical complex known as the Pain Management Clinic. How we understand LLCP in the workplace, how we as individuals with LLCP understand ourselves and learn to resist or simply manage expectations, in both the organizational and medical contexts, will find its best expression through Foucault's concept of govermentality, a construct that makes patent the bond between power, knowledge and subjectivity. Governmentalty provides a conceptual framework for identifying the pain management clinic as an emerging nodal point in identity formation and social control while exposing some of the unique phenomenological and practical challenges LLCP creates. The incipient nature of the pain management clinic makes premature a detailed genealogy of the sort Foucault for asylums, hospitals and prisons, an exploration of governmentality and the management of LLCP can engage the conditions of possibility for a genealogy to come. Rethinking LLCP through governmentality provides a productive insight into the possibility of identity formation for those with LLCP and even an identity politics that can create an avenue for resistance.

Foucault's sense of 'bio-politics' explains how society and social institutions operate through the creation of a self-regulating consenting individual. Supplanting the liberal notion of the singular self—the independent free and self-determining individual—Foucault understands the 'subject' through a 'bio-politics' of institutionally conditioned expectations that eventually implants in that subject's consciousness a sense of right conduct. By internalising the 'Master's Gaze', the individual navigating modern institutions, at school, work, in hospital or prison, learns to act, and self-correct, in a manner conducive to the institution's operational needs. A 'conduct of conduct' arises from this bio-politics and replaces the master's panopticon with a self-policing that assures organizational efficacy. This is the nature of identity formation and organizational control through 'governmentality' that can best frame our understanding of LLCP.

Foucault sees the individual subject as a product of continuously evolving institutions that create the boundaries and possibilities for identifying who we are and what we can become. Some wish to move beyond speaking of identity. However, there is still much to be done, particularly where the fight itself is just beginning to take place. In particular, cashing out the nature of 'disability' as an identity produced by techniques of practice within modern, even nascent, parts of the governmental-medical-pharmaceutical complex is a process still in the very early stages. Disability Theory has received much attention recently, but the discussion of diverse identities is hardly exhausted. To drill down, different types of disability produce very different senses of identity. One portion of the group we refer to as 'the disabled' that will be the focus of this chapter is those living with LLCP. Why examine this one particular sub-group of the 'disabled'? Discussion of Foucault, disability and identity already ranges from those with paralysis to patients suffering from severe psychosis (Tremain 2005). The answer is, as it frequently is, personal.

Scholars often choose to study issues of concern to our own self-expression and the barriers that keep us from living 'the good life' philosophers find so fundamental to the ongoing human discussion. Much of what has been known as 'identity theory' began by scholars exploring the political implications of their own identity, be it race, gender, sexuality and more recently disability. My interest in coming to understand what it means to own my disability, compounded by the fact that chronic and breakout pain is phenomenologically inscrutable, compels a significant level of reflexivity. Reflexivity has a place in any scientific method (Alvesson & Sköldberg 2009) and with a phenomenologically singular object of study, chronic pain, reflexivity can be essential. For evidentiary purposes, I will often unapologetically fall back on my own experience of living with LLCP.

In short, during college, my roommate and I jumped onto my motorcycle on our way to the library. Moments after leaving the garage my headlight went out and a pickup truck struck us, more specifically me, crushing my left leg and sending us airborne. Instantaneously a certain truth became clear—the 'disabled' is the only 'minority' group anyone can join at any moment. My roommate had only minor injuries. Fortunately I had a backpack full of philosophy books and managed to slide on F. M. Cornford's translation of Plato's *Republic* for about thirty yards down the street; in what must have been the most 'practical' use of philosophy imaginable (Plato 1941). After two years I re-learned to walk, do martial arts, travel and live well. But three decades and nineteen surgeries later, with more to come, each day brings constant chronic pain that gives way only to crippling breakout pain attacks. Neurological outbreaks, arthritic joints, replacement parts and more combine to make daily living, and the duties required of the modern academic, a serious challenge that only deteriorates over time. I have seen the pain management industry grow first hand from an anesthesiologist in the basement of a hospital decades ago to large business operations offering a range of treatments, some previously vilified. Caveats aside, I do not offer a genealogy of the modern pain clinic in this short work of philosophy. Rather, I intend to isolate the *emerging* identity of those with LLCP through governmentality.

Why Governmentality?

Foucault provided us with tools, concepts and sketches for understanding institutional development and the differential distribution of social privilege. In his genealogies, particularly *Discipline and Punish* (1977), Foucault, while famously claiming to 'cut off the head of the king', still proposed a view of the exercise of power as fundamentally repressive. Exploring the metaphorical use of Bentham's Panopticon model for a prison, where the structure allows all inmates to be closely and constantly observed, Foucault paradoxically reinforced the sense of power as a top down means to control behaviour. This would change as the logic of the panopticon evolved from an expression of external observation as a means of social control to the internalised panopticon of the master creating a self-regulating individual.

While the rudimentary ideas can be found in his earlier work, it was not until his lectures at the College de France that Foucault began to develop the notion of bio-politics, where the active subject is imprinted with a 'conduct of conduct' (Foucault 2010). Governmentality entailed a sense that management of the self through creating modalities of social control where the self, as locus of disciplinary activity, internalises the Master's Gaze and becomes self-regulating. Disciplinary institutions, through organizationally developed techniques of practice, create the self-regulating character that gives rise to the 'docile body' and an individual who consents to act in a manner conducive to reinforcing institutional control and minimising the need for overt coercive practices. Foucault's expression of governmentality provokes a call to conscience to resist repressive techniques of practice, while maximising the freedom-creating capacity of institutional enhancements. Governmentality has the elasticity to account for both the freedom restraining and the emancipatory capacities of social institutions in cashing out how techniques of practice create a subjectivity that is self-regulating and compliant with the demands of all manner of institutions.

Subject formation is a relatively new phenomenon. Simon Critchley reminds us that the 'Subject', the self or ego, first comes into English usage in 1796 (Critchley 1999: 53). 'Subject' derives from the Latin *subjectum*, literally, 'that which is thrown under' (Critchley 1999: 51). This foundational substrate is cast down, much like the sand beneath the paving stones of a brick porch. Critchley proceeds to say that the Greek origin of the term subject, 'hupokeimenon', or 'that which lies under', brings to the word 'subject' the sense of 'subject of study'. Etymologically, the 'subject' is understood as the 'foundation' of a given field of inquiry. Critchley tells us that 'philosophy after Descartes, is that this metaphysical foundation no longer claimed to reside in a form, substance, or deity outside of the human intellect but is, rather, found in the human being understood as subject: Heidegger writes "Man has become the *subjectum*"' (Critchley 1999: 53). For our purposes, we might read this, *pace* Heidegger, referencing the Greek origin of the term—'Man has become the *hupokeimenon*'—the subject of study.

For Foucault, population calculations systemically replace the sovereign discipline: punishment and discipline now target the mind, moving away from conditioning the physical body. This is not to suggest that what we think of as 'government', the institution that 'has a monopoly on the legitimate use of physical force' as Isaiah Berlin's commonly accepted definition suggests (Berlin 1958), does not play a central role in the process of studying the human subject and building institutions that form a 'conduct of conduct'. But the state is only one of many nodal points of power studying and defining the human subject: 'The state is only an episode in government' (Foucault 2010: 325):

> I intend this concept of governmentality to cover the whole range of practices that constitute, define, organize and instrumentalise the strategies that individuals in their freedom can use in dealing with each other.
>
> (Foucault 1984: 300)

Towards Medical Governmentality

Foucault left us with only a sketch of what he meant by 'governmentality'. Understanding the challenges faced by those with LLCP involves finding the point where managerial and medical governmentality intersect. Engaging the governmental-medical-pharmaceutical complex through the Pain Management Clinic entails compliance with a medicalised governmentalism needed to manage LLCP. Beginning with managerial governmentality and moving to medical governmentality produces the emerging identity of LLCP.

The great institutionalizations Foucault studied translate directly into organizational studies as the business world has the greatest influence on identity formation during our professional life. Much like the modern prison, the business organization survives through employee internalization of supervision, embedding a sense of right conduct in order to 'self-correct' work behaviours. Governmentality and the cognitively subsumed panopticon of managerial oversight differ with the organizational need. More generally, governmentality emerges historically with the rise of the modern state. The development of managerial governmentality can be located in as part of an emerging liberalism.

The liberal state battles to reconcile an open-ended concern with the populations' well-being with a determination that the state should be frugal, constantly seeking to curtail its activities in the interest of cost and liberty.

(McKinlay et al 2012: 8)

Panoptic control was 'about efficiency, transparency and legitimacy as much as surveillance'. As the welfare of the population becomes a central state concern so,

the growth in the state's administrative knowledge of its population, census, mortality, education, productivity, becomes both a source of knowledge *about* welfare and the measure *of* the efficacy of the specific state interventions and governmentality in general. That is where social statistics become central to the political debate and social interaction, measurement etc. . . .

(McKinlay et al 2012: 9)

This governmentalist logic becomes part of business organization: the sovereign consumer, the active citizen and now the 'empowered-employee', entail practices that 'mobilize, measure, and manage' these identities through incentives and sanctions that encourage self-directed behaviour (McKinlay et al 2012: 9). The 'conduct of conduct' begins to emerge in the modern organization, where skilled involvement from qualified subject matter experts, guided by standardised methods and processes, build an internal sense of right conduct and self-management. Foucault's rejection of Marxist and structuralist determinism placed him in a post-foundationalist position centering on the construction of compliant individual identities. This fundamental shift to the process of identity formation and the creation of the self-regulating employee is what makes managerial governmentality so useful.

Understanding the implications of the tenuous organizational identity of LLCP must begin from the point where managerial and medical governmentality meet. The business of managing pain brings together the techniques of practice forming this new subjectivity, peculiarly in the developing Pain Management Clinic. More specifically, before the creation of the singular pain clinic, a person with LLCP was a patient where pain was considered a secondary effect of a physiological problem. Working with a specialist, an LLCP patient with pathology in the cardiac or neurological system had their pain treated by that systemic specialist. Over the past few decades, pain management clinics emerged with the sole purpose of treating chronic pain, irrespective of the etiology. Walking into an orthopaedic office one sees immediately that patients share many outward characteristics. Crutches, braces, surgical scars create a commonality, a shared identity created by clinical practices. Enter a cancer facility and it is not hard to see how many features each patient shares—they immediately know one another and share a pathos. However, in a pain management clinic no two people look the same. Each patient comes to the clinic from a different systemic place, neurological, cardiac or oncology: yet each struggles to develop a shared identity since what they share is neither visible nor easily communicated. They are *all* chronic pain patients—the object of study and treatment often completely distinct from their systemic etiology. The techniques of practice in pain clinics that will eventually create a pattern for internalised conduct ingrained in the patient remains in its infancy. Contradictory legal requirements, pharmacies manipulating supply, insurance companies denying benefits in an attempt to mitigate risk and control costs, constitute a primordial soup of identity formation.

Moving to the medical component of governmentality allows a better understanding of the peculiarities related to subject formation and the 'conduct of conduct' in the therapeutic context. Shelly Tremain introduces her *Foucault and the Government of Disability* (2005) by defining how Foucault's notion of governmentality might help understand the identity formation of the 'disabled' individual. Tremain looks at events and accommodations, such as the Americans with Disabilities Act, redesign of urban affordances, closed captioning and more as a 'growing recognition that disabled people constitute a marginalized and disenfranchised constituency' (Tremain 2005: 2). Here, Tremain overlaps with a Marxian sense that given the functional need of productive technology, certain groups are exploited and others marginalised. The able bodied poor, people of colour, women, and people who work low-wage jobs differ from those considered unfit for productive labor. It is no accident that attitudes towards the disabled are changing rapidly as the information society now renders economically otiose many types of disability. Digital work can often easily accommodate many differentially abled workers, making the formerly economically unnecessary disabled member of the community a fully functional participant in the work-force, ready to move from 'marginalised' to 'exploited' labour.

Reading the development of Foucault's thought in terms of medicalised governmentalism, Tremain explains 'bio-power' through understanding the 'subject' as the object of medical and public health studies.

> In his lecture of 17 March 1976, Foucault remarked that this new technology of power, this bio-power, this bio-politics that begins to establish itself in the late eighteenth century, involves a set of measurements such as the ratio of births to deaths, the rate of reproduction, and the fertility of a population. These processes, together with the whole set of related economic and political problems, becomes bio-politics' first objects of knowledge and the targets that it seeks to control. It is in this historical moment, Foucault noted, that the first demographers being to measure these phenomena in statistical terms.
>
> (Tremain 2004: 4)

A new type of medicine came into being, one directed at public hygiene, normalising knowledge through data, creating public health education. Through bio-politics Foucault understands that institutions seek rational solutions, involving insurance, retirement plans, etc., that invest in the long-term health of their employees. Tremain notes that 'bio-politics involves the introduction of mechanisms whose functions include forecasts, statistical estimates, and overall measures' so that in the past two centuries the 'vast apparatus, erected to secure the well-being of the population, has caused the contemporary disabled subject to emerge into discourse and social existence' (Tremain 2005: 5).

A focus on the 'conduct of conduct', of identifying one's self with the norm of efficiency, emerges: to be treated requires a certain way of behaving and thinking about oneself. 'Human kinds' emerge as classifications in a self-reflective manner (Hacking 1999). 'Human kinds' differ from 'natural kinds' in science as people who come to identify as members of that human kind change their self-perception in what Ian Hacking calls a 'looping effect'. As new 'human kinds' are created, individuals of that 'kind' reflectively understand themselves in new ways and can shape the definition of the kind itself—something that does not happen in the a-conscious world of natural kinds. Identifying with a new kind of norm changes normalisation itself as the sublated synthesis of the self-reflected contradiction makes manifest the protean nature of the identity dialectic.

This shaping of conceivable choices allows the discursive formation in which people circulate to be normalised and legitimated. The 'social model' of disability in the UK makes the intuitive, if problematic, distinction between impairment and disability. The former may be inconvenient but the latter is detrimental to economic participation. 'Impairment may be seen in the lack of a limb, but disability involves a disadvantage, something imposed on top of the impairment caused by social organization' (Tremain 2005: 9). Social organizations create social affordances that favour some physical bodies and not others, those with an impairment that renders them unfit for labour. Disability is not a necessary consequence of impairment; impairment is not a *sufficient* condition for disability. Impairment on the UK model then is a *necessary* condition for disability (2005: 9). And yet, regarding directionality in causal relations, Tremain suggests something different:

> An argument about disability that takes Foucault's approach would be concerned to show that there is indeed a causal relation between impairment and disability, and it is precisely this: the category of impairment emerged and, in many respects, persists in order to legitimize the governmental practices that generated it in the first place.
>
> (Tremain 2005: 11)

The fabricated group, or 'human kind', called 'impaired', is created and persists over time in order to make sensible the concept 'disabled' as a category required by extant forms of expertise and institutions. Rather than understanding impairment as an individual lack, the missing limb or absent hearing, 'the impaired' as a social category is read epistemologically. We might idiomatically refer to one missing a limb to be 'impaired' in some sense. However, the social construction of the now named social group, 'the impaired', becomes apparent when looking at impairments we know to be fictions in themselves. It seems that every exploited or marginalised group suffers from language expressing beliefs that 'these people' need to be controlled or excluded as they lack some necessary constitutional condition. Be they allegedly organically less intelligent, by nature less motivated, or perhaps more violent, these contrived notions of 'impairment' exist to create the illusion of an organic deficiency overlaid with social affordances that legitimise extant power relations. The Foucauldian causal link lies not with taking an extant organic impairment and elucidating how that lack, overlaid by social affordance, creates a disability that produces exclusion. Rather, it is the socio-economic requirement for the disability not to impede the productive process that creates an appellation, and even an often complex self-appellation, of 'organic impairment' to come into being and persist. Fabricated impairments, functional for economically oppressing or marginalising certain 'kinds', illustrates from the extreme the epistemological and economic reading of 'disability' and suggests that 'impairment' is *not* a necessary condition for 'disability'. A similar epistemic reading is offered by Tobin Siebers: 'Identity is neither a liability nor a disability. Nor is it an ontological property or a state of being. Identity is, properly defined, an epistemological construction that contains a broad array of theories about navigating social environments' (Siebers 2008: 42).

Understanding identity, and *a fortiori* disability identity, formation epistemologically, is less controversial than one might expect. To be sure, this process undermines the ontological status of impairment held even by Merleau-Ponty, the sage of the philosophy of the body:

> The environment affords human beings to behave in a certain way whereas other ways are less supposable. For instance, chairs afford sitting on them just because human beings' knees, kneecaps, and thighs enable movements like bending the legs and sitting down. This relation between agent and environment can also be interpreted from the perspective of chairs: they are built in a certain way in order to afford and match certain embodied capabilities.
>
> (Merleau-Ponty 1962: 144)

This suggests that having two legs with knees that bend is 'normal'— expected—the way things naturally are placed in 'embodied capabilities'. Only 'abnormal' thighs are incapable of making the knee bend suitably for the 'normal' chair. Implicit in Merleau-Ponty's existential phenomenology is a sense of the normal and its relation to an idealised, 'normal' human body.

Interpreting the individual from the perspective of the chair assumes that chairs somehow exist in a 'normal' state contained in 'the given'. From the chair's view any significant deviation from that norm makes for an abnormal 'impairment' resulting in a 'disability'. Fortunately, chairs do not have 'views'. Chairs, tables and other social affordances are designed for economic and political reasons. That chair, so easily used by those who have knees that bend 'normally' as Merleau-Ponty suggests, may be a small table for someone, like myself, who has knees that do not bend well; or equally a chair may be an effective table for an 'able-bodied' person who happens to be smaller in stature. I traveled often with a colleague who was quite tall with very long legs and would be, on any account, considered 'able-bodied'. Yet an economy seat on an aircraft was terribly cramped and unpleasant for him. However, even with my disability, I fit quite comfortably into the next seat, given my height and considerably shorter legs. Standing side by side anyone would identify me as the one with a disability. However, which of us is disabled when confined for a long period of time to the extraordinarily restricted 'affordance' of flying in coach? Perhaps Merleau-Ponty only flew business class.

As much as Siebers' epistemological sense of disability identity formation rings true, I would take issue with his dismissal of pain itself as a possible locus for identity.

> Pain is a subjective phenomenon, perhaps the most subjective of phenomena. It is therefore tempting to see it as a site for describing individuality. This temptation is troublesome for two reasons. First, individuality, whatever its meaning, is a social object, which means that *it must be communicable as a concept*. Individuality derived from the incommunicability of pain easily enforces a myth of hyperindividualty, a sense that each individual is locked in solitary confinement where suffering is an object of narcissistic contemplation. People with disabilities are already too politically isolated for this myth to be attractive.
>
> (Siebers 2008: 60, emphasis added)

For those of us who live with LLCP this is an astonishing statement. Given Siebers' strong stand on the moral imperative to see disability not as an individual defect, but as a matter of social injustice, it is rather 'painful' to hear him suggest that the incommunicability of pain makes us narcissists. There is a serious challenge of hyperindividuality raised here that must be taken up, and it becomes the central objection to my claims about LLCP as an identity in formation. In response, I will try to sketch how pain can be communicated *sufficiently* to form an adequate sense of social identity such that an identity politics can emerge. Certainly, pain is phenomenologically singular and something that cannot be directly communicated. But the risk of hyperindividuality does not waive what is right in front of us. A new subjectivity is emerging from the techniques of practice in the developing pain management clinic. That people with LLCP should be left out of the democratic discussion simply due to the phenomenological complexity of inter-subjective discourse seems patently unjust as well as conceptually unnecessary.

Pain

The phenomenological singularity of pain is that its physiology cannot be seen, heard or measured in any way other than by indirect physical cues or analogies. To be sure, the concern for hyperindividualization is problematic for the LLCP individual, but perhaps not insurmountable. Verbal expressions tend to be limited to analogies: 'it feels like a hot drill boring into the bone'. Non-verbal cues are even more problematic. In any organization, the LLCP individual faces the constant necessity of obscuring those visual cues as pain expressions make others uncomfortable and carry a stigma. Seeing someone in pain produces a natural sympathy, or a repulsion. An accurate outward expression of the amount of pain I typically experience might be best displayed by grasping a knee and rolling on the floor moaning pathetically. This would make any kind of productive discourse, particularly in the workplace, somewhat challenging. Why is pain phenomenologically unique? I will then take issue with the seemingly self-evident view that an individual with chronic pain must always know how much pain he or she has—before going one step further. The LLCP individual may momentarily wonder if the pain exists at all. That may seem counterintuitive. Given the phenomenological challenge to inter-subjective communicability, the task of LLCP identity construction is uniquely difficult.

The Phenomenology of Pain

One of the most important works on the phenomenon of pain, Ellen Scarry's *The Body in Pain* (1985), suggests that:

> When one hears about another person's physical pain, the events happening within the interior of that person's body may seem to have the remote character of some deep subterranean fact, belonging to an invisible geography that, however portentous, has no reality because it has not yet manifested itself on the visible surface of the earth.
>
> (Scarry 1985: 3)

While I agree that pain exists in this invisible geology, I am unsure about her seemingly Cartesian form of phenomenological knowing,

> So, for the person in pain, so incontestably and unnegotiably present is that 'having pain' may come to be thought of as the most vibrant example of what it is to 'have certainty,' while for the other person it

is so elusive that 'hearing about pain' may exist as the primary model of what it is 'to have doubt.' Thus pain comes unsharably into our midst as at once that which cannot be denied and that which cannot be confirmed.

Physical pain does not simply resist language but actively destroys it, bringing about an immediate reversion to a state anterior to language, to the sounds and cries a human being makes before language is learned.

(Scarry 1985: 13)

Scarry is right in that 'for physical pain—unlike any other state of consciousness—has no referential content. It is not *of* or *for* anything. It is precisely because it takes no object that it, more than any other phenomenon, resists objectification in language' (Scarry 1985: 5). However, this does not make pain a private language where the phenomenon is encountered in an unmediated state of internal, albeit incommunicable, certainty.

Inevitably, this leads us to Wittgenstein. In his private language argument, pain is an exemplar since Wittgenstein agrees with Scarry. Wittgenstein's aphorism 246 in *Philosophical Investigations* asks:

In what sense are my sensations *private*?—Well, only I can know whether I am really in pain; another person can only surmise it.—In one way this is wrong, and is nonsense. If we are using the word 'to know' as it is normally used (and how else are we to use it?), then other people very often know when I am in pain.—Yes, but all the same not with the certainty with which I know it myself!—It can't be said of me at all (except perhaps as a joke) that I *know* I am in pain. What is it supposed to mean—except perhaps that I *am* in pain?

Other people cannot be said to learn of my sensations *only* from my behaviour—for I cannot be said to learn of them. I *have* them. The truth is; it makes sense to say about other people that they doubt whether I am in pain; but not to say it about myself.

(Wittgenstein 1958)

Wittgenstein supports much of what has been said about the nature of pain and inter-subjective communication. I would agree that others can come to know that I am in pain through indirect language, pre-linguistic utterances and visual cues; we will return to this. But, like Scarry, he also makes the strong claim that one cannot doubt that one is in pain. Wittgenstein goes so far as to say that even the word 'know' when speaking of pain is redundant.

Those with LLCP can doubt both that they have pain, at least for a short time, and quite often have difficulty knowing what their 'pain level' actually is. LLCP individuals have nothing to compare their current pain levels to, other than a recollection of a mental state sometimes long passed. When the only modality of comparison lies in relating a present mental state to a recollected previous mental state, extensive distortion is possible. Sometimes pain can be so common, so much a part of daily life, one begins to doubt, momentarily, if one even has that pain at all. That doubt will not last long; but it does exist. Of that I am certain. How can I communicate this 'truth'? Understanding pain mental-events as a *palimpsest* may clarify some of the distortion endemic to pain mental-events occurring over time. And still, the fear of hyper-individuation returns. When one lives in constant pain all day every day for decades, it is fairly simple to see how differentiating between greater or lesser degrees of pain may be difficult. But how can one not know that one has any pain at all? At times, chronic pain can become so familiar that it cannot be distinguished from normal everyday discomfort. It can take a moment of reflection to self-examine and ask oneself, 'where is the pain'? And while the pain is quickly located, and the comforting assurance that the pain that has become a life-partner has not left us, it does not obviate that momentary doubt. The difficulty of understanding our own pain mental-events compounds the challenge of how to communicate pain mental-events to others—a charge that gives rise to the challenge of hyperindividuality and the indictment of narcissism that must be addressed if we are to overcome this phenomenological objection to LLCP identity formation.

Further compounding the unique nature of pain mental-events are the interactions of other kinds of mental events that can be very closely associated with pain experience. Patrick Wall, in *Pain: The Science of Suffering* (2000), suggests that,

> Pure pain is never detected as an isolated sensation. Pain is always accompanied by emotion and meaning so that each pain is unique to the individual. The word *pain* is used to group together a class of combined sensory-emotional events. The class contains many different types of pain, each of which is a personal, unique experience for the person who suffers.
>
> (Wall 2000: 30)

Pain, stress, anxiety, fatigue, can combine to make phenomenological uncertainty all the more relevant. One need not go as far as Wall and suggest that pain supervenes on, or is of necessity associated with, a different set of mental-events. Pain phenomenon, in its many forms, can be *moderated* with an increased or decreased intensity by other 'sensory-emotional' events. When chronic pain becomes associated with tension, anxiety, stress and exhaustion, these mental-events serve to compound the individual's ability to manage pain. Hence, these other sensory-emotional events effect the LLCP individual's ability to deal with the pain experience and perhaps phenomenologically intensify the event. However, one can have pain in isolation such that substantial pain is possible to experience without being muddled by exogenous sensory-emotional events. A sudden crippling attack of neuralgia can emerge when one is in a relaxed state, stress-free and happy. Neuralgia attacks, the intense cramping of muscles and distortion of digits, where signals are sent telling muscles to cramp, digits to pull out of joint or bend in unnatural ways, can be among the most hideous of sudden pain attacks and may be entirely independent of other mental events. These kinds of neurological attacks can happen randomly at even the most peaceful moments. Pain, though it manifests in different forms, can exist in isolation even though it is typically compounded by related mental-events.

Communicating Pain

Attempting to cross the phenomenological chasm with regard to pain communication, three possible approaches seem productive. First, pain mental-events often provoke pre-linguistic visual and auditory acts. These events provide a cue to others that a pain mental-event has occurred and are a simple form of inter-subjective communication. Next, understanding pain mental-events over the long periods involved with LLCP can be productively understood as a palimpsest. The intertextual nature of reading pain-mental events makes the inter-related historicity of pain occurrences essential. Knowing pain through a trace, a remainder of what was, affords indirect access to pain mental-events over time. With these three approaches to inter-subjective communication and the deconstruction of pain mental-events we may clear some phenomenological space for LLCP identity formation.

Wittgenstein asks how far we can go using language to mediate pain and the external appearance of pain (Wittgenstein 1958: aphorism 245). For Scarry, pain lies beneath the crust yet has to be seen on the surface of inter-subjective experience. Physical pain, she says, 'destroys' language as the pre-linguistic utterances of suffering, cries that were ours before we learned to speak, makes language impossible. However, we might suggest that pre-linguistic utterances have inter-subjective meaning prior to language use. Even if we assume that such an utterance 'destroys' language, pre-linguistic signification can provide an avenue for communication and identity formation. Emoting pain through facial expressions, perhaps combined with holding the affected area, shaking, sweating, limping, creates an understandable language. The auditory primitive utterances in themselves communicate a pain state. Others understand that we are in pain and know 'pain sounds'. These pre-linguistic visual and auditory cues are part of our everyday experience. When my foot gives way and I stumble, often provoking a slight pain sound, adequate information is provided to the other to amount to 'language' as the event itself has the *perlocutionary* property of a speech act (Austin 1962). Seeing the mechanical failure and hearing the primitive pain response often provokes in the other a sense that a pain event occurred. The perlocutionary property of pain-related pre-linguistic acts and utterances creates an inter-subjective experience that amounts to communication. Phenomenologically we may call this 'pre-linguistic', but words may not always be needed. To a great extent people know the natural pre-linguistic meaning of these cues and do not need language to recognise a request for assistance.

These pain expressions clearly have meaning and can be a form of inter-subjective communication.

Taking this line of thinking a step further, while the primitive utterances or actions of a child emote pain experience in an unmediated manner, the adult, particularly the individual with LLCP, learns to control these primitive pre-linguistic utterances and physical cues that express pain in ordinary social interaction. Learning to handle pain and suppress primal pain reactions is part of the maturing process for any person. Learning to control the cues peculiarly associated with pain is a practice that LLCP individuals must perfect if they want to interact in a complex social and organizational context. Visual cues are often misleading. Shaking hands and sweat are often taken as signs of nervousness, irritability, uncertainty, disagreement or even a lack of understanding. However, all communication is open to distortion and impoverished interpretation. Hence, these pre-linguistic utterances or visual cues, far from 'destroying language', seem to amount to a level of inter-subjective communication perhaps adequate to begin to build an identity for those with LLCP.

Through the phenomenological challenge of comparing pain mental-events over time, pain experience may profitably be understood as a palimpsest. The ancient text that has been written on vellum, a material too valuable to simply discard, is then scrubbed for reuse but never completely cleaned, only partially erased, and then written over again. Elements of the text past remain and create an intertextual reading as a palimpsest. 'Reading' pain experience as palimpsest profitably expresses the governmentalist evolution. Pain mental-events can be read in terms of a new attempt to control the primal need to express the pain mental-event in a manner disadvantageous to social interaction as a partial erasure of similar previous pain mental-events and a rewriting within the current event's historicity. Unlike 'peeling back the layers of an onion', where each coat is layered on top of the last such that we must remove the outer layers to find the more meaningful inner coats, the palimpsest tells us of the intertextuality of pain mental-events within the historicity and governmentality of each occurrence. Perhaps if we see how new pain mental-events overwrite, to a greater or lesser degree, previous mental-events, the nuance of controlled rethought will provide greater insight. Of course, this analogous notion derives, in part, from how Kristeva (1980) and others understood intertexuality as a palimpsest of interacting layered literary events living within their historicity. The notion of seeing pain events as a phenomenological partial erasure and rewriting over pain events from the past, social interactions that conditioned the disciplining of the cues layered and partially re-rewritten at varying points in time, pain as palimpsest is a substantial advance in understanding the ontological nature of pain. This approach to pain can help the LLCP individual learn to 'read' the intertextual mental-events and express pain in the nuanced fashion needed to relate the governmentalist overlay. Understanding extant phenomenological features of pain mental-events as a palimpsest, created through repeated partially overwritten historically conditioned prior pain mental-events, may take us further down the road towards a detailed account of inter-subjective communication adequate for LLCP subject formation.

Beyond pre-linguistic pain expressions and the palimpsest, we might productively look to understand pain communication by showing where it is not. In some sense pain can be understood and communicated as an erasure, as a trace left to be understood. I will resist the temptation to go down the Derridean path of the 'trace' as contradiction not present.

Consider instead a more ordinary language use of the term 'trace', communicating pain mental-events by knowing the remainder, the effect, perhaps what it has left behind. I know that I am often unaware of the limp pain produces to the point where I insist that I am not limping at all. Of course, my wife will then gently ask me to remove my left shoe. The wear on the outside left part of the shoe's heel demonstrates that again she is right about most things. I now know that I have been limping from pain by the trace, the part of shoe's sole that is no longer there. Strangely, I am consistently amazed by that fact. Limping from pain, much like pain itself, becomes so much a part of the LLCP experience that one can simply forget it happens, deny it, and only when faced with the effects, the trace left by the pain mental-event, come to see the self-in-pain for what it is. The logic of the trace, knowing by the effect, gives credence to the notion that chronic pain can be communicated effectively, albeit indirectly.

The unique phenomenological nature of pain challenges our ability to have an identity founded on a linguistically incommunicable phenomenon. In response I would suggest that the pain experience is *adequately* communicable if directly inexpressible through codified language. Perhaps we do not need to find an *optimal* means of linguistic communication for identity formation. A *satisfactory* minimal level will have to do, for now. It may be possible to conceive of effective pain communication both in terms of relating the experience in primal pre-linguistic verbal and physical cues as language, and deconstructing pain mental-event texts as a palimpsest, or look to the simple trace, a remainder indicative of the pain that was.

The Emerging Governmentality of the Pain Clinic

The rise of the modern pain clinic presents a new nodal point for identity construction within the social. Over just the past few decades, the singular point of contact for a patient dealing with chronic pain consolidated into a clinic with only modest techniques of practice. It is too early in the development of the pain clinic for genealogy. The modern pain clinic is now where the LLCP patient engages with the governmental-medical-pharmaceutical complex, and as such, needs to be seen in terms of governmentality in order to understand, and where needed and possible resist, the developing forms to 'conduct our conduct' needed to receive the treatment that makes our participation in the governmentalised work environment possible.

In today's environment we take for granted that relieving pain is desirable and that physicians and everyday people should try to realise this end as much as possible. Richard Rorty borrows the definition of a traditional 'liberal' from Judith Shklar, 'who says that liberals are the people who think that cruelty is the worst thing we can do' (Rorty 1999: xv). Stopping the infliction of cruelty implies the imperative to relieve suffering. And the command to alleviate suffering, having its roots in the Aeschelepian imperative to 'do no harm', has long been part of the medical profession. Yet in practice, these values have not always been embraced.

For much of human history pain has defined the human experience, and is, as Marcia Meldrum (2003: 1) puts it, 'the central metaphor of Christian thought: the test of faith in Job, the sacrificial redemption of the crucifixion'. Similarly, the pain of childbirth was seen as the price paid to expunge original sin. To alleviate that pain was to interfere with the will of the almighty. In terms of emerging pain treatments, anaesthesia violated the religious need for pain as a way of strengthening faith and deepening maternal self-sacrifice (Meldrum 2003: 1–2). Not everyone valued controlling pain through the emerging use of chloroform in the mid-nineteenth century, in childbirth, surgery or elsewhere.

Pain plays an important diagnostic role for the physician, as a symptom of a pathology. That said, the use of anesthesia in surgical settings became commonplace in the late nineteenth century. Opioids by this time were in wide use, treating acute and chronic pain, and palliation for those dying of incurable and painful diseases. Laudanum, for all the dangers of abuse, found widespread acceptance by the end of the century. While in the early twentieth century, the Bayer Company developed a form of diacetylated morphine that they trademarked as Heroin (Meldrum 2003: 2).

Where pain mental-events become even more complex, the most crippling of all pain attacks, neuralgia, has seen validation only quite recently. Meldrum relates the misery of chronic neurological pain, those with phantom limb pain and neuralgia that persisted long after the physical wounds healed, first encountered clinically during and after the American civil war. Unfortunately physicians began to develop diagnostics and classifications that labeled unexplained neuropathic pain as something other than 'true' pain: 'By the 1920's . . . those who suffered from unexplained chronic pain syndromes were often regarded as deluded or were condemned as malingerers or drug abusers' (Meldrum 2003: 3). Sadly, this attitude persists to this day. A better understanding of neuralgia, if not treatment, has moved to remedy that thinking to some extent. Nerve blocks allow anesthesiologists to, at least temporarily, calm the offending nerve. The first nerve block pain clinic was opened in 1936 (Meldrum 2003: 4). Society began to develop a sense that we are not malingerers any more than we are narcissists.

After World War II John Bonica began building multi-disciplinary pain clinics and creating cross-departmental research into pain management. His

1953 book, *The Management of Pain*, created a sensation that started much of modern pain management thought (Meldrum 2003: 4). In the field of pain management, it was not until 1965 that the 'gate control' model of pain changed the way physicians thought about neuropathy, validating its existence medically and confirming that pain without seemingly adequate external etiology could be explained by neural mechanisms. It is here that the modern pain management industry, as we are coming to know it today, truly begins. It was in the 1970s that the journal *Pain* was established and an International Association created for the inter-disciplinary study of pain began its work. The pain management clinic as a centralised place to handle diverse pain pathologies is, then, a novel phenomenon.

It is clear how the pain management industry has developed. And with that comes the contradictions that will, in time, form the governmentality of managing chronic pain. Until the fight for governmentalist control abates and profit maximisation and organizational efficiency is assured through a well-developed 'conduct of conduct', we will continue to see a chaotic scramble for control through colliding and colluding institutions. This leaves the LLCP individual, among the most vulnerable of patients, unprotected and severely underserved. The insurance companies often still subscribe to the outdated 'specificity theory' of early pain management rather than the more advanced 'gate theory'. The lack of clear etiology, particularly with neuralgia, the incommunicability and phenomenological singularity of the pain mental-event, gives reason for insurance companies to deny or delay claims for those with LLCP. The refusal to reimburse inter-disciplinary pain management programmes flies in the face of proven approaches to working with chronic pain patients (Schatman 2011: 418). This part of the governmental-medical-pharmaceutical complex conditions the possibilities for treatment needed for participation in the workplace. Delaying service through pre-authorizations effectively postpones treatment, often making treatment unavailable or less effective. Ordering slow, often odious, independent medical examinations throws up another barrier: 'there is little doubt that the health insurance industry has developed numerous strategies for limiting the scope and the quality of care that chronic patients receive, with these strategies serving to perpetuate suffering in what is already a very vulnerable population' (Schatman 2011: 420). Our vulnerability is an obvious opportunity to begin to embed a 'conduct of conduct'. These painful, useless delaying tactics create a protocol we must follow to assure risk reduction and maximised profit for insurers. The patient learns to go along and accepts that reality as there simply is no other choice. We conduct ourselves as the insurance company says we should as the legitimate therapeutic treatment is available to us only if we consent to a protocol advantageous to the industry in terms of aggregate cost control but often of no therapeutic value to the patient. A crude governmentality is coming into being.

Nothing in the pain management world better exemplifies the chaos in creating a chronic pain governmentality better than the regulatory and economic flux surrounding opioid use. Opioids have been the central modality in treating pain for millennia. On the reasoning that non-pain patients abuse narcotics with sometimes fatal implications, limitations placed on the availability of these pharmaceuticals has had a tremendous impact on the LLCP patient's ability to control pain. And while the National Institute for Health Director, Dr. Francis Collins (Collins 2015), is clear that opioid painkillers have a role in managing chronic pain caused by severe injuries, she admits that there are no long term studies of its efficacy. Without any clear science behind long-term opioid treatment, hyper-regulation easily becomes a reality. Of course, that physicians may have just discovered the need to do studies on long-term opioid use for LLCP patients does not obviate the evidence known to those who have had long-term success. Without the requisite 'science' to back up the need, the burden is placed solely on the LLCP patient to demonstrate drug efficacy and defend treatment choices until the right physicians find the time to write for the appropriate research grant. Given what we have learned regarding the nearly insurmountable challenge of communicating pain mental-events, placing the evidentiary burden solely on one with LLCP creates a significant vulnerability and creates an encumbrance no patient should endure.

Most critically, the use of opioids, historically the most fundamental tool used in pain management, inserts a sense of 'vice' into the discussion. The stigma so often associated with disability (Goffman 1963) is radically compounded by the puritanical sentiments conditioning the discussion of opioid treatment. No other patient must live in a constant state of self-justification to others in order to receive needed medication. In the puritanical mind, pain medication needed by LLCP patients is a weakness born of vice that must be central to the panopticon—justified through odious scrutiny of the patient and health care provider. The palpable sense of guilt until proven innocent exists where science has not adequately tread and where demonstrating innocence, if such a thing is possible, makes the communicative challenge substantially more disturbing. What other patient faces the constant accusation of 'addiction' and contributing to social 'depravity' for seeking a treatment on which they 'depend'? Dependency is not addiction. Heart patients are dependent on their nitroglycerin but are not considered addicted malingerers. To the point, we might have established possible grounds for inter-subjective communication adequate for identity formation, but the same cannot be said for communication with government regulators and the insurance industry.

Beyond the stigma, beyond the association with vice, in the larger governmentalist conflagration examples are made of outlier unscrupulous physicians who prescribe for money. Patients who take their medication can now be convicted of driving under the influence and can face harsh penalties if their medication is misused. However, the legal persecution of physicians, duty bound to relieve suffering, LLCP patients exasperated attempting to find care, resistance organised by the American Society of Consulting Pharmacists against the pharmaceutical companies themselves, contradictions between the interests of doctors, pharmaceutical companies, pharmacists, insurance companies and the government as they battle it out over profit maximisation, public health and the benefits of being the locus of governmentalist control of a highly lucrative industry, has created a situation of tremendous uncertainty. LLCP individuals are simply baffled as to how they should 'conduct their conduct' in order to simply manage day to day living. Gradually an orderly system of profit maximisation and control will emerge, the confusion will ease and a clear 'conduct of conduct' will come forward. The networks of colluding and colliding institutions are barely beginning to integrate to the point where the individual with LLCP can identify let alone internalise conduct conducive to the operations of the pain management industry. This is an emerging governmentality and until the dust settles, attempting a genealogy is premature and the LLCP identity produced by this nascent governmentality must be understood as existing in a primitive and unstable state.

Conclusion

The governmentality of managing pain is beginning to provoke some resistance, or at least a small form of direct organization putatively advocating for those with LLCP. If we accept the claim that hyperindividuality and a concomitant 'narcissism' derive of necessity from an attempt to found an identity on putatively incommunicable pain mental-events, then we would be forced to ignore the LLCP advocacy groups that are just taking root. Outside of the medical societies for pain management and those with vested economic or professional interest, non-profit support organizations for LLCP are beginning to form. The US Pain Foundation, a non-profit support organization, developed the 'Invisible Project', which disseminates thought provoking photographs of those with LLCP. The images connect the viewer to the pre-linguistic component of pain mental-events we all share to 'create pain awareness, empower survivors and generate change'. The American Chronic Pain Association has a similar mission, providing useful information in order to help the individual with LLCP become 'a well informed consumer'. By no means are these organizations warriors for LLCP identity politics. Even a 501(c) 3 non-profit corporation is still a corporation. It is not a matter of which, if any, of the new operations truly has the LLCP patients' interests fully at heart. That organizations are working to develop an LLCP community, advocate for LLCP rights and create channels for action suffices to show that an LLCP identity must exist as well. How genuine or effective any of the extant organizations are is open for discussion. Their existence, however, is not. And if a rudimentary LLCP identity politics exists, then a basic LLCP identity must exist, as nothing can be phenomenologically impossible if it is socially actual.

As a concluding thought peculiar to the American self-understanding and its relation to disability simpliciter, the Foucauldian approach to the governmentalism of disability challenges the deeply held liberal notion of the self-contained, able-bodied and naturally autonomous individual so critical to American self-identity. Rosemary Garland Thomson (1997) expresses this elegantly by turning to Ralph Waldo Emerson's quintessential nineteenth century American Transcendentalist's work *Self-Reliance*:

> And now we are men . . . not minors and invalids in a protected corner, not cowards fleeing before a revolution, but guides, redeemers, and benefactors . . . advancing on chaos in the dark.
>
> (Thomson 1997: 134)

The vision of 'real men' as strong, able-bodied and capable of being the self-reliant American who conquers the western frontier to achieve a manifest destiny that casts the disabled as living in a protected corner, impotent and of no more assistance to the economic task of building America than a child or a coward. 'Thus translated', Thomson comments, 'physical difference yields a cultural icon signifying violated wholeness, unbounded incompleteness . . . susceptibility to external forces. The body's threat of betrayal thus compartmentalized the mythical American self as unfolded, unobstructed and unrestrained, according to its own manifest destiny' (Thomson 1997: 26). The 'disabled' self becomes a threat to our idiosyncratic nationalistic ambitions and our sense of who we are as Americans. Engaging this 'unpatriotic' stigma daily, those of us with LLCP must be mindful of the extant ordoliberal governmentality of the pain management clinic as it grows within its historicity. Michel Foucault's governmentalist method of understanding power in the social underlies the institutions leveraging the LLCP stigma after herding us into this new singular institutional point of social control. Finding robust modes of communication such that we can build solidarity and perhaps create social hope (Rorty 1999) is the challenge we must meet.

References

Alvesson, M. & Sköldberg, K. (2009), *Reflexive Methodology: New Vistas for Qualitative Research*, London: Sage.

Austin, J. L. (1962), *How to Do Things with Words*, Oxford: Oxford University Press.

Berlin, I. (1958), 'Two Concepts of Liberty', in I. Berlin (1969), *Four Essays on Liberty*, Oxford: Oxford University Press.

Collins, F. (2015), 'Managing Chronic Pain: Opioids Are Often Not the Answer', posted on 27 January 27, NIH Director's Blog.

Critchley, S. (1999), *Ethics, Politics, Subjectivity: Essays on Derrida, Levinas & Contemporary French Thought*, London: Verso.

Foucault, M. (1977), *Discipline and Punish*, New York: Pantheon Books.

Foucault, M. (1984) "the Ethics of Concern for the Self as a Practice of Freedom." In Foucault M. 1997. Ethics: Subjectivity and Truth, the Essential Works I. Ed. P. Rabinow. London Penguin Press, 281–301.

Foucault, M. (2010), *The Birth of Biopolitics: Lectures at the Collège de France, 1978–1979*, New York: Picador.

Goffman, E. (1963), *Stigma: Notes on the Management of Spoiled Identity*, Englewood Cliffs, NJ: Prentice-Hall.

Hacking, I. (1999), *The Social Construction of What?* Cambridge, MA: Harvard University Press.

Kristeva, J. (1980), *Desire in Language: A Semiotic Approach to Literature and Art*, New York: Columbia University Press.

McKinlay, A., Carter, C. & Pezet, E. (2012), 'Governmentality, Power, and Organization', *Management and Organizational History* 7/3: 3–16.

Meldrum, M. (2003), 'A Capsule History of Pain Management', *Journal of the American Medical Association* 290/18: 2470–2475.

Merleau-Ponty, M. (1962), *Phenomenology of Perception*, London: Routledge & Kegan Paul.

Plato (1941), *The Republic*, translated by F. M. Cornford, Oxford: Oxford University Press.

Rorty, R. (1999), *Philosophy and Social Hope*, London: Penguin.

Scarry, E. (1985), *The Body in Pain: The Making and Unmaking of the World*, Oxford: Oxford University Press.

Schatman, M. (2011), 'The Role of the Health Insurance Industry in Perpetuating Suboptimal Pain Management', *Pain Medicine* 12: 415–426.

Siebers, T. (2008), *Disability Theory*, Ann Arbor, MI: University of Michigan Press.

Thomson, R. (1997), *Extraordinary Bodies: Figuring Physical Disability in American Culture and Literature*, New York: Columbia University Press.

Tremain, S. (2005), *Foucault and the Government of Disability*, Ann Arbor, MI: University of Michigan Press.

Wall, P. (2000), *Pain: The Science of Suffering*, New York: Columbia University Press.

Wittgenstein, L. (1958), *Philosophical Investigations*, New York: MacMillan.

Part IV

Expertise, Experts and Governmentality

8 'Bottled Magic'

The Business of Self-Knowledge

Alan McKinlay and Scott Taylor

Introduction: Testing, Testing

'Governmentality' refers to the ways that the social is imagined and governed. The term originated with Michel Foucault, who provided only glimpses of what he meant. Nikolas Rose and Peter Miller are central figures to the 'London governmentalists', who have used this approach to mapping the social by various accounting and psychological techniques. Following Foucault, Miller and Rose have examined the ways that accounting numbers and psychological metrics have simultaneously created a social *and* individuals that are knowable and manageable. Above all, they insist that 'governmentalization' is a type of process that is not monopolised by the state but has become increasingly ubiquitous. The 'London governmentalists' entreat us to trace the activities of those 'little engineers of the soul', who translate broad philosophies of governing into local measurable practices. We take this appeal seriously to look beyond the programmatic level and examine the work and experience of one group that translates spiritual abstractions into material practices. The organization is 'Psyche', a multinational consultancy that provides, among other things, psychometric testing and counselling. Secondly we consider one of Psyche's products, a psychometric test and its associated counselling for individuals, as an ambiguous 'technology of the self'.

Psyche is a multinational consultancy organization with offices in around forty countries. The firm has grown from a small regional operation to a highly profitable limited company in less than twenty years. It concentrates on blue chip clients and provides them with a range of psychological, mentoring and teambuilding services. Psyche's mainstay business is psychometric testing. The company's history is bound up with its founder's lengthy and worldwide search for personal enlightenment. This ended with his encounter with the psychology and philosophy of Carl Jung. This personal encounter was transformed into Psyche's 'USP', infusing psychometric testing techniques with Jungian terminology. There are two paradoxes to be explored in understanding what Psyche promotes. First, there is a clear tension between the technical, statistical expertise that underpins and validates psychometric testing, and the important undercurrent of Jungian mysticism evident in the organization and management, the techniques promoted and the working environment. Second, key members of Psyche's staff were attracted to the organization by a combination of its charismatic founder and possibilities for self-improvement that their work offered. Respondents during data collection were unusually deliberate in how they participated in interviews, self-conscious about how they presented themselves and as fluent when talking of personality, meaning and spirituality as they were of client satisfaction and market dynamics. In practice, however, for at least some of the Psyche respondents, the dominance of the statistical has squeezed out much of the space for applying Jungian psychology to their own working—or personal—lives.

Psyche deploys psychometric testing as an ambiguous, limited 'technology of the self'. Every test conducted generates a lengthy report on the individual's preferences, separated into four domains, each denoted by a point on a compass. In turn, this report is further refined into a multitude of more specific sub-categories. Through reflecting on the report, the initial response encouraged is to confirm its accuracy and to identify those surprises whose truth is revealed by reflection. The end of the report identifies how each personality trait is *actually* deployed in one's work role, and then proceeds to compare this everyday use of the self with the 'real' self identified by the test. Inevitably, this comparison demonstrates degrees of harmony and dissonance. For instance, the analytical 'northern' personality on the compass is most comfortable at the margins of organizational life, but may be in a work role that compels—uncomfortably—accentuation of the supportive, collegial aspects of their personality; that is, the 'eastern' elements. The comparison between the 'real' self and the workaday self provides space—perhaps shock—of identification of dissonance. Counselling—a form of one-to-one facilitation—deepens the individual's self-awareness and allows them to become more skilled, more disciplined in the use of Psyche's analytical tools. In this way, Psyche contends, the individual can become a more effective therapist of the self. Psyche is, however, careful to refute any suggestion that it provides therapy. However, the post-test counselling sessions assume the form of therapeutic intervention, at least for some. Psyche does not attempt to repair damage—real or imagined—or to reduce abject misery to commonplace unease, but only to *prepare* the self for work. Although Psyche's employees are careful to distance from any suggestion that it offers therapy, preferring—albeit hesitantly—the term coaching, Psyche's intervention does require the individual to become her or his own therapist, however momentarily. Or, rather, the individual has first to pathologise the self, then to analyse this condition and finally to intervene. Individual salvation is always a work in progress. As an important part of the counselling process is to return the individual to their organization's objectives and thereby to maximise their individual effectiveness, any shift in the relationship between the individual and the organization must be infinitesimally small: self-awareness provides only a temporary balm for the distressed soul, a moment that has to be endlessly replicated both as a discipline and as a technology of the self.

Practising Governmentality

Governmentality's central insight is that neoliberalism should not be seen so much as the shrinking of the state, more as the construction of new institutions and techniques that produce, regulate and sustain markets. Moving towards a neoliberal state reduces direct provision which, in turn, necessitates institutions and techniques to increase the transparency, efficiency and security of markets. Governmentality does not accept neoliberalism at face value, but it *does* take its central conceit of increasing and dispersing individual freedom seriously, rather than dismissing this as so much ideological smoke screen. This does not mean that we—or Foucault—approve of neoliberalism or accept that it delivers on its impossible promises, but it does imply acceptance that it produces effects. 'The new governmental reason', insists Foucault, is shot through with tensions, paradoxes and contradictions (Foucault 2008: 63–4):

> [This form of reason] consumes freedom, which means that it must produce it. It must produce it; it must organize it. The new art of government . . . appears as the management of freedom. . . . I am going to see to it that you are free to be free. . . . Liberalism must produce freedom, but this very act entails the establishment of limitations, controls, forms of coercion, and obligations relying on threats, etc.

Similarly, organizations may both reduce hierarchy *and* produce or be dependent upon a range of technologies that develop new forms of employee identity that stress their psychological involvement and capacity for self-management. Just as the liberal state always seeks frugality, so the lean enterprise has to deploy ways of encouraging ever greater, and so ever more efficient, forms of self-management. Whatever the intuitive appeals of team-working or self-management, they require the management of new technologies of organization, new systems of quality measurement, corporate culturalism and seek to increase the scope and depth of individuals' active involvement in these new logics of organization (Styhre 2001). The penetration of accounting numbers is a pervasive feature of this everyday organizational life, as individual legitimacy is gained through demonstrating their fluency in this new social accounting for the self.

Organizations may self-represent as places that create the conditions necessary not just for individuals to go beyond contract but where they regard and—perhaps—experience this as personal development. Here it is impossible not to hear distant echoes of motivation theory and self-realisation. It is not that the neoliberal enterprise aspires to deliver the sustainable material security that Abraham Maslow regarded as a base-line accomplishment, but that these needs could not, indeed should not, be met by corporate employment. Rather, the reverse: employment security was produced by enhanced corporate competitiveness that was, in turn, dependent upon the depth of emotional commitment of individuals. In other words, Maslow's iconic hierarchy of needs is turned upside down.

Psyche, then, can be read as part of a much wider movement in management development that seeks to re-enchant the rationalised workplace through personal change or the re-discovery of authentic selves masked by restrictive work roles (Acker & Preston 1997: 682). But there is deep paradox here in that working on the self inevitably teeters on the cusp of being either and both a technology of the self *and* deeply disciplinary. Developing and managing corporate cultures is based around embedding high-end abstractions—integrity, fairness—with performance targets—productivity or quality improvement, customer satisfaction and competitiveness. These are intended as unitary cultures. This becomes even more problematic when performance targets are transformed into proxy measures of self-worth and collective meaning. It is difficult to see how these unitary cultural goals can be reconciled with forms of management development that surface and celebrate difference.

Psyche is organised around a headquarters that provides the survey technology; produces, validates and publishes the results; and pursues product development. Services are delivered through consultants who operate under license. Headquarters also provides back-office functions, such as accounting, training and compliance. Work is organised through a matrix structure, 'a moving, changing hierarchy with mind games'. Psyche's results are not delivered to the client organization either in the form of individual reports or overall populations. In other words, the client organization does not acquire the knowledge to centralise and normalise its population. Although it is capable of producing populations and norms that would recast diversity as deviance, the tests are not used for this purpose. Nor are they used as a personnel selection tool, only as part of an organizational development programme. For instance, the personal inventory is not correlated to job profiles or to performance. In these important respects, Psyche does not deliver a disciplinary technology to the organization but a technology of the self to the individual.

Statistics and Markets, Mystics and Myths

Industrial psychology has long provided expertise about workers as individuals and team members, constituting forms of knowledge about how they should be managed. Psyche's services are delivered *through* client organizations, but the recipient is the individual. Psyche therefore offers a different, twofold possibility from that of industrial psychology. First, the psychometric measurement provides the individual with a sense of his or her psychological preferences and, perhaps, some sense that others have different preferences and priorities. This provides at least the possibility of improved self-management and team participation. To be an effective organizational citizen, one must first accept this psychological pluralism. Second, by allowing deeper self-discovery, the individual can know themselves better. Greater self-awareness is a necessary precondition to improved self-management. The self becomes a more knowing subject and an external object to be managed externally, objectively and differently:

> My job is statistics, the *hard* technology but it's underpinned by this very spiritual psychology, which is a very *soft* technology. Jon, the founder, is driven by a passion, a love for Jung: it has given him so much that he wants to share it with the whole world. Surveys, data, reliability—the *hard* technology—is our way of sharing something of that passion. The statistics are behind, the engine that allows the archetypes to becomes a part of a conversation inside client organisations. We don't go into this with clients but basically we're selling a dream: how to allow people to realise their own potential.
>
> (Macey, statistician)

Jung's admixture of scientific formalism and mystical archetypes is echoed in Psyche's obsession with maximising the statistical rigour of its tools and the symbolism of its facilitated sessions. Even when Psyche's objective is defined more prosaically, in terms of what will be delivered to the client, these are rendered in Jungian language: 'we want to be alchemists of commitment' (co-founder). Indeed, transforming base metal into gold was a recurring motif in Jung's writing: dreams were data to be understood archetypally and transformed into knowledge; an event transformed into a meaningful experience. Alchemy was a widely used term in Psyche. Both types of transformation were possible through the deployment of Psyche tools and personnel.

Jung provided a psychological framework that was based on a fundamental binary between introversion and extraversion: 'an essential bias which conditions the whole psychic process, establishes the habitual reactions, and thus determines not only the style of behavior, but also the nature of subjective experience' (Jung 1933: 88). These base types were overlaid by four categories: thinking, feeling, sensation and intuition. This psychological complex was pre-behavioural but was amenable to some degree of self-management. 'One thing I must confess: I would not for anything dispense with this compass on my psychological journeys of discovery. . . . I value the type-theory for the objective reason that it offers a system of comparison and orientation which makes it possible something that has long been lacking; a critical psychology' (Jung 1933: 96). Here Jung is hinting at a process which is therapeutic but which can be taken further, to allow the individual to come to the edge of the sublime. This is why Jung's work attracts so much theological commentary. It is also why Psyche's appropriation of Jung, or, at least, the way that the organization understands itself, combines the analytical and the spiritual.

A crucial element of Psyche is the self-conscious mythologising that surrounds the father and son who founded the company. The father-son dynamic was not a tale of generational tension, far less a reprise of a Freudian Oedipus myth but, following Jung, was depicted in terms of contrasting, complementary energies: instinctive versus rational, caring versus competitive. These organizational myths were utterly psychologised and poetic rather than expressed through the language of markets, opportunities and competitive advantage. Again, this is consistent with a Jungian privileging of the experience of archetypes as the way to avoid the lure of intellectualism. All respondents referred to the company's founding myths as *their* way of understanding the organization, its history and purpose. Individuals had assimilated Psyche's founding myths so deeply these were understood as their own personal interpretation, their own Jungian reading of the organization. Several respondents referred to the dynamics between the founders in explicitly Jungian terms. The father represented the spirituality of Jung while the son embodied modern rationality. These were not regarded as tensions but as evidence that recognising these archetypes allowed the organization to benefit from harnessing the energy of both the dominant and shadow.

Central to the organization's founding myth was Jon senior's journey from a lengthy, if ultimately successful, struggle to rescue his financial services company which had been imperiled by the collapse of his underwriters. Physically and emotionally drained by this process, Jon senior stumbled through a series of self-help and management gurus until he discovered Jung. The accidental nature of finding Jung is, of course, also significant. 'We could have had a pick and mix of gurus, philosophers, psychologists. We chose Jung; or, rather, Jung found us. We love the singularity, the particularity of Jung and *only* Jung' (Jon junior). This account suggests extensive intellectual research and spiritual dissatisfaction that legitimates the ultimate discovery of Jung as a source of psychological rigour and redemptive possibility. The meaningful accident of finding Jung, or of allowing himself to discover Jung, echoed the account of Katharine Briggs and her daughter, Isabel Briggs Myers (Myers with Myers 1995: xi–xv). Katharine Briggs had an established intellectual interest, expressed in language suggestive of a vocation, but Jung's *Psychological Types* triggered her interest in measuring and comparing personality. Jon senior found Jung, *then* the Myers-Briggs testing regime. In both cases, Jung is represented as an intellectual and spiritual touchstone, but both sublimate Jung's debt to astrology and alchemy, preferring to highlight the practical and scientific value of their statistical psychology (Case & Phillipson 2004: 477). Importantly, for Jon senior much more than for Myers or Briggs, statistical psychology was not just a veneer of scientific authority but was also the vehicle for returning spirituality to the disenchanted workplace. In parallel, his son became increasingly disenchanted by his own successful career in banking, where his success turned on his forensic attention to tiny movements in exchange rates. The implication was clear. However well rewarded, this was a task that could never become a vocation: working with Jungian psychology was both intrinsically more meaningful and offered the prospect of a more significant impact upon the world. Working together, father and son built a business around selling management development products under licence and organised business guru events. This experience is portrayed as a prelude, a period in the wilderness, before they began to develop their own management development tool. Of course, this prelude provided them with vital experience about organising events, the market for management development products, and knowledge about licencing contracts.

The discovery of Jung is depicted in quasi-religious language. Jung's combination of science and magic, the mythical and the everyday, the collective and the individual is revelatory. Personal revelation comes through a journey from despair and a loss of certainty about rationality to a gradual awareness that business need not be stripped of the very possibility of meaning. A visit to Jung's hand-built retreat and library becomes a kind of pilgrimage. The founder's process of self-transformation now produces a purpose: to package Jungian insight for the management development market. The bridge from personal experience to an organised business was Jon senior's completion of the Myers-Briggs test and, indeed, becoming an accredited tester himself. A more extensive reading of Jung opened up doctrinal and technical differences between Jon senior and Myers, Briggs, and Myers-Briggs. The doctrinal difference was that Myers-Briggs privileged Jung's judgement category in ways that foreclosed complex interactions of other categories and their shadows. Not only did this foreclosure 'dishonour Jung', more importantly it limited its complexity: 'There is more to personality than Myers-Briggs. It's not about being faithful to Jung but about opening up the *more*' (Jon snr.). Again, there is a claim to authority here. Where Psyche's founding myth was based on the founder's spiritual quest, this was bound up with a deep reading of Jung that was both philosophically and technically superior to Myers-Briggs.

Psyche's founders understand and project their purpose as a way of improving lives and, as a consequence, increasing the productive capacity of individuals (Hook 2007: 26).

> We understand ourselves as part of the history of industrial psychology. Those traditions—Taylor, Hawthorne—were about extracting the maximum value from the human machine. They took an instrumental, external view. Jung, on the other hand, saw there was no cure except with the person themselves. We ask people to look at performance from the inside out. We encourage ourselves and our clients to think of our tools as performance management of the self.
>
> (Jon jnr.)

This is more insightful than Jon junior fully appreciated. After all, Elton Mayo, often portrayed as the humanist antidote to the brute engineering logic of Taylor's 'scientific management', was trained in Jungian therapy (Trahair 1984). Mayo transferred the logic and practices of Jungian therapy from the individual and the family to the corporation (Smith 1998; Illouz 2007: 14–15).

Mapping the Territory: Points of the Compass

Jung's archetypes are intended as universal categories that we can use to frame our understanding of the world. Our unconscious experience of the world is, in a Jungian frame, only possible through these archetypes. In the same moment, archetypes both enable and constrain our subjectivities. The intensity and balance between archetypes establishes deep emotional, intellectual and behavioural scripts. Jung's psychological types begin from two 'attitude types': introvert and extravert, defined in terms of the relationship between the individual and the object. For Jung, the object is the other. The introvert withdraws into abstraction to reduce the other's power, whether that be an individual or an institution. Conversely, the extravert defines themselves in terms of the other, seeking involvement in, and the approval of the other, of power. These attitude types are then overlaid in personality testing by four basic 'function-types': sensation, thinking, feeling and intuition. Each type and sub-type is defined along a continuum. In matrix form, the MBTI translation of Jung therefore produces sixteen psychological types. Developing an understanding of our individual script is the first step towards the management of dysfunctional elements of those scripts and the enhancement of others. Self-awareness is also the precondition to an appreciation of the personality types of others. For management development, in principle, self-awareness makes a positive dynamic of difference possible rather than incomprehensible, misunderstood and disabling interactions. Understood in this way, archetypes do not establish imperatives for acting so much as the possibility for understanding and acting more deliberately and differently. More important than an interpretation of archetypes, however, is the experience of how they operate, and how they operate differently.

The notion of an endless journey is, of course, inherent in contemporary management narratives and practices such as quality improvement. Jon senior's journey towards personal enlightenment was a root metaphor for Psyche. Equally, Psyche's founder drew on Jolande Jacobi's, one of Jung's most ardent followers and a key interlocutor, imagery of Jungian therapy as a troubling but rewarding journey that could be given direction and plotted (Anthony 1990: 60). The appeal of Jungian ideas for management development is that they do not just create a record of why attitudes and behaviours happened, but allow adaptation and purposeful change. The circle is a Jungian commonplace, but the Compass suggests both wholeness and almost limitless difference. Each point of the Compass was defined in terms of personality traits: 'north' suggested a cold, deliberate, somewhat cautious, formal personality; 'south' represented dynamic, enthusiastic and social personality; where 'east' was caring, relaxed and nurturing, 'west' was demanding, ends-driven and competitive. Each vector represented a unique combination of dominant and secondary characteristics: primaries such as 'north' or 'west' were pure ideal types, and never encountered; whereas 'north-west' represented someone who was primarily analytical, tempered by competitiveness. Recognising the relationship between primary and secondary traits permitted an individual more nuanced insights into the tensions, complementarities and dynamics of their personality.

The great number of sub-categories also made individual profiles more fine-grained: the algorithmic statement generator that lay behind the personality inventory simply had more categorical scope. The intricacy of Compass sub-types consolidated its image as complex, subtle and scientific. The Compass vectors are easily translated into a range of familiar managerial tropes: for 'north' read 'observer' or 'co-ordinator'; for 'yellow' read 'helper' or 'inspirer' (Case & Phillipson 2004: 485–6). To be defined as 'north-west' is to be curious, reserved, practical, creative, very organised and to prefer structure. To be a dominant 'north', with a secondary 'western' characteristic, is to be 'intensely individualistic'. For someone who sets unattainably high personal standards, this combination leads to 'withdrawal when stressed. He prefers to remain emotionally free of the other person's point of view. He tends not to care how he is seen as measuring up to others' standards as it is his own standards that are important to him'. This can result in indecisiveness, a reluctance to offer honest criticism of others and the tendency to excessive self-criticism may hinder his ambition.

This kind of spiritual management development is explicitly about recasting the self, 'to produce a different state of being, rather than specific knowledge or skills indicative of a more general shift away from skills training and towards a more informal, open-ended approach to personal growth' (Bell & Taylor 2004: 461). Compass generates a 'unique personal map' drawn from 'many hundred thousand permutations'. Again, there is a paradox between the secular technology and the spiritual sub-text: 'We have to codify this "magic" but every time we improve the survey, make it more precise, make it more reliable, the danger is that we lose a little bit of the "magic". My job is to take care of the "magic" statistically'. But, Macey continues:

We can't talk to clients about listening to your dreams or collective unconscious. We absolutely don't ram that stuff down people's throats. But our tools—the Compass—allow people to grasp some of the fundamentals of Jung even though they don't know that's what's happening. Most people instinctively understand that our tools are to make them self-aware and so work better together.

This elision is the central paradox of Compass. That is, the paradox between revealing innate diversity of psychological types and developing individual awareness becomes not just unproblematic but *necessary* to make the collective function better. Or, reflecting on wider trends in management development, as Emma Bell and Scott Taylor (2003: 336) put it: 'By constructing workplace spirituality as an important organizational phenomenon, the contemporary experience of work is mystified and its meaning is suggested to be elusive. Paradoxically, the subsequent representation of workplace spirituality as something to be managed, measured and modelled contributes towards the subsequent demystification of spirituality and the self'. At first sight, Compass is an invitation exclusively for individual reflexivity, but that is not all. Compass *can* produce 'a good understanding of the self, both strengths and weaknesses, enables individuals to develop effective strategies for interactions and can help them better respond to the demands of their environment' (Compass, Personal Profile). The use of the conditional tense signifies that compass is an invitation to self-knowledge, a sense that this is now available to the individual to use. However, this is *directed* self-government by a more knowing subject, *always* to be used with reference to the external order of the organization. In such processes any distinction between *homo oeconomicus* and *homo psychologicus* collapses, as the former colonises the latter: *Homo oeconomicus* is 'the person who accepts reality or who responds systematically to modifications in the variables of the environment, appears precisely as someone manageable . . . *Homo Oeconomicus* is someone who is eminently governable' (Foucault 2008: 270).

Working on the Soul

> To be skeptical about profiling is to both erect a barrier against self-knowledge and a form of narcissism, a refusal to imagine that the self needs management.
>
> —(Neil)

> To remain silent is to defend oneself from others and from self-awareness.
>
> —(Sandra)

The Compass can, following Nikolas Rose (1990: 257), be interpreted as a technology of freedom because it helps the individual assume greater responsibility for themselves and their work performance. It is not about external control or aligning identity with a corporate mission. The Compass, like confession, entails the labour of self-improvement. Psychological exams may usefully be understood as a ' "confessional technology" ', suggests Majia Holmer Nadesan (1997: 206), since:

They provide the individual with a system of statements, a vocabulary, for knowing him or herself. However, this process of self-identification is simultaneously a practice of subjectification: the individual is identified by the personality variables and norms of identity used for self-recognition (eg, as Introverted, Sensing, Thinking, Judging) and is subjectified because the individual becomes a subject of the discourse used in this process.

It is clear that the Compass completely depoliticises the relationship between the individual and the organization: fabricating the self is wholly the business of the individual. Confession works only if the individual moves beyond doubt and skepticism. Confession works because the individual believes that there is a truth in us which needs to be revealed and cleansed. To hold onto doubt is to make absolution impossible. Doubt therefore has to be suspended if self-revelation and absolution are to be possible, set aside lest the individual precludes the possibility of genuine revelation. To be wholly effective, use of the Compass requires something similar: 'You don't want to break people but they have to become vulnerable, and they have to admit that vulnerability. You can't reveal yourself *without* allowing that vulnerability' (Rhona).

Ron, one of the self-styled 'organizational mystics', spoke of his 'sense of release, of possibility' that he experienced during his first 'personality inventory'. This interview was extremely intense. After a couple of opening questions, through tears, the respondent insisted that he would only proceed if I answered the same questions about my own 'emotional experience' of the personality inventory. Ron's tears were a claim to Compass' legitimacy, to the intensity of the experience and its lasting effects. All exchanges, however mundane—however emotionally charged—should be treated as moments for self-evaluation and self-development. He refused the distinction between the interviewer and respondent as one that privileged the detachment of one actor over the emotional commitment of the other. This allowed 'an emotional dialogue, not just words'. For Ron:

> The methodology spoke to me. [long pause] Actually, it *forced* me to investigate myself; *who* I was; *what* I was; *what* I might *become*. It was a powerful moment in my life, transforming. I could never be the same person again. This was the moment from which I developed as a person . . . in every sense: professionally, in relationships, spiritually.

Before his personal inventory Ron had not been religious, nor had he been attracted to any forms of personal development beyond the strictly professional. Professionally, his strength had been analytical. His experience had been of detachment, distance not just from the organization but from his peers and himself:

I had worked in values driven organisations—*good* organisations. I had contributed to those organisations and held with their values but they were still *outside* me. Psyche allowed me to work on myself, to work out what I was—not just live up to someone else's values but to live up to myself. . . . *Me* is a moving target, something that I'll never really hit. It's the journey, it's the process that's really important. *Me* is a tough, demanding boss, . . . the toughest boss of all.

Here Ron is reflecting on his experience of the paradoxes of corporate attempts to re-enchant the workplace, to re-invest rationalised organizations and tasks with meaning (Taylor & Bell 2011). For almost thirty years, soft capitalism has acknowledged and addressed the tension between hollowed out work processes and individual and collective meaning (Thrift 1997). The reality of—in Ron's words—'corporate value engineering' is acknowledged for how meanings were projected by the organization, to be expressed, lived and policed by the individual. However compliant he was with these corporate values, they remained somewhat abstract and external. Equally, there is the sense that the measurement of how thoroughly Ron lived those corporate values was imposed on him and reflected a corporate pursuit of collective compliance more than the personal growth of the individual. For Psyche staff, '*the* privilege of working here is that every intervention with a client is an intervention with yourself':

The organization is a place where we work on ourselves and each other every minute of every day. That's true of every organization whether or not people appreciate it. Here (pause) we *know* this. *That's* demanding. You have to live up to yourself, . . . not always consciously: that's the point—you have to absorb this process so that it becomes automatic.

The knowledge of self gained through Compass can be double-edged, and is not always a burden lightly borne: 'Your whole life is touched by the knowledge you have about yourself and others. You can't unlearn this knowledge. It's very difficult to put this knowledge aside, even for a short while. It is a gift, but sometimes it's a gift you wish that you had never received' (Rowan). The intensity of this process of self-improvement was recognised by all Psyche respondents, but others countered any impression that this process was, or could be, ever-present.

Quietly, inside the organization, people will tell each other very intimate, emotional things about their life. This is what they mean—I think—by 'magic': it's those moments of clarity. We try to help each other to sustain those moments beyond the here and now. That's work. Perhaps not work as we'd normally talk about it but it's about learning the skills necessary to see yourself more clearly.

For only a small minority of Psyche employees and licenced practitioners, Jung was little more than a backdrop, concentrating instead on statistical validation of the product.

It's all about the numbers, the charts, the Compass points. Jung matters in-house, but it's the numbers that matter to the clients—that's our USP. We're all the same, and we're all different: that's the basic message. Some of our consultants see the methodology as the compass for their spiritual journey. Once upon a time that was true of most of our consultants. Now, our consultants are increasingly client-focused, (rather than) seeing every contract as an experience *for them*.

(Robert)

Compass' objective is that the individual recognises their own uniqueness; recognises and accepts the uniqueness of others; understands the complexities, dynamics and inter-connectedness of self, team and organization. Finally, through this enhanced understanding of self, the individual will be able to manage themselves and others more effectively. As Jon jnr. put it, 'we all have a hinterland. Now, we don't—can't—provide a map of that wilderness. *But*—and this is an important but—we can provide a compass for people to use. They can then draw their own map of themselves'. To suggest that the self is, at least in part, a 'wilderness' is to suggest that the unknown is knowable, and that its dangers can be reduced through knowledge. Not only can the hinterland of the self be mapped—routes chosen, dangers avoided—the scope of the known can be expanded so long as Compass is used. By taming the everyday wilderness, the spiritual adventurer can venture beyond. So this is not a reassuring, far less a self-soothing therapy. Quite the opposite: the Compass inventory is intended to be unsettling, and, after some modest practice, a probing auto-therapy. Compass allows the individual to have a structured dialogue with themselves rather than through an interlocutor, a therapist. 'We provide data *for* the soul; data *of* the soul' (Jon snr.).

All of this begins with the Compass personality inventory questionnaire, which takes between forty-five minutes and two hours. Completion of the personality inventory is followed by the corporate production of an extensive personalised report. This ritualised moment is carefully stage-managed. Each individual is handed their Compass profile and asked to open them simultaneously. Distributing participants' individual profiles was highly ritualised, a moment that was intended to be reverent, revelatory and joyful. As they read through their profiles, there are gasps, exclamations, laughter as the participants recognise themselves in the text. This is a secular epiphany, a moment in which the individual is revealed and connected to others, all unique but all different. That this epiphany is achieved through a survey, algorithms and a database does not so much dispel the magic as underscore it. This, then, is a thoroughly modern scientific epiphany. Then there are three one-to-one debriefing and mentoring sessions. These sessions typically last between thirty minutes and one hour and follow a carefully managed process led by a Psyche practitioner. There are four stages: a recognition of the truth of the results; an acknowledgement of the results' consistency; an acceptance of the rounded picture produced by the inventory; and finally placing oneself in a work context and analysing one's behaviours in terms of self-management and the management of others. The first three stages require the respondent to confirm and accept their psychological typing, an acceptance of the power and authority of Psyche and the Compass. The final stage requires the individual to become active, autonomous and responsible: to appropriate this new sense of themselves and imagine themselves back at work. Revelation comes to the individual if they read themselves through, and only through, Compass. Equally, others are read through, and only through, one's projection of Compass categories. To interpret the behaviour of others is to render their psychological make-up visible. A colleague becomes an object of knowledge, not just their skills or technical competence but their psychology, drivers and behavioural triggers. This is the end of liminality, the moment that the individual re-enters the world of work.

During these groups and individual sessions there are very few asides about Jung and any notion of smuggling spirituality into the workplace slips from view. The final questions are explicitly and exclusively about work. The analytical circle is closed: what begins with self-examination is completed, at least temporarily, by the reconciliation of the individual with the psychological adjustments necessitated by their work role and corporate culture. How to consolidate this new self-awareness and channel it knowingly, instrumentally? This is the paradoxical promise of Psyche: through knowing themselves a little better, the individual can more effectively lead and manage others. Of course, it is an open question as to whether in practice the more psychologically informed manager improves their performance not through empathy or by objectifying themselves and others. As Psyche's introductory brochure puts it, 'Every time you meet someone you have the opportunity to practice your skill of recognizing and adapting to their colour energies'. So, the newly self-aware individual can glimpse again something of the sublime in their everyday, instrumental use of Compass categories. This is not a contemplative, comforting or dialogic project but wholly practical. How to mobilise—to valorise—Jungian categories in the workplace?

Working on the self is liminal work, as a task that can never be completed nor understood as immediately or measurably value-adding. Such liminal work was performed in a liminal space in which work tasks were suspended as work roles and behaviours were considered (Foucault 2006: 67–8). Completing the personal inventory is embedded in a series of workshops designed to be intensive, immersive and to reveal individuals to themselves and others through story-telling, painting scenes from one's past, and play.

> The workshops provide a safe place for individuals to challenge themselves. People learn best when they play. Play takes away most of our inhibitions. . . . The workshops are very structured and we really try to keep to that structure. We try to keep the atmosphere friendly, supportive, almost playful. Play makes work feel like not work. (Q: Are you playing?) No, absolutely not. We're the only ones who know that *everyone* is working. It's our job to hide the work inside all the games. The people only really understand the work they've done at the very end of the workshop.
>
> (Daniel)

Psyche games were structured to make it impossible for anyone to exempt themselves from participation. Some games involved physical movement in response to questions or cues by a facilitator. Other games were based on call and response, again led by a facilitator. There were three types of games: those in which one revealed something about oneself to the group; others that required individuals to allocate and so group themselves according to Compass categories; and still others in which participants acted out the organising characteristics and management styles of Compass personality types. The games produced tableaux vivants of psychological typing. One key Psyche 'process designer' confirmed that all was carefully choreographed. The games were not just about developing the participant's knowledge of Compass categories but were 'a stripping bare' of the individual inside a 'safe space'. All of Psyche workshop exercises were to depict the self and life-history so that they could be discussed and analysed. Responsibility for the success of the workshop—represented as a temporary sanctuary from the everyday—was with the individual. Responsibility for increasing self-awareness was solely the responsibility of the individual (Bell & Taylor 2004: 458–9).

Psyche's four-day process was designed to erode any skepticism. Questions of accuracy, utility and meaning of the personal inventory are determined solely by the facilitator. Similarly, the readiness of the subject to begin the next phase—and the overall pace of the process—is at the discretion of the Psyche facilitator. To move through the debriefing and analysis process, then, the subject has to conform to Psyche's process design. The end point is the subject's reflection on whether they have a different understanding of work relationships and whether this could improve their own performance and those around them. Unavoidably, by completing the test, individuals have to objectify themselves. This objectification is confirmed by recognition of the personal inventory's accuracy. By refracting themselves and their relationships with others through the testing process, the possibility of assessment, improvement and management becomes possible.

Along the way, people inevitably gain some degree of self-awareness. The difference is that we use tools that do not judge. People understand themselves a little more without being judged or by judging themselves. I'm proud of the shadow work that we do. We help people know and value the parts of themselves that they either don't know about or banish to another room. We don't boast about doing Jung's shadow work but that is the most important thing we do.

(Doug)

Psyche provide technologies of autonomy that are wholly consistent with the neoliberal insistence on individuation and personal, never collective, responsibility. Neither the personality profiling nor the workshops permit any space to explore shared, collective or relational dimensions of identity. This was a promise of self-mastery inside the—unacknowledged—dependencies of the wage relationship. No other cultural resources for individual identity projects were referenced. The workshops may have based around group participation but identity work was solely the responsibility of the individual. Pulling identity in line with the demands of work and organizational strategy was for the individual alone.

Organising Psyche and the Compass

Psyche programmes are delivered through a web of independent consultants working as 'licenced practitioners'. Consider the ambiguous status of the 'licenced practitioner'. They are trained in Psyche facilitation and scripts but have only the most limited input into their writing. 'Licenced practitioners' adhere closely to Psyche scripts; they do not necessarily have anything more than the sketchiest version of the Jungian taproot of Psyche's knowledge base, which is itself not exposed to intellectual or practical challenge from external experts. Jon senior is the only connection between Psyche, the 'licenced practitioners' and Jung. If the 'licenced practitioner' enjoys a form of professional legitimacy then this is strictly limited to the organization or, more accurately, to the temporary sanctuary of a Psyche workshop.

Perhaps all of this is no more than another example of the creativity of power, a means of teaching how to interrogate the self to put it to good use at work. Understanding the self has no value in itself, only in the organization and only if consistent with work rules and corporate culture. It is not that Jungian psychological typing is inherently managerial: it *could* be a 'simple' technology of the self, a way of improving ourselves that had no other purpose than that. In practice, of course, the distinction between the production of the self through various power relations and technologies of the self is blurred. In both, as Michael Behrent (2013: 90–1) observes, 'the individual is the object of technical practices (such as subjecting behaviour to norms, regulating movements, surveillance, etc). Yet with technologies of power, these practices are ultimately exercised on individuals from outside; with technologies of the self, individuals make themselves the object of their own technical practices'. Foucault was aware of this practical ambiguity which implied that technologies of the self were often inherent in, or even central objectives of, disciplinary powers: to govern others in ways that teaches them to better govern themselves. Ironically, given his ill-deserved dystopian notoriety, in his final decade Foucault's commentary on ancient ethics was about 'best to speak of' moments, only moments, of self-direction within disciplinary powers but without recourse to a transcendental vocabulary. Compass encouraged reflection of the experience and the nature and limits of the self, although this is only in the most circumscribed manner (Bennet 2001: 146). Freedom is not to escape external constraints but to work with, through and against an inescapable web of discipline. In this sense, Jungian psychology is neither necessarily disciplinary nor liberatory, irrespective of the motives of the client organizations.

A governmentalist method requires us to set aside motivations and interests as determinants in favour of examining the technologies that produce social effects. Psyche collected individual statistics to construct a statistical population to validate their technology, rather than providing a psychological assessment for client organizations. Nor did Psyche collect longitudinal panel data to analyse whether the known self is altered through self-management. Indeed, there is very little evidence of the long-term impact of psychological typing on individual identities or of populations. It may be that psychological typing, like cultural change programmes, have a half-life that requires sporadic renewal. One extensive Australian study of the impact of psychological testing, embedded in an organizational change programme, concluded that MBTI provided a robust language for individuals in terms of their sense of themselves and their place in the corporate structure (Garrety et al 2003: 225–6). There was no suggestion, however, that this was a permanent, immutable or irreversible change in the categories and language used to understand and express the self and the organization. Even in its most extreme carceral form, Foucauldian discipline may require something more than the compliance of the individual. But discipline is typically built into the architectures of buildings and designed into the incentives and sanctions of bureaucratic rule. The logic of personality typing may share this pursuit of efficiency, the combination of centralised oversight and devolved operations. While there is a central oversight of an organization's population, this is not paralleled by any attempt to manage the cultural or operational risks associated with the spread of different personality types.

Conclusion: The Breathtaking Ambition of Technologies of the Self at Work

Developmental technologies such as the Compass promote individual assumption of responsibility for the self at work. The alignment of the individual with organizational culture and objectives is framed as a task that only the individual can complete. Companies such as Psyche deliver an indirect, oblique intervention on behalf of the client organization in which the individual is coaxed, but never conscripted, to identify with organizational goals. It provides a very partial, very seductive form of individualization. There is an important limitation: the use of the Compass inventory in terms of the HRM practices of client organizations is neither tracked nor measured. We cannot know what effects, if any, Compass has on the long-term development of the self. However, this lack can be read as consistent with the individualization noted in the use of the questionnaires and reports. If the individual employee or team leader interprets the technology as effective, then by definition it is. The component parts, including those that are absent, of the Psyche schema are self-supporting and mutually reinforcing.

The sheer ambition of Compass as a technology is breathtaking. Its sub-text is that of a spiritualised psychology that suggests the possibility of mastery of the Jungian cosmology of the self. Even if we discount for hyperbole, Compass clearly both measures populations the better to ensure its validity and renders its subjects calculable and calculating by themselves. Again, this is a technology of the self that is consistent with a neoliberal version of individual freedom. More accurately, Compass provides a targeted form of self-knowledge, the *working* self. Techniques of self-knowledge empower the individual, by the individual, for the individual. The therapist, industrial psychologist, personal development provider (in corporate and individual forms), are all legitimised by their professional status, mathematical competence and how convincing they are. Appropriately, in the Psyche programme, the individual is exposed to themselves but with little or no guidance of how to proceed. There is counselling, but this goes no further than to ensure that the individual has understood their personal inventory. The purpose—and limit—of the programme is revelatory, and Psyche accepts no responsibility for how the individual responds to this revelation. That, as all else does, rests with the individual, who is expected to continue an endless cycle of soul-searching, armed only with limited techniques to do this in an orderly, disciplined way. And all the while, this individual must respond to sometimes capricious organizational expectations as to behaviour, productivity and action.

Acknowledgements

Our thanks to the people of Psyche for their time and candour. The name of the organization, its tools and respondents have been anonymised. Psyche's operational details have been altered. Both authors experienced the Compass personal inventory as part of separate research projects.

References

Ackers, P. & Preston, D. (1997), 'Born Again? The Ethics and Efficacy of the Conversion Experience in Contemporary Management Development', *Journal of Management Studies* 34/5: 677–701.
Anthony, M. (1990), *Valkyries: The Women around Jung*, London: Element.

Behrent, M. (2013), 'Foucault and Technology', *History and Technology* 29/1: 54–104.

Bell, E. & Taylor, S. (2003), 'The Elevation of Work: Pastoral Power and the New Age Work Ethic', *Organization* 10/2: 329–349.

Bennet, J. (2001), *The Enchantment of Modern Life: Attachments, Crossings, and Ethics*, Princeton, NJ: Princeton University Press.

Briggs Myers, I. with Myers, P. (1995), *Gifts Differing: Understanding Personality Type*, Mountain View, CA: CPP.

Case, P. & Phillipson, G. (2004), 'Astrology, Alchemy and Retro-Organization Theory: An Astro-Genealogical Critique of the Myers-Briggs Type Indicator', *Organization* 11/4: 473–495.

Foucault, M. (2006), *Psychiatric Power: Lectures at the College de France 1973–1974*, London: Palgrave Macmillan.

Foucault, M. (2008), *The Birth of Biopolitics: Lectures at the College de France 1978–1979*, London: Palgrave Macmillan.

Garrety, K., Badham, R., Morrigan, V., Rifkin, W. & Zanko, M. (2003), 'The Use of Personality Typing in Organizational Change: Discourse, Emotions and the Reflexive Subject', *Human Relations* 56/2: 211–235.

Hook, D. (2007), *Foucault, Psychology and the Analytics of Power*, London: Palgrave Macmillan.

Ilouz, E. (2007), *Cold Intimacies: The Making of Emotional Capitalism*, Cambridge: Polity.

Jung, C. (1933), *Modern Man in Search of a Soul*, New York: Harvest.

Nadesan, M. (1997), 'Constructing Paper Dolls: The Discourse of Personality Testing in Organizational Practice', *Communication Theory* 7/3: 189–218.

Rose, N. (1990), *Governing the Soul*, London: Routledge.

Smith, J. (1998), 'The Enduring Legacy of Elton Mayo', *Human Relations* 51/3: 221–249.

Styhre, A. (2001), 'Kaizen, Ethics, and Care of Operations: Management after empowerment', *Journal of Management Studies* 38/6: 795–810.

Taylor, S. & Bell, E. (2004), 'From Outward Bound to Inward Bound': The Prophetic Voices and Discursive Practices of Spiritual Management Development', *Human Relations* 57/4: 439–466.

Taylor, S. & Bell, E. (2011), 'The Promise of Re-Enchantment: Organizational Culture and the Spirituality at Work Movement', in D. Boje, B. Burnes, and J. Hassard (eds), *The Routledge Companion to Organizational Change*. Abingdon: Routledge.

Thrift, N. (1997) 'The Rise of Soft Capitalism', *Cultural Values*, 1/1: 29–57.

Trahair, R. (1984), *The Humanist Temper: The Life and Work of Elton Mayo*, New Brunswick, NY: Transaction.

9   Governing Knowledge
The Siemens Experience

Nancy Richter

Introduction

This chapter describes how the relationship between organizations and the worker has changed since the rationalisation movement of 1930s Germany. Drawing on Nietzsche's categories of material, symbolic and imaginary power, we examine how managerial practices manufacture employees in different historical contexts. Siemens serves as an example of how knowledge is governed and how power relations changed within German organizations through the twentieth century. Contemporary work is portrayed—and often experienced—as less constrained through rigid structures compared to the Taylorised offices and factory floors of the early twentieth century. However, work is still regulated, albeit by 'soft' forms of managerial power. Power becomes less visible the more dispersed it becomes in everyday routines. The paradox is that 'soft' management methods now explicitly target the subjectivities of employees, understood as technologies of freedom, where Taylorism focused on employees' bodies. Drawing on extensive archival research, this chapter asks how has Siemens imagined the organization, the individual and knowledge as territories to be governed? How did Siemens shift from targeting the individual worker's body to creating the intangible knowledge of the organization as a whole, as a population? This chapter aims to provide not simply an account of the Siemens experience through an application of Foucault but to contribute to the theory of governmentality in terms of conceptual and practical innovation.

After 1918, scientific management gained huge popularity among German enterprises. Scientific management emphasised the rationality of the organization and the rationality of the people in it, managers and workers alike (Taylor 1913; Albrow 1992). The main objective of scientific management was maximising the efficiency of human labour. Management was about the transformation of personal knowledge into explicit scientific knowledge and to install exact routines (Clegg et al 2006). The German efficiency—or rationalisation—movement represented an attempt for the systematic implementation of scientific management knowledge within organizations. Rationalisation was a powerful economic and cultural force in inter-war Germany. The main argument for the implementation of rational approaches within organizations in Germany was the improvement of the economic situation for all, for individual employees, for the enterprise and society as a whole (Türk et al 2006).

Between the wars, Siemens was heavily engaged in the technical rationalisation of the production processes (Homburg 1983). The firm was founded by Werner von Siemens in 1847 and since 1907 Siemens was the largest German electrical engineering firm. Siemens was not only engaged in internal 'rationalisation' but played a prominent role in various organizations established after 1918 to promote scientific management (Eidenmüller Chronik ND). A central vehicle for scientific management was 'Reichskuratorium für Wirtschaftlichkeit (RKW)' (Board of Trustees for Economic Efficiency), which was founded by Carl Friedrich Siemens, the 'Reichsministerium' (the Reich's Ministry of Economics), and the association of German engineers (VDI) in 1921. The RKW defined rationalisation as 'the adoption and employment of all the means of increasing efficiency which are furnished by technical science and systematic organization. Its aim is to raise the general level of prosperity by cheaper, more plentiful, and better quality goods' (Hinnenthal 1928: 11). The term 'individual' is absent from this definition, but this is due to the fact that the working individual was not regarded as important for organizational success.

From the late 1980s there has been a discourse about fundamental organizational changes in Germany that gains much of its legitimacy through its criticism of rationalistic approaches to management and organization. This amounts to a theoretical and practical paradigm shift towards a postmodern trend of de-rationalisation (Lemke 2000; Türk et al 2006: 262). Organizations are described as less rational and less hierarchic while focusing more on personal responsibility and the exploitation of individual knowledge. These approaches underline the decline of the rational organization. With network forms of organization and electronically connected work the organizational boundaries seem to fade. New work identities evolve which are orientated at artistic work and production (Boltanski & Chiapello 2006). At the same time, organizational culture, creativity and knowledge management have become increasingly popular topics. Siemens has been at the forefront of this knowledge revolution, just as it was during the rationalisation movement of the inter-war years.

Siemens has long been renowned for its strong hierarchy and bureaucracy (Davenport et al 2001: 220) and focuses on encouraging cooperation, as well as sharing information and knowledge. From 1995 Siemens publicly embraced a new business concept: knowledge management. Reflecting these changes, the German 'RKW' changed its name, adding innovation to its established rationalisation programme ('Rationalization and Innovation Centre of the German Economy'). Rationalisation is not regarded as antithetical to innovation. Quite the reverse: rationalisation is regarded as strongly aligned with innovation, creativity and entrepreneurial spirit.

Innovation and rationalisation are understood as two sides of the same coin. For Ingrid Voigt, RKW's deputy chief executive, innovation now demands constant rationalisation: 'In a knowledge society the competitiveness of firms is strongly connected to the creativity and commitment of employees' (Voigt 2006: 30–1).

To move to an innovation-based organization is not, then, a rejection or even qualification of rationalisation but an intensification. In contrast to early conceptions of rationalisation, the individual growth and learning is now in the centre of political and organizational efforts. Recent managerial discourses often underline the creativity, freedom and self-responsibility of the working individual. This view is supported by knowledge management initiatives in organizations like Siemens. Flexibility and dynamism are recurring tropes within these programmes (Siemens 1996: SAA 23627). There are, of course, tensions and ambiguities in contemporary discourses of flexibility, innovation and creativity. Recent organizational developments are often presented as opposed to the established rational organization. They are presented as allowing more freedom and fulfilling perfectly the needs and wishes of individuals, especially their wish for self-actualisation.

I want to make the case that this dualistic conception of rationalistic and non-rationalistic organizational concepts is not very instructive. The notion of 'less bureaucracy', 'less hierarchy' or 'less rationalisation' (including the notion of 'more freedom') says nothing about how organization and management work. Furthermore, such distinctions inherently serve to legitimise contemporary organizational developments, even to accelerate or deepen structural and cultural changes that do not go far enough or fail to deliver greater individual freedom. I therefore want to call the very distinction between rationalisation and de-rationalisation itself into question. To argue about the degree to which contemporary organizations are less rationalised or permit greater individual freedom and chances for self-fulfilment is to accept the logic of this managerial discourse.

The organization of knowledge can be better understood in terms of power relationships. To understand new management approaches is to reject the question as to whether there are unparalleled opportunities for freedom, but that they seemingly consist of power relations which are less visible and less transparent than ever before. One productive way to make these power relations visible is to apply the power approach of Friedrich Nietzsche: 'Knowledge works as a tool of power' (Nietzsche 1968: 338). He insists that: 'the measure of the desire for knowledge depends upon the measure to which the will to power grows in a species: a species grasps a certain amount of reality in order to become master of it, in order to press it into service' (Nietzsche 1968: 338). Power cannot only be seen in terms of repression and suppression, but as a set of practices which positively produce ways of thinking and behaving (Saar 2007). In this case, power is closely linked to knowledge. Similarly, Michel Foucault understood knowledge relations always implicate power relations and vice versa. Both Nietzsche and Foucault denied believing that subjects are behind social practices. Rather, both took on the opposite view: historically and culturally determined practices precede and form the subject. The individual is, therefore, to be seen as an effect of power. Both Nietzsche and Foucault used the concept of genealogy as a 'historical investigation into the events that have led us to constitute ourselves and to recognize ourselves as subjects of what we are doing, thinking, saying' (Foucault 1984: 416). Rather than treating the needs and wishes of working individuals as autonomous realities as often underlined in modern management approaches, the subject itself can be viewed as an effect of a cultural constitution. Management must be seen as a specific cultural technique. To understand the employee one should not begin with an idealised notion of meaningful work but instead research those different notions of power which *manufacture* the employee, as a category and as a subject (Jaqcues 1996). Management and managing—no more than worker and working—cannot be deduced from abstract, idealised categories or ascribed to coercive and suppressive forms of power.

Friedrich Nietzsche: Power, Knowledge and Genealogy

How might one write a history of management, organization and the working individual through Friedrich Nietzsche's critique of modern morality, especially his 'Genealogy of Morals' (Nietzsche 1887; Pippin 2004)? For Nietzsche, a critique of morality implies that the value of moral values themselves must be called into question. To this end it is necessary to provide a history of morality. Nietzsche supposed that modern morality and the moral subject developed into their current form through certain power relationships.

In his 'Genealogy of Morals', Nietzsche provides us with three different forms of power to show how social realities and a moral subject are constituted (Saar 2007). They can be interpreted as material, symbolic and imaginary forms of power. In the first essay of the 'Genealogy', he describes the power of the master over the slave, which can be interpreted as a material power. It is a form of power that acts directly on the slave's body and guides his behaviour. In this case, the master experiences himself as determining values, following his personal will to power. Or, as Nietzsche puts it: The powerful 'arrogated to themselves the right to create values, to stamp out the names for values' (Nietzsche 1887). The slave morality revalues the master's morality through a symbolic power which constructs and projects meaning. Symbolic power speaks of the relationship of the powerless to the powerful. Symbolic power shapes the way individuals think and how they understand themselves and their way of live: 'To breed an animal that is entitled to make promises—is that not precisely the paradoxical task nature has set itself where human beings are concerned? Isn't that the real problem of human beings?' (Nietzsche 1887). Symbolic power is not material and it does not primarily work on the body. It is symbolic power which shapes realities, social orders and social actors. But this form of power is not only interesting because it shapes realities or how we conceive reality: 'The real genius of the slave rebellion, according to Nietzsche, lies in its going beyond a simple inversion of value types, and in the creation of a new way of thinking about human beings: the creation of a subject [or soul] "behind" the actual deed' (Pippin 2004). Symbolic power not only influences the ways individuals think but also how they understand themselves. Symbolic power is a precondition for constructing responsible subjects: Nietzsche's third essay in the 'Genealogy' analyses the ascetic ideal as an imaginary form of power. Like the symbolic form of power, it is not visible, but in contrast to that, its origins lie in the individual itself: 'The ascetic procedures and forms of life are the means whereby . . . ideas are freed from jostling around with all the other ideas, in order to make them "unforgettable"' (Nietzsche 1887).

Individuals are willing to assume certain roles and ideas which shape their self- understanding and their behaviour. However, while taking over these roles they produce and reproduce existing social power relationships: 'They are not free spirits—not by any stretch—for they still believe in the truth' (Nietzsche 1887). The ascetic ideal is a form of power which involves the notion of self-sacrifice in the name of a higher ideal—to be found in the next world perhaps—but also within any idea of truth, objectivity or justice.

Analysing scientific management and knowledge management as an aggregation of interacting power regimes aims to identify their specific underlying assumptions about organization and the working individual. Which behaviour should be regulated by the material forms of organizational power? Which self-understandings are provided through which concepts of symbolic power (e.g. social politics, organizational culture)? Which roles are provided and how should these roles be translated into actions? How do these forms of power interact to manufacture 'working individuals' in relation to a given historical and cultural context? Management becomes 'will to power' which changed its form and focus according to social and cultural developments. In this way management is analysed on how it aims to establish certain power relationships within organizations.

The remainder of this chapter will investigate how managerial and organizational power relations in Siemens changed over time and engaged in the constitution of appropriate employees. The first regime I want to focus at is the rationalisation movement in Germany, which can be seen as a starting point for the systematic implementation of scientific management knowledge within organizations in Germany after 1918 (Höpner 2004). We then turn to the regime of knowledge management which has gained popularity in the two decades since 1990. Knowledge management clearly focuses on notions of motivation and self-fulfilment and relies largely on Nietzschean imaginary power relationships.

Governing Knowledge: Siemens after the First World War

In the first phase of German industrialisation from 1830 to 1870 there was little interest in abstract, far less scientific management knowledge (Kocka 1969: 335). Organizations were seen as highly individual and unique. Organizations were understood as organic and natural. In 1915 Wilhelm v. Siemens (1855–1919) insisted: 'A company is comprised of billions of processes which cannot be rationalised or organised in a homogeneous way' (Kocka 1969: 355). Organizations remained small and dominated by proprietorial or personal forms of administration. The founder was often the company's operational director. Most of these founders had a practical education and were little interested in theoretical concepts about organization. From 1900, however, there was a growing interest in general management methods (Kocka 1969: 347). This was due to economic crisis, intensifying global business competition, technical developments, a tendency towards a rise in joint-stock-companies and the growing scale of companies (Kocka 1969: 348). Management became an important practice for planning and shaping rational organizations. To achieve greater efficiency not only must the organization operate like a machine, but so must the body of the worker. The organization and the worker's body both became the focus of a form of material power.

Material Power: Management of the Body

The US served as a model for the rationalisation of organizations and work processes in Germany, especially after the First World War (Kocka 1969: 357). In Germany, the American engineer Frederick W. Taylor (1865–1915) was one of the first and most influential to develop a coherent approach of the objectives of personnel management. Specifically, Taylorism was appropriated as techniques to produce the most efficient use of the human body (Homburg 1983: 138). After the First World War, German industrialists and engineers visited the US to accelerate the development of management knowledge.

Siemens staff regularly visited the US and reported about American methods to regular 'Technical and Operating Conferences' (eg.Siemens 1925/1926). In 1924 Siemens and Westinghouse, the American Electric and Manufacturing company, signed a contract to routinely exchange of product and process knowledge and patents. At Siemens' technical and operating conferences, engineers regularly presented the detailed reports on administration, plant and workplace labour management at Westinghouse. The American model set targets for the reduction of costs for wages and materials (Köttgen 1926).

Siemens' personnel management also started to be recognised as an important management function. In 1919, Siemens introduced a centralised, hierarchically structured administration and institutionalised an integrated system of direct managerial control (Homburg 1983: 146). This structure was constantly refined according to the American model. This privileged Siemens executives in personnel politics and reduced the autonomy of the plants (Ernst ND). Secondly, plant and workplace labour was centralised and direct managerial control was installed. Thirdly, the foreman's autonomy on the shopfloor was severely curtailed. A new managerial hierarchy of production engineers was introduced. This was accompanied by the general implementation of the 'work office' to reorganise and intensify work (Homburg 1983: 150–1). In 1919 the 'work office' started to carry out time, motion and fatigue studies to measure the performance of machine tools and workers on the shopfloor (Eidenmüller ND). This new knowledge was then used to increase the productivity of every single movement of the worker's body. This new knowledge constituted a form of material power, guiding the actions of the bodies of the worker and of production as a whole. These developments were accompanied by a more or less permanent performance screening. This systematic approach of avoiding wasteful movements was not restricted to the shopfloor, but also applied to office work. New knowledge was transformed into new organizational routines and working practices. In 1922 Siemens introduced daily control and reporting sheets for employees, identity cards and annual performance ratings. Further, Siemens launched three anti-waste campaigns between 1920 and 1930. Part of these anti-waste campaigns included the installation of photographs aimed at line workers. Untidy workplaces were photographed and these images were displayed in the relevant division. Sometimes they were accompanied by photographs which provided images of how workplaces *should* look (Le Vrang 1930). Following Nietzsche, then, Siemens management was concerned with the creation, representation and manifestation of values.

Siemens' increasingly wide-ranging innovations in systematic management intended to produce efficient bodies by observing, calculating and fixing human behaviour. Despite the separation of thinking and doing between engineer and worker, the engineer did not experience himself as determining values, exercising his personal will to power. Management installed a power regime governing behaviour based on objective and 'scientific' principles and economic rationality. Power was inscribed in the routines and processes. However, Siemens' will to power was accompanied by employee resistance. Workers mistrusted the dissolution of the foreman's direct, personal power, expressed through spoken rules and arbitrary methods. Supervisory power was understood and negotiated with the workgroup. The new rationalising organization did not have equivalent negotiating points at which workers' informal bargaining power could be deployed. Siemens' vision of a rationalised workplace left it unclear where worker voice would be expressed, far less heard. Increasing worker protest was one important factor in a growing management awareness that efficiency could not only focus on the body but also had to shape new cultural realities in which economic progress was understood as serving all parties. Siemens had created a new object of knowledge—the worker's body: the task was now to shape a disciplined soul.

Symbolic Power: Management as the Production of 'Disciplined Souls'

Organizational rationalisation at Siemens was paralleled by the articulation of a form of power which attempted to construct and shape meaning: a symbolic power. To shape the employee's soul, Siemens had to counteract the impact of the increased degradation of work and increasing worker resistance. Normalising rationalisation into obedience needs to produce not only appropriate body movements through monetary incentives but also to produce an appropriate soul (Clegg et al 2006). Siemens had to reform the worker socially, morally and culturally in order to normalise rationalisation.

Siemens' managers were trained to use psychological methods and to behave respectfully when dealing with employees (Bolt 1928). In the 1920s psycho-technical ideas were gradually linked more explicitly to industrial problems. This was due to labour shortages, workers rebellion and the rise of female workers during the First World War (Türk et al 2006: 219). Theoretical approaches—and 'psychotechnic' practices—were primarily concerned with aptitude analysis and the planning of worker training. In industrial practice certain apparatuses were used for testing workers' abilities like memory and perception and for the registration and analysis of movements: for example, hearing acuity apparatus; apparatus to register and analyse hand movements; apparatus for examinations into perception, association and memory (Rupp 1931).

In Siemens, industrial psychology tested memory, for example. Several tests were supposed to examine the worker's abilities to remember words and numbers (Siemens 1930). Siemens tracked workers' psychological and physiological capabilities over the long-run. This was to inform company policy and the selection procedures for technical labour training. For Siemens, the overall goal of industrial psychology was to capture and shape the worker's inner life according to industrial principles (Bolt 1930: 125). Industrial management was to be supplemented by leadership. The ideal was the so-called 'Betriebsmensch', or organization man (Fricke 1950). In 1925 the German Institute for technical labour training (DINTA) was founded (Fricke 1950). Its main focus was to analyse mental states of workers and nurture human labour. In 1926 DINTA launched a series of publications whose aim, in the words of its chief executive, was to 'conquer the worker's soul' (Osthold 1926). This was part of a social disciplining campaign to shape a new type of worker. This new ideal—the 'organization man'—was motivated and committed. Training programs for workers and company social policy were both aiming to reshape the working man and women on the shopfloor, in their private life, in their behaviour and thought.

Before 1922 the following instruments of social engineering were intro-duced at Siemens: scholarships for highly qualified apprentices, training of commercial apprentices, a monthly published company journal, the open-ing of a sanatorium for workers, the construction of company dwellings, the introduction of a further internal differentiation of status for middle and higher salaried employees, recreation areas and programmes aimed at specific groups, such as female workers (Homburg 1983: 151). Further-more, Siemens introduced internal training programmes, provided lectures on social and technical topics, administrated internal company careers and promoted company-sponsored social activities after working in the second wave of rationalization between 1925 and 1928. 'Siemens clubs covered almost every possible leisure time occupation from sports to stamp collect-ing' (Homburg 1983: 151). In the third phase, the training and allocation of labour developed into a primary function of management.

Social programmes served to 'promote integration and commitment to the company'. In a report on the Siemens 'work community' in the 1930s, Carl v. Siemens announced: 'We are human beings, not machines therefore collaboration needs a spirit of connection' (v. Siemens nd). Symbolic power can be seen as an expansion of managerial power focusing on shaping a new moral economy of the subject. The Siemens experience demonstrates that power was not restricted to the single body, but extended the focus to the worker's soul. Management as a symbolic form of power is, therefore, not only about shaping realities. It is rather creating a subject or soul *behind* the actual deed.

Imaginary Power: Managing Identity—The Manager-Engineer

Managerial activities are difficult to control and coordinate, due to their non-standardised nature. The efficiency of managerial work is difficult to standardise or to evaluate in real-time. Organizations depend on managers to actively self-regulate their self-image, their feelings, identifications and behaviours. The manager, following the ascetic ideal, shapes himself ac-cording to given social roles without external prompts. According to man-agerial tasks of installing efficiency and motivation within organizations, they were expected to be engineers and managers the same time (Reckwitz 2006). While engineering as a material will to power was concentrating on efficiency, managing, as a symbolic will to power was more focused on mo-tivation. The manager-engineer recognised himself as being the expert for organizations and human resources (Wupper-Tewes 1995: 282).

As a coordinator of a machine-like-organization, the manager-engineer was invested with an overview and the technical/coordinative skills nec-essary to optimise all organizational processes. The engineer's diagnostic gaze was directed at micro processes of work: 'A precondition for judg-ing working motions according to their functionality was the nurturing of the manager's gaze' (Wupper-Tewes 1995: 284). The engineer's gaze was supported by modern media like the stop watch, the camera or a film. All of these instruments made new individual and social objects visible. The organizationally and technically augmented managerial gaze created new objects to be governed. These techniques and the resulting new way of seeing and shaping workers' movements was a precondition for scientifically reforming the whole production process. The manager-engineer was represented as someone with complete insight and overview of the company and the capacity to produce efficient organizations and workers.

Due to their social tasks, manager-engineers were expected to have motivational and communication skills (Bolt 1928). Siemens published psychological guidelines for those responsible for evaluating, controlling and training workers. For Siemens' industrial psychologists, the perfect manager derived part of their authority from as an expert for observing and evaluating people in organizations. Manager-engineers should train themselves to be everyday diplomats: every worker had to be known scientifically *and*, much more prosaically, according to their personal character. Industrial psychology complemented the personal authority of the Siemens manager-engineer. At Siemens, industrial psychologists and manager-engineers worked closely together in developing assessment sheets, guidelines for dealing with individual workers and evaluating the technical and psychological qualifications of the worker. The manager-engineer's role was to believe in—and increasingly to embody—the truth and justice of the rationalisation movement, to assume responsibility for the welfare of individual workers, for Siemens and for society as a whole. Manager-engineers were manufactured to willingly assume roles and ideas which shaped their self-understanding and their behaviour. Through these roles, manager-engineers reproduced the existing social power relationships of the efficiency movement in Germany.

Governing Knowledge: Siemens Since 1990

Siemens is now a global corporation in heavy engineering, energy, information technology and healthcare. Siemens has long been known for its strong hierarchy, bureaucracy and its expertise, characteristics established by its part in the rationalisation movement from the early 1920s (Davenport et al 2001: 220). The company now focuses on encouraging cooperation, sharing information and knowledge (Siemens 1996). From the mid-1990s, Siemens has embraced a new business concept, knowledge management: 'For today, companies like Siemens have to exploit their expertise more systematically and more intensively than ever before. Between 60 and 80 percent of the value added we generate is directly linked to knowledge—and the proportion is growing' (Pierer 2000: 5).

Material Power: Managing Embodied Knowledge

Despite the proclaimed organizational and cultural changes, knowledge management still works like a material will to power because knowledge is in part treated as an objectified commodity which has to be captured, developed and reused (Alvesson & Karreman 2001: McKinlay 2005). Knowledge management produces routines which result from acquiring and codifying what was formerly embodied knowledge. Knowledge management can be seen as a material power (Nietzsche 1887). In 1999, Siemens introduced ShareNet, a knowledge sharing system (Nielsen & Ciabuschi 2003). ShareNet is a top down approach to mobilise knowledge through prescribed routines. It is one part of the corporate project for capturing knowledge in order to evolve into a knowledge-based company. The system allows employees to exploit knowledge within the company from anywhere in the world. Codified knowledge provides users with ready solutions. Examples are sales projects, technical solutions, customer and competitor information (Nielsen & Ciabuschi 2003). Personalised knowledge includes urgent requests and news. It is meant for installing prescribed routines for global co-operation and social networks that criss-cross formal hierarchies. Ratings by re-users are intended to improve the quality. Uploading poor quality leads to poor ratings and reputational damage for the individual poster. Other quality control instruments are ShareNet managers and the global editor. Beyond these system-wide systems, quality guidelines provide the framework for a self-monitoring system.

Compared to Taylorism the will to power through knowledge has been transformed. Instead of a panoptical form of control, knowledge management installs a 360 degree control (Lemke 2000; Bröckling 2007). As a result, this control is visible to all actors within the corporate network. Its impact is tremendous because it influences the reputation and future prospects of employees. Neither the individual task nor a single ShareNet performance is the object of control, but the whole person over time, which increases the imperative for sustained identity work. Employees are permanently compelled to recognise themselves as an object of improvement and to regard themselves as subject/objects to control. It is not that they internalise the managerial gaze: they *become* the managerial gaze. Control is becoming less hierarchical, but ever more encompassing. This indirect form of control is exercised mostly through peers and self-evaluation (Bröckling 2007). Adjustment of employees in Taylorism was one-dimensional. Control is no longer reduced to reaching a certain goal. It is, rather, a dynamic form of permanent self-optimisation.

Symbolic Power: Management as the Production of 'Autonomous Souls'

Knowledge management concentrates on symbolic forms of power to motivate the worker's cooperation. For the rationalisation movement the employee had to be integrated into the organization as a subjected and not as a resistant individual. Management needed to produce an appropriate soul through constructing and embedding meaning. From 1923, Siemens renounced their reliance upon psychotechnical approaches like aptitude tests (Homburg 1991). Universal social welfare for all employees became less important. Analyses of the company's self-descriptions in company magazines, for instance, suggest a slow erosion of the intimacy of Siemens' relationship with employees. Until the 1970s, the company regarded—and projected—itself as a benign paterfamilias that provided help concerning questions of security, finance and health (Vogt 2005). Until 1963, for example, in-house-magazine articles preset the company's role as a close supporter of the family's breadwinner. Through the 1970s, Siemens shifted from being a well-meaning relative into behaving like a stranger who only provided useful, generic tips. This thinning of the social politics of Siemens increasingly used financial rewards to incentivise employee compliance (Vogt 2005). For example, Siemens offered a Development Promotion Reward (EFA) programme that insists that the performance and success of every employee be rewarded individuaoly (Siemens 1996). The EFA system puts an employee in charge of their own professional development by letting the employee suggest what training courses will enhance their skills and negotiate their individual targets for the coming year with their line manager, supported by an HR manager. Siemens promotes open communication by offering regular development and mentoring sessions, in addition to the annual employee survey (Siemens 2016). Such developments suggest a turning away from the notion of producing obedient employees the company has to care for. Instead, Siemens has become an institution which underlines its dependence on its self-managing employees (Vogt 2005). However, financial or material rewards are not viewed as sufficient for achieving legitimacy and subjected employees. Each division offers a variety of benefits to the employees: financial incentives, training and education in promoting innovation and leadership roles in creating, managing and sustaining innovation. There are, for example, on-line training programmes for new software and project management that are regarded as essential innovation skills for employees (Siemens, Knowledge Management 1995, 1998). Siemens also gains its legitimacy through promoting these new possibilities of motivation and creativity for employees (Siemens 2010). The focus of management stories is the self-actualisation of employees. The ambiguous character of knowledge work and organizations implies that the necessity of a symbolic power to tell workers who they are and what they are doing has become essential. Symbolic power therefore relies largely on a form of cultural control as a set of ideas, values and emotions for guiding employees (Alvesson 2005).

Imaginary Power: Managing Identity—We are all Managers Now!

Siemens' focus on innovation means that it expects its employees to be creative even if their creativity is tightly framed in terms of efficiency (Clegg et al 2006). Siemens' (1995) annual report proclaims: 'We are striving for a culture where creativity and ideas are encouraged, where productivity and the customer are in the center of all our efforts'. Instead of passive obedience, organizations need employees to be actively creative and entrepreneurial (Siemens 1997b). Not only the manager, but also the employee is expected to take on the initiative and personal long for continuous improvement. The ascetic ideal as a form of power which involves the notion of self-sacrifice in the name of a higher ideal is now employed on the knowledge worker. Knowledge workers have to actively incorporate the managerial discourses into narratives of self (Alvesson & Willmott 2002): 'In the past, as the work of Frederick Taylor illustrated, motivation theory linked very closely to pay and output. Individuals now need to be motivated in a completely different way. They have higher order needs. . . . Self-fulfilment is about working to one's full potential. This would involve doing something challenging, creative or interesting' (Siemens 2010). Maslow's humanistic theory of motivation serves as a discursive pillar for the deal of self-fulfillment (Maslow 1943). Self-actualisation can be seen as an ideal for motivating creative knowledge workers. Another important ideal is the claim to being an entrepreneurial subject. The ideal is a rational, self-interested and sovereign subject that is not embedded within given rules, but able to make its own choices (Reckwitz 2006). These choices are to be made within unstable and permanently changing environments. The context is one of general competition between active, risk taking, self-interested and self-responsible individuals: 'We have to make pro-active suggestions about where our customer's business may go and in which field he may be operating the next years' (Gibbert et al 2000: 23). This implies taking over new and more entrepreneurial roles: 'We have to play the role of a strategy-management consultant who is able to interpret trends and to design new business opportunities together with the customer' (Gibbert et al 2000: 23). The consulting role implies 'a continual refining of competencies, to keep pace with market developments' (Gibbert et al 2000: 23) The role implies constant improvement and behavioural training as an entrepreneurial subject. Individuals transform—and—transform themselves—into a form of capital. Competencies form this capital and are subjected to permanent improvement and observation. Siemens represents executives as coaches who support autonomous working processes and enable employees to be entrepreneurial: 'We are looking for characters not for grades. We are not looking for cogs in the machine. We are looking for employees dedicated to success for themselves and the company' (Siemens 1997a). Contemporary managerial and organizational interventions concentrate more on using and shaping imaginary forms of power which are less visible but more connected with forms of the 'ascetic idea'. Employees feel free and self-determined. The shift in in management approaches to identity work is not synonymous with *less* managerial power. Indeed, the most pervasive form of power is that which makes its subjects cooperate in their subjection to it.

Conclusions

The central aim of this chapter is to provide a positive logic of governance. Which power techniques, which discourses and which technologies of self are governing modern organizations? Management plays a central role as a form of government and shapes the relationship between organization and the subject. Here we draw on certain power relationships identified by Nietzsche's 'Genealogy of Morals'. Power regimes consist of different forms of power which serve as an analytical instrument for researching management approaches. Power ceases to be something that can be usefully discussed in terms of more or less. A power approach to management allows us to identify affinities between apparently quite different regimes. However, there are important differences. Contemporary organizational power relationships are less visible than those of the early twentieth century: because power is more de-centered and individuals play an active role within processes in which symbolic and imaginary forms of power assume greater importance than material power.

Acknowledgements

I am grateful to the Siemens Archive, Munich.

References

Albrow, M. (1992), 'Sine era et Studio—Or Do Organizations have Feelings?', *Organization Studies* 13/3: 313–329.

Alvesson, M. (2005), 'Knowledge Work: Ambiguity, Image and Identity', in K. Starkey, S. Tempest and A. McKinlay (eds), *How Organizations Learn: Managing the Search for Knowledge*, London: Thompson Learning.

Alvesson, M. & Kärreman, D. (2001), 'Odd Couple: Making Sense of the Curious Concept of Knowledge Management', *Journal of Management Studies* 38/7: 995–1018.

Alvesson, M. & Willmott, H. (2002), 'Identity Regulation as Organizational Control: Producing the Appropriate Individual', *Journal of Management Studies* 39/5: 619–644.

Bolt, R. (1928), 'Vortrag für die V. Internationale Konferenz für Psychotechnik' (SAA/ 10508).

Bolt, Richard (13.09.1928): Geschichte der Psychologie bei Siemens. Vortrag für die V. Internationale Konferenz für Psychotechnik vom 10–14. September 1928 in Utrecht. Siemens-Archiv München. SAA/ 10508.

Boltanski, L. & Chiapello, È. (2006), *Der Neue Geist des Kapitalismus*, Konstanz: UVB Verlagsgesellschaft.

Bröckling, U. (2007), *Das Unternehmerische Selbst. Soziologie einer Subjektivierungsform*, Frankfurt am Main: Suhrkamp.

Clegg, S., Courpasson, D. & Phillips, D. (2006), *Power and Organizations*, London: Sage.

192   Nancy Richter

Davenport, T. H. & Völpel, S. (2001), 'The Rise of Knowledge', *Journal of Knowledge Management* 5/3: 212–222.

Eidenmüller Chronik (n.d.), 'Die Epochen des technisch-organisatorischen Wandels im Produktionsbereich', (Siemens AG, SAA 12138).

Ernst, S. (n.d.), ' Schrift zum Führungsverhalten bei Siemens', (SAA 49/ Lb 445).

Foucault, M. (1984), 'What Is Enlightment?' in J. Appleby (ed.) (1996), *Knowledge and Postmodernism in Historical Perspective*, New York: Routledge.

Fricke, F. (1950), 'Die Rechtfertigung des DINTA.' Online unter: http://library. fes.de/cgi- bin/arb_.pl?year=1928&pdfs=291x292x293x294x295x296x297x2 98x299. Abgerufen am: 10.09.2011

Gibbert, M., Jonczyk, C. & Völpel, S. (2000), 'ShareNet—The Next Generation Knowledge Management', in T. Davenport and G. Probst (eds), *Knowledge Management Case Book: Best Practices*, Munich: Wiley & Sons.

Hinnenthal, H. (1928), *Die deutsche Rationalisierungsbewegung und das Reichskuratorium für Wirtschaftlichkeit*, Berlin: Reichskuratorium für Wirtschaftlichkeit.

Homburg, H. (1983), 'Scientific Management and Personnel Policy in the Modern German Enterprise 1918–1939: The Case of Siemens', in H. Gospel and C. Littler (eds), *Managerial Strategies & Industrial Relations*, London: Ashgate.

Homburg, H. (1991), *Rationalisierung und Industriearbeit: Arbeitsmarkt-Management-Arbeiterschaft im Siemens-Konzern Berlin 1900–1939*, Berlin: Haude & Spener.

Höpner, Martin (2004), Der organisierte Kapitalismus in Deutschland und sein Niedergang. Unternehmenskontrolle und Arbeitsbeziehungen im Wandel. In: Politische Vierteljahresschrift : Zeitschrift der Deutschen Vereinigung für Politische Wissenschaft, Sonderheft (34).

Jaques, R. (1996), *Manufacturing the Employee: Management Knowledge from the 19th to the 21st Centuries*, London: Sage.

Kocka, J. (1969), 'Industrielles Management: Konzeptionen und Modelle in Deutschland vor 1914', *Vierteljahresschrift für Sozial- und Wirtschaftsgeschichte* 56: 332–372.

Köttgen (1926), 'Niederschrift über die 'Betriebstechnische Konferenz, Amerikaberichte', (SAA 64/ Lc 511).

Lemke, T. (2000), 'Gouvernementalität, Neoliberalismus und Selbsttechnologien: Eine Einführung', in U. Bröckling, S. Krasmann, & T. Lemke (eds), *Gouvernementalität der Gegenwart. Studien zur Ökonomisierung des Sozialen*, Frankfurt am Main: Suhrkamp.

Le Vrang (1930), 'Verminderung des Ausschusses und Erweckung der Interesses der Arbeiterschaft für die Arbeit, Niederschrift über die, Betriebstechnische Konferenz', 5 and 6 May (SAA 64/ Lc 511).

Maslow, A. H. (1943), 'A Theory of Human Motivation', *Psychological Review* 50: 370–396.

McKinlay, A. (2005), 'Smart Workers, Dumb Organizations', in K. Starkey, S. Tempest, & A. McKinlay (eds), *How Organizations Learn. Managing the Search for Knowledge*, second edition, London: Thomson.

Nielsen, B. & Ciabuschi, F. (2003), 'Siemens ShareNet: Knowledge Management in Practice', *Business Strategy Review* 14/2: 33–40.

Nietzsche, F. (1887), *Zur Genealogie der Moral. Eine Streitschrift*, Leipzig: Naumann.

Nietzsche, F. (1968), *The Will to Power*, London: Random House.

Osthold, P. (1926), *Der Kampf um die Seele des Arbeiters*, Düsseldorf.

Pierer, H. V. (2000), 'Knowledge as a Competitive Advantage', in T. Davenport & G. Probst (eds), *Knowledge Management Case Book: Best Practices*, Munich: Wiley & Sons.

Pippin, R. (2004), 'Lightning and Flash, Agent and Deed', in O. Höffe (ed.), *Zur Genealogie der Moral*, Berlin: Akademie Verlag.

Reckwitz, A. (2006), *Das Hybride Subjekt*, Weilerswist: Vellbrück Wissenschaft.

Rupp, Hans (1931): Psychotechnische Zeitschrift, Vorwort, Wien. Siemens & Halske Berlin. Siemens-Archiv München. SAA 10508.

Saar, M. (2007), *Genealogie als Kritik. Geschichte und Theorie des Subjekts nach Nietzsche und Foucault*, Frankfurt: Campus.

Siemens (1925/1926), 'Niederschrift über die Betriebstechnische Konferenz, Amerikaberichte', (SAA 64/ Lc 511).

Siemens (1930), 'Gedächtnistest aus dem Jahr 1930, Betriebspsychologie', (SAA/10508).

Siemens (1995), 'Knowledge Management', (SAA 18264).

Siemens (1996), 'Siemens', (SAA 23627).

Siemens (1997a), 'Die Einführung neuer Mitarbeiter', (SAA H43/ 3355).

Siemens (1997b), 'Goth Pressegespräch', (SAA 23627).

Siemens (1998), 'Wie man besser wird. Ein Selbststudium', in 9 Minuten (SAA 15630).

Siemens (2010), 'Motivation within a Creative Environment', *The Times* 100 Business Case Studies.

Siemens (2016), 'Siemens in dialog'. Retrieved November 22, 2016, from http://www.siemens.com/about/sustainability/en/sustainability-at   siemens/siemens-in-dialog.htm.

Taylor, F. W. (1913), *Die Grundsätze wissenschaftlicher Betriebsführung*, München/Berlin: Oldenbourg.

Türk, K., Lemke, T. & Bruch, M. (2006), *Organisation in der modernen Gesellschaft*, Wiesbaden: Verlag für Sozialwissenschaften.

Vogt, B. (2005), *Wir Gehören zur Familie: Das Unternehmensleitbild der Siemens AG anhand der Selbstdarstellung*, Marburg: Tectum Verlag.

Voigt, I. (2006), 'Rationalisierung—Definitionen, Vorstellungen und Zitate von Gestern und Heute', www.rkw-magazin.de, Nr. 2, Mai 2006.

Wupper-Tewes, H. (1995), *Rationalisierung als Normalisierung. Betriebswissenschaft und betriebliche Leistungspolitik in der Weimarer Republik*, Münster: Westfälisches Dampfboot.

Part V
Conclusion

10 Making Governmentality I
An Interview with Peter Miller

Alan McKinlay

ALAN MCKINLAY (AM): Today I'd like to discuss the development of 'governmentality' as a concept over some thirty years and more: the career of a concept from its birth in Foucault's lectures through an early phase of conceptual experimentation, innovation and application to what we might call today's mature state where some of the main terms are widely used across many disciplines. But let's start with a sense of where you started your own academic career and how that became entangled with Foucault and governmentality.

PETER MILLER (PM): I was reflecting back on this the other day and I realised that—if you like—the bits and pieces that ended up as 'governmentality' started off in 1981 when Nik Rose and I separately were moving in the same direction. There was my doctoral thesis which was a broad social science discussion of power but with a focus on subjectivity and subjectification: why the Frankfurt School got it wrong about subjectivity; why Lukacs got it wrong about subjectivity. Basically, it started out as quite a theoretical piece of work but as I got more into counterposing Foucault's approach to subjectivity with the Frankfurt School and so on, the more I realised that I had to read Foucault's histories. Governmentality didn't exist at this time. We were in the aftermath of structural Marxism—of relative autonomy, of ideological state apparatuses—but to understand Foucault you had to read his histories, particularly *Birth of the Clinic* and *Histoire de la Folie*. You had to use the French original because the English translation was so abridged and virtually without references. For me, that was revelatory. All of a sudden, you realised that you had to read the history of medicine and the history of psychiatry to *really* appreciate Foucault. I was moving from set of debates that were dominated by very abstract debates about structuralisms in all their different forms, to pretending to being a historian. Then realising that what you had to do was *histories*.

That was when and how Nik Rose and I hooked up. Actually, we were teaching a quite quirky—off the wall—set of seminars under the University of London external programme. He had always had an interest in applied psychology and psychiatry. Somehow we had the idea that it would be good to put on a series of seminars that we thought would attract something like five people. Instead the room was packed. This involved us in an encounter with radical psychiatry that paralleled Foucault's interests. So, I was exiting from a heavily theorised post-Marxist intellectual tradition, then reading these local histories, and radical 'psy' practitioners. All of this was being put together bit by bit. Nik had already published his first book, *Psychological Complex*, which was a history of applied psychology; and I was dabbling with bits of the history of psychiatry: the psychiatrisation of unemployment and so on. We started picking things up—it was completely opportunist and unsystematic. We then did some work on the Tavistock in *Sociology*; other pieces appeared in other journals. In the introduction to *Governing the Present* we look back on that process as a somewhat sporadic examination of little histories, that we now recognise as laboratories of governmentality. Of course, we didn't call it governmentality at the time. So it was all very uncoordinated, unplanned, unsystematic: in fact, that was the beauty of it. It was around this time that I met up with Ted O'Leary and we presented our 'Governable Person' paper in 1984. So, there was this funny sort of temporality with very different things going on in parallel. At this point, I was just starting to dabble in the history of accounting but still doing these histories of psychology. And Nik was coming more from a kind of applied psychology. We started to realise that there was something in common between things that looked completely different. This was a gradual process. Don't forget, I was also trying to get a job and trying to explain a curriculum vitae that included a book on Foucault and critical theory, studies of the history of British psychology and then starting to do studies of accounting as well.

AM: Why accounting? How did that come about?

PM: I was exiting from a broadly structuralist Marxism; there were some big problems facing Marxism about economic calculation. The set of people that were relevant to me as I finished my doctorate were Paul Hirst and Barry Hindess who, with Tony Cutler, put together *Marx's Capital and Capitalism Today*; Jim Tomlinson who was talking about the importance of understanding different forms of economic calculation; Graeme Thompson whose work on the nature of the firm was very important for me. And so at this point this was nothing specifically to do with accounting but all about forms of economic calculation and how these were done and their effects—what everyone now calls performativity. A lot of that impetus came from that group of people and especially from *Marx's Capital and Capitalism Today*. We *have* to look at forms of economic calculation and their impact, or their variable impacts, and their constitutive powers. This offered a way of moving beyond Marxism's struggle to move from value to anything observable.

Actually, *Marx's Capital and Capitalism Today* does have a chapter about accounting.

I had been struggling within this structuralist Marxist framework to understand something called 'ideology' and ended up worrying that this notion of 'relative autonomy' was a bit of a cop-out. So worries about that sort of dimension; worries about economic calculation. This was a genuine insight: all of a sudden, we realised that we *need* to look at particular forms of economic calculation and what they do and what effects they produce. And then completely out-of-the-blue, but not since, of course, networks are real: through a friend who was working with Anthony Hopwood on one of their long-running projects. Anthony was at London Business School at that point. And asked me to teach a doctoral course on theory and methodology. Anthony insisted that you should not start such a course with Aristotle and just about get up to the eighteenth century but start with relevant materials about things that are interesting *now*. Before I knew it I was teaching *Discipline and Punish* and *The Order of Things* at London Business School. And in a crazy way it worked: partly because it was so off-the-wall but also because it forced the students to really question what they would otherwise have treated as purely technical. Ted O'Leary was visiting LBS that year—1982 and 1983; and Ann(e) Loft was studying with Anthony as well. And Anthony suggested that Ted (O'Leary) and I write a paper together. Anthony just had this brilliant way of spotting possible pairings: it didn't always work, but often worked. And that was the start of the 'Governable Person' paper.

The move into accounting was not as weird as it looked because of those worries—that had been going on for several years by that point—about how do we analyse forms of economic calculation and what they do, from a radical left position? That worry—that question—predated anything about accounting. Accounting, in that sense, was a natural fit. It seemed to me a very natural move from the history of psychiatry to the history of accounting. I don't know that that trajectory would be so likely today. I was effectively an unemployed sociologist doing bits and pieces that were interesting and a few things with Nik. But governmentality didn't exist at this time: we just had several studies of different things. We were not even trying to be Foucault scholars. One lovely little story is that we had written a paper about something to do with the Tavistock for *Sociology*. The reviewers' feedback was that they liked the empirics, liked the paper, but that the theoretical framing was low-key and did we know that there was this guy called Michel Foucault whose work would be very useful to us. So, we were not banner-waving Foucauldians. For people who had spent a lot of time worrying about how to make structural Marxism work in a way that didn't rely on get-out clauses, part of the liberation was that you studied things simply because they were interesting. Now, there were certain themes such as how subjects were made up, and so on, but without any theoretical shackles. It wasn't naïve empiricism but it wasn't very structured theoretically.

AM: You have had an interest in accounting as a technology, as a technology that *does* things. Conventional accounting thinks of itself as a technology that reports. Now, that all makes sense. You explain that you came from an intellectual milieu—structural Marxism—that was running out of steam, and that its increasingly abstract nature did not allow it to easily ask relevant questions about contemporary capitalism. But there were other theoretical alternatives: Gramsci; or 'history from below'. So, by choosing to make concepts stimulated by Foucault involved not choosing, say, Gramsci.

PM: You're quite right. We acknowledge this in *Governing the Present*. We were reading Gramsci. The appeal of Gramsci was that he offered a less constrained way of framing questions: you did not have to worry about 'relative autonomy' and other get-out clauses. Gramsci was always seen as a sort of fellow-traveller. But the importance of Foucault's histories was that it allowed a framing of subjectivity, the formation and enabling of certain subjectivities. That was the absolute punch-line for me: that the appeal to subjectivity is so central to Foucault's histories. Now, of course, those themes *are* in Gramsci but they are *absolutely* in the foreground of Foucault. And that provided the most obvious hook with the accounting because if you go in via management accounting, not financial reporting, then the minute you see Taylorism and standard costing from a Foucauldian perspective, it's such a perfect example of acting or managing at a distance or the conduct of conduct. It just seemed such a perfect illustration of how devices like that make up people. It was just such an ideal fit. We took a firm decision that you could not get there by hanging onto structural Marxism because of all the problems with Althusser and caveats like 'relative autonomy'. That said, Althusser did prompt us to look to subjectivity but—for me—that was where you hit a brick wall because that didn't help—*really*—how subjects got made up and what does that making up. Jumping from the super-theoretical register to the empirical, Nik had done various studies in psychology and education and we started doing work on various forms of Tavistock interventions: industrial psychology, the psychotherapy of unemployment. And you then start seeing all these very different sites We're not very temperamentally suited to 'the voices of the underdog' approach. Rediscovering the voices of the dispossessed was *not* the register we were using. We *were* interested in how people's lives are interfered with. We start from forms of intervention or forms of power and then just looking at how those play out and how they operate in quite low-level settings. But it was never a matter of recapturing voices, it more trying to examine *how* are those voices framed and articulated and to some extent constrained.

AM: So it was almost about those devices that provided the vocabulary for living?

PM: Yes, exactly. There are quite serious misconceptions in many of the readings of Foucault and Foucauldian type writings. But, that vocabulary is about making people and giving them certain capacities to act. There's a very nice phrase of Foucault's in his Afterword to Dreyfus and Rabinow (1982) *Michel Foucault: Beyond Structuralism and Hermeneutics*, where he says that devices such as these forms of intervention are bad in and of themselves but that everything is dangerous. This points us the operationalisation of these devices but not from a presumption that forms of autonomy are necessarily evil; nor that forms of autonomising are necessarily positiv.e or liberatory either. Nik expresses this in the title of one of his books, *Powers of Freedom*. That idea—coming from Foucault—that we borrowed, was that freedom can be a form of the exercise of power.

AM: One of the curious aspects of the way your work became entangled with governmentality is that, initially at least, Foucault provided you with a general sensibility, new ways of looking at things, an open approach rather than a theory whose conclusions are written before any historical or empirical work begins. Althusserian Marxism cranks out certain, almost pre-determined results. Foucault, at that juncture, provided you with new concepts that was looser—much looser—in terms of what could be examined and the connections that could be made between quite different institutions or quite different forms of expertise.

PM: That's absolutely the case. Foucault's lecture on governmentality we published in *Ideology & Consciousness* long before it got any wider currency. That essay was republished a decade later in *The Foucault Effect*. If you had wanted a theoretical framing to reassure you then it just did not exist initially. When we started in the early 1980s governmentality didn't really exist. Even if you look at the lecture on governmentality there's not a huge amount in there. There were gentle hints at something like governmentality in *Histoire de la Folie* or in his essay on public health in the eighteenth century where he looked at epidemics and notions of population. In doing empirical studies what we were doing was thinking about important problems about expertise and how that framed the ways that people lived their lives. Only after a decade of empirical work we started to think about the loose categories that we found useful. *Science in Action* had just been published and we were enamoured with certain ideas, such as action at a distance and stable combining with mobile. Ian Hacking has always been very important, especially the notion of devices that both represented and intervened.

AM: Perhaps with governmentality Foucault is having another attempt to cut off the king's head. Discipline can be too easily read as a form of social control. There are too many forms of government to be captured under the single term, discipline. Governing means something more, something else. Clearly, governing means something different when we are talking about families from when we are talking about asylums. However, there are moments when one can see those sorts of connections. Cultural Marxism's greatest insight was that capitalism was remaking itself before our very eyes. Jimmy Airlie, a former leader of the 1971–72 UCS work-in and national union organiser, credited Ford Motor Company with enough intelligence to recognise that you catch more files with honey than you do with vinegar. Management was being rethought at the same time as government was being reimagined. Management was now a cultural form—a language and set of practices—that cannot be reduced to a logic of capital.

PM: And this is why all these peculiar connections are so important. Robert Castel's histories of psychiatry were very important: his first book (1973) *Le psychanalysme: l'ordre psychanalytique et le pouvoir* was a follow on to *Histoire de la Folie*. Jacques Donzelot's writing on the family was also crucial. Castel's next book, with Françoise Castel and Anne Lowell (1979) *La société psychiatrique avancée: le modèle américain* looked at libertarian psychotherapies in the USA. Those were people writing in the penumbra of Foucault. So it was quite a mixture of writings and not at all a fine-tuned theoretical apparatus. We drew on this range of literatures not because we thought we could combine them into 'a theory' but because they seemed helpful ways of doing things. And it was those things that got brought into management in various different forms. Again, it was getting a handle on how techniques that were supposed to liberate people but which were about power in one way or another. Much of the Foucauldian writings up to that point had focused on the 'psy' disciplines but had not engaged with the economic world or with management. But it became so obvious that there was that route into management for all of these devices. And, of course, it was obvious to us simply because we had researched the Tavistock which has both pillars, management and organization, on the one hand, and the family, on the other. And so it was incredibly important to see how those devices were retraining management. This was a management that was at odds with the Taylorised factory and speeded up production lines. Part of the appeal—and part of the success of this research—was what was happening at the time. The other thing was that we were moving into a period in which the state was being dismantled, rolled back. Markets were being celebrated and freedoms trumpeted.

AM: There was an incoherence in Thatcherism. It was absolutely not a fully-fledged neoliberal project. Far from it: initially, Thatcherism was little more than a list of things that the Tories were against. Neoliberalism gained shape over the first decade of Thatcherism. In parallel with your work on governmentality, neoliberalism was gaining a shape—not just instincts hostile to the state—that the state should be used proactively to construct different kinds of market inside the state and beyond the state.

PM: That's absolutely correct. We very gently suggest that rough chronology in 'Politics . . .' That the thing called 'neoliberalism' has feeder roots from the left. Demands for transparency and accountability were not unique to neoliberalism. The power of the medical profession, their intransigence and their unwillingness to be open was criticised from the left. More generally, a suspicion of the state: all of this was a broad current on the left. Ironically, calls for autonomy—also from the left— ended up becoming part of neoliberalism. The culture of transparency and accountability that is central to neoliberalism was not the case in the 1970s: indeed, it was the other way around. Transparency and accountability have become appropriated, annexed by neoliberalism. In terms of our practice, we did not have a checklist for neoliberalism. We just studied things that seemed important and relevant at that moment, which seemed relatively open-ended about where it would end up.

AM: Just as you say, through the 1980s there were numerous attempts to develop theoretical languages that could come to terms with the new management and the turn to flexibility. Was this flexible Fordism or flexible specialisation or something else besides? There were two strands to this. First, how to work with the grain of flexibility to produce more skilled, better jobs. Second, to lament the passing of a world of mass production in which inherited assumptions about the nature of management and work organization were becoming increasingly irrelevant. Both, of course, were about preserving *something* of the past.

PM: Again, we now live in a world in which everyone is quantified; in which everyone can be benchmarked against everyone else in six different ways. But some of those demands for quantification and comparability came from more democratising ambitions that became part of the bandwagon of neoliberalism. One of the reasons we do the sort of research that we do is to not forget that things can be changed and can end up going in quite different, unexpected directions over a relatively short time span.

AM: That takes us on to the thorny question of the state. Perhaps the thing that has created the most controversy about your work which is that your version of governmentality goes too far. That is to say, it's one thing to state that the state does not exhaust politics and, as you have quite rightly insisted, that new ways of governing have become the ways that all sorts of institutions operate, and that this was not initiated or

prompted by the state. The state is not unique, it's certainly not shel-
tered from these new ways of managing. But at the same time, to look
at political power beyond the state suggests that the state continues to
play an important role, not least as a vehicle for neoliberal ideas and
practices.

PM: It is a headache. We have always made that we say, quite unambigu-
ously, that this is not to say that the state does not exist or that the
state is not important. But that is certainly how it has been interpreted.
But all we were trying to say was that there is a huge amount of law
outside and beyond those domains. Much of what we were interested
in interventions in domains that were officially or formally private or
personal: *that* was our starting point. Again, if you traced back the affiliations and how these unfold then you do not end up back at the state.
If I were to be a little reflective then it would be valuable to trace how
linkages and connections that produce effects that *are* beyond the state
are mobilised around the state; or, give the state a role in articulating
the desirability of those effects. One of Donzelot talks about mobilising
languages and practices in relation to the state where the state is not the
core actor. The state, then, becomes the effect rather than the primary
cause. But I do think in relation to the question what is neoliberalism,
it would be very interesting to reflect on how these connections get
established between the state and things that are certainly beyond the
state. So, that's something that we haven't done. But, on the other hand,
we did ask what forms of intervention; how are they being articulated;
how is it being organised. Much of what we were looking at just did
not come from the state. So, that has been a bit of a problem but we
have also been wilfully misunderstood in that people still want to hang
onto a notion of there being an essential human asset called subjectivity
rather than that subjectivities are being made up by a whole range of
ways by a whole range of devices. The same holds true for 'the state':
people seem offended if you argue that this other stuff matters and may
even come to matter more than the state. Don't forget that before we
formulated the notion of political power beyond the state we were simply doing studies of this, that and the other. When we started to frame
our practice, only then we realised that much of what we had been
studying was partly empirical and that these interventions had not been
coming from, or related to or organised by something called the state.
Now, some people found that very difficult to accept.

AM: Of course, there is a more primitive refusal to attribute everything to
Thatcher: that's just too easy. In that sense, what the notion of political
power beyond the state offered was a way to cut off the queen's head.

PM: I've been using more of Deleuze's ideas, especially the idea of assemblage. An assemblage is the putting together of a lot of disparate elements, sometimes complementary, but often contradictory, where these
have stabilised for long enough to operate and do something. That is a

helpful way of understanding what is neoliberalism: it's absolutely not a coherent thing. And what we were looking at was not coherent but there were still connections and affiliations.

Initially, when we framed out empirical work we talked about 'rationalities', 'programmes' and 'technologies'. 'Programmes' was a category that allowed us to address somewhat more empirical, somewhat localised, low-level projects. 'Technologies' was about the devices that were formed around these programmes. 'Rationalities' was supposed to allow us to engage with quite abstract political theory but quite quickly got edited out. Colin Gordon, whose work is very important to me, speaks to these issues. What we were trying to do was tease out whether there were things in common, that were useful. We ended up by saying that these things seem to have some sort of family resemblance, but they are not the same but they can work jointly or in the same direction. So 'governmentality' came late to the game. For me, what was at issue was an insistence on the pairing of certain devices, how these are mobilised and legitimised through certain sorts of programmatic ambition. Anthony Hopwood used to talk about similar things: the relationship between costing and costliness. He had a Foucauldian spirit to his writing without being a card-carrying Foucauldian. But the one thing that I would have liked us to emphasise a bit more was the multiple, differentiated—possibly contradictory—nature of programmes. It would almost be against the spirit of what we have argued to talk of a hierarchy. So, programmes can be multiple because there is a danger at times that they become invested with a bit more coherence than they really merit. It's relevance because if, for instance, you're studying factory reform processes in the USA then you have national level debate about forms of economic citizenship and that's a meta-level debate. There will also be corporate level formulations about what is being done in the name of competition with Japan and so on. You will also have factory-level articulations of those questions. In health care and social care, for instance, you have a modernising ambitions that then come into contact with a whole range of different things, particularly a very strong sense of professional identity; and then people at the front-line who have deliver pressure-relieving mattresses to an individual. The task is to hang onto the idea of programmes but to look at them on a number of levels, including a rather lower level. The worry I have is that when people then go to study a social worker going to get this particular mattress then people end up studying reality. So, programmes cannot be treated as hard-line definitions. Programmes—and the idea of programming—works through many more levels.

AM: Let me be clear. It would be wrong to understand the delivery of a mattress, say, the reality on the ground, as derived from a programme.

PM: Exactly. Now, it *could* be that particular act was derived in that way. But you would have to look at are real and are top-down and relatively organised to build in much, much less organised, much less articulated processes. It's effectively what people keep calling resistance and then complain that they don't find enough resistance in Foucault's writings. So, it would be about that, it would be about counter-arguments, counter-programmes though they may not even merit the word programmes: to pluralise the notion of programmes.

AM: Would there be a danger that you may smuggle in relative autonomy?
PM: That's true: although it would be relative autonomy in terms of a whole range of things, not just the economy.

AM: It would be about extending that sense of openness, contingency, to different levels, different types of programmes.
PM: This has been prompted by the current worry that by saying economising or quantification you are saying that it's all the same. That forms of quantification by actuaries and health economists that produce league tables are very different from forms of marketising. Some forms of tables do have economising behind them but others are rather old-fashioned bureaucratic resource allocation models. So, one must be careful to pluralise quantification. In practice, because you want to say something useful you do not want to talk as if they were infinite programmes because they have to have a certain ability to link up, mobilise and so on. For those reasons, you would not expect to find infinite numbers of programmes. To see programmes as interacting, sometimes contradictory. To study and write across those different registers is actually very difficult. The danger is that one programme is privileged and you lose that sense of plurality, of connectedness and contradiction. If it were just a morass of unrelated things, then it wouldn't be terribly interesting. But what is interesting is that quite disparate programmes do gain a consistency and a connectedness. That consistency seems to be necessary if a programme is to have an effect.

AM: One theme that has run through all your work with Nikolas Rose and others has been an insistence that your work is empirical and historical but never theoretical. You have explained that's partly to do with your own biography: of having emerged from a tradition that was exclusively, excessively theoretical. Equally, and your notion of programmes speaks to this, you deliberately chose not to investigate the lived experience of working people, patients or inmates.
PM: It was something of a reaction against theory: that's true. We do emphasise the empirical, the historical. Here and there, we do talk about how these things get articulated and mobilised as projects. We do return again and again to a very small number of organising categories:

programmes and technologies; assemblages; action at a distance; representing and intervening; chains of calculation is another. More recently, the notion of mediating instruments I've found very helpful to think about things that embed different and sometimes contradictory things in one metrical instrument. And, by so doing, connect up languages and processes that were previously not connected up. So, there is a relatively long list of concepts and categories that we've used repeatedly because they are helpful. But the attitude is not wanting to turn that into some sort of theoretical apparatus which can only be bought into wholesale. This is not anti-theory so much as a theoretical eclecticism that is much more permissive than the theoretical tradition that prevailed in the 1970s and 1980s. The main driver is to be permissive and useful: categories can be used, or not, depending on the problem at hand. There is, of course, Foucault's comment that my work should be used as a tool-box. Regardless, of whether or not Foucault actually said this or quite what he meant by it, I feel that there are a set of categories which are a useful tool-box, which are sort of complementary and have some very loose affiliation but you can use some of them but not necessarily all of them. You can use one conceptual tool but not another. This is not a hierarchical arrangement, nor does usage necessarily suggest that one tool is always more useful than another. Any notion of a theoretical hierarchy, of a completeness was exactly what I was trying to get away from.

AM: Until the last thirty years, all craft apprentices, whether an engineer or a building worker, would quite literally make their own tool-box; and often make some of their own tools as well. Now, some tools were made to certain standards but then might be personalised to the individual and to the tasks they met. These were toolkits that were standard but that were also personalised and modified according to the types of work being done.

PM: That's a very apt metaphor. To summarise: it's more of a push, not towards theory but away from theory. It's about concepts and categories which are useful but which do have some affiliation with each other.

AM: In terms of methodology, Foucault listens to debates amongst experts. He listens to debate amongst criminologists and penologists rather than to gaolers or convicts. This means he interrogates public archives, for expert knowledge has to be public, to some extent. Now, for historians, Foucault's methodological choice not to burrow deep into the private archives of prisons or asylums is a failure. Foucault listens to the formulation of programmes where one can hear experts developing their expertise. The difficulty is that it is much easier to represent knowledge than it is to represent power.

PM: That would not be so true of some of Foucault's work, especially *Histoire de la Folie*. Both Nik Rose and I had a similar feeling. But don't forget that neither of us are philosophers. We were working at a slightly lower level effectively: working with welfare policies—programmes, if you like—rather than political philosophy. So, I don't think that's entirely true of all of Foucault's writings and *Histoire de la Folie* was fairly intricate although it was working at a fairly abstract level. That would be consistent with my focus on programmes. This is something that organization theory has always struggled with: loose coupling, uncoupling and so forth. If I thought that the idea of 'economic citizenship' that I studies with Ted O'Leary in the Caterpillar case was completely divorced from, and meaningless to, people on the shopfloor it would not have been worth studying. We did interviews, we did go around shopfloors and it is interesting how the narratives that employees create have some resonance with the meta-narratives that management were creating. For me, that's the issue, the meeting point. In some case, dismissing 'economic citizenship' completely; in some cases, selecting some parts. For instance, the ways that employees appropriated management language of autonomising; or spoke of their own business on the shopfloor. It becomes a question of performativity: to what extent do these things have effects? So, I feel very strongly that the things that we have studied do have effects on the ways that people live their lives. The study of those effects is tremendously difficult because they require the skills of a social psychologist or an ethnographer. There is sufficient evidence that people start reorganising and reframing what they do, rearticulating why they do it, and what it means in terms of some affiliation to some broader programme.

AM: A final question: where next for governmentality, given that you have established a certain family of concepts, a certain way of doing research? Since governmentality is so bound up with neoliberalism will the concept expire when neoliberalism expires?

PM: I don't think the governmentality project will expire if, or when, neoliberalism expires because the technology is durable. A parallel would be standard costing which is equally at home in Taylorised factories in the USA and now in hospital resource allocation mechanisms. The stability of the technologies will guarantee that this way of studying governmentality will continue. Some of the concepts and categories—programmes, technologies, calculative chains—are being used quite widely and would continue to be useful. Now we have a little toolkit that we have some experience with and have found to be of some use. Personally, I hope that there would be to continue the spirit of the early studies: to look at problems that are interesting and relevant: to unpack what is going on beneath the neoliberal headlines of economising, quantifying, marketising and consumerising. Our understanding of neoliberalism needs to be unpacked and pluralised.

References

Donzelot, J. (1979), *Policing of Families: Welfare versus the State*, London: Hutchinson.

Foucault, M. (1972), *Folie et Deraison: Histoire de la Folie*, Paris: Gallimard.

Foucault, M. (1976), *Birth of the Clinic: An Archaeology of Medical Perception*, London: Tavistock.

Foucault, M. (1977), *Discipline and Punish: The Birth of the Prison*, London: Penguin.

Foucault, M. (1982), 'The Subject of Power', in H. Dreyfus & P. Rabinow (ed.), *Michel Foucault: Beyond Structuralism and Hermeneutics*, London: Harvester Wheatsheaf.

Foucault, M. (2001), *The Order of Things: An Archaeology of the Human Sciences*, London: Routledge.

Hacking, I. (1983), *Representing and Intervening: Introductory Topic in the Philosophy of Natural Science*, Cambridge: Cambridge University Press.

Latour, B. (1987), *Science in Action: How to Follow Scientists and Engineers through Society*, Cambridge, MA: Harvard University Press.

Miller, P. & O'Leary, T. (1987), 'Accounting and the Construction of the Governable Person', *Accounting, Organizations and Society* 12/3: 235–266.

Miller, P. & Rose, N. (1988), 'The Tavistock Programme: The Government of Subjectivity and Social Life', *Sociology* 22/2: 171–192.

Miller, P. & Rose, N. (2008), *Governing the Present: Administering Economic, Social and Personal Life*, Cambridge: Polity.

Rose, N. (1985), *The Psychological Complex*, London: Routledge & Kegan Paul.

Rose, N. (1999), *Powers of Freedom: Reframing Political Thought*, Cambridge: Cambridge University Press.

Rose, N. & Miler, P. (1992), 'Political Power Beyond the State: Problematics of Government', *British Journal of Sociology* 43/2: 173–205.

11 Making Governmentality II
An Interview with Nikolas Rose

Alan McKinlay

ALAN MCKINLAY (AM): Governmentality has become synonymous with histories of the present, Foucault's over-arching project. And, since the present is dominated by neoliberalism, governmentality has become the favoured way of understanding how neoliberalism plays out in different domains of economic, social and personal life.

NIKOLAS ROSE (NR): I am actually rather hostile to the way that the term neoliberalism has emerged, and how it is taken to be an adequate description of what is going on, of the political rationalities of the present. Neoliberalism is much too simple a term, to general a term, to capture what is going on. This is an argument that is very current in Latin America where the term is used unquestioningly by critics of the contemporary political situation. These blanket terms make it almost impossible to understand where the handholds are, where the fault-lines are: the things that one might want to latch onto and try to intensify as opposed to the things that one might want to criticise. We—that is Peter Miller and myself—used the term neoliberalism initially but later on chose to use the term 'advanced liberalism' to try to indicate the changes that were happening: changes to the form of the state, the emergence of the new distantiated technologies for governing, like the new public management, the devolution of responsibilities as close as possible to the individual, responsibilisation and all that. These ways of thinking about transforming regimes of governing were not just the property of the right; they took up themes that had emerged in liberal and left-wing critiques of the overweening welfare state. There was something of a consensus that something had to be done—that is to say, of the problem to be addressed—and there were some similarities in the solutions being proposed. But that didn't mean that all the solutions had similar implications when it came to power. The proliferation of audits, for instance, can be used both to impose certain targets on entities—government at a distance as we would say—but also to do, for instance, environmental audits: audits *can* be used for very progressive purposes.

AM: Let me backtrack. A key question is how you found Foucault, before you found governmentality. Clearly, this is something about how Althusserian Marxism had run its course, and you were one of a group of people that were looking for new ways to ask new questions, without the theoretical straitjacket of structural Marxism.

NR: I started reading Foucault as an undergraduate in 1966 or 1967 when I read the shortened English translation of *Madness and Civilisation*. I started working with those concepts in the early 1970s when I began to work on the genealogy of the 'psy' disciplines. My first book, *The Psychological Complex*, was a way of trying to think about the emergence of these new types of authority figures, in particular authorities of the 'psy'. On the one hand, at the role that those played in the constitution of the human sciences, in particular the psychological sciences; and, on the other hand, the centrality of these new governors of the soul to the forms of welfare government that had emerged in most European societies and, to some extent in the United States, in the twentieth century. So, it wasn't a case of finding Foucault and then finding governmentality; it was a case of trying to think how some of the concepts that Foucault developed—or, as I prefer to put it, his ethos of investigation, of fieldwork in philosophy—could then be deployed in relation to the questions that then concerned me: a critical analysis of 'psy' experts in the welfare state and beyond. And that was the subject of my first three books: *The Psychological Complex; Inventing Ourselves; Governing the Soul.*

Peter Miller and I arrived—from different directions—at an understanding of the fundamental role played by these small, petty authorities who base their legitimacy on a claim to knowledge in a whole diversity of domains: psychologists, social workers, those giving advice to parents and so on, all infused by the 'psy' disciplines. Independently and together, we came to the conclusion that if you were going to understand forms of political power in contemporary liberal democracies then you had to look beyond the conventional analyses that focused on the state, not least because most of these petty authorities who managed businesses and schools and so on originally derived their authority not from the state but from other domains. Only across the twentieth century did they get lashed up in various ways into the networks of governing that we call the welfare state. So our view was that states could govern only on the basis of the emergence of those authorities who base their claim to manage individual and collective lives on forms of expertise grounded in knowledge. It was from that perspective that we started to wonder what would happen if we took that kind of perspective and focussed it on what was conventionally understood as the authority of the state. In the late 1980s we wrote a long paper that we originally called,

'Cutting off the King's Head', looking at the 'conduct of conduct' in complex liberal societies. That paper was widely circulated—and criticised—and eventually became 'Political Power Beyond the State' which was published in the *British Journal of Sociology*. Before that came to fruition, we wrote 'Governing Economic Life'—published in *Economy and Society*—which tried to show that questions at the very heart of Marxist theory, questions about economic organization, could be illuminated in important ways by this approach to knowledge, power and technologies of intervention.

When it came to governmentality, Peter and I arrived from different directions. My late, dear friend Paul Hirst, and several others, those who had been Althusserian Marxists, in the British Althusserian Marxist tradition, and had gone through the phase of the critical analysis of capitalism represented by *Marx's Capital and Capitalism Today* had come to the view that the apparatus of Marxism, even in its Althusserian form, was inadequate to understand contemporary state forms and forms of politics. Paul set up a closed workshop called 'State and Politics', of around twenty to twenty-five of us and in the course of that, that I came to wonder if one could not build on Foucault's work on governmentality to address these issues. I actually came upon 'governmentality' in a rather ad hoc way. In the mid 1970s, together with some friends, I had set up a journal, initially called *Ideology & Consciousness*, but later because we didn't believe in the utility of either the notion of 'ideology' or 'consciousness'—renamed itself *I&C*. Some of our colleagues who were working with *Radical Philosophy* at the time—Graham Burchell and Colin Gordon—left that journal and joined *I&C*. We started to publish some translations of Foucault, largely either translated by Colin Gordon or acquired in various ways from his many contacts. In a roundabout way, we published a translation of one of Foucault's lectures on governmentality in the Autumn of 1979—we translated it from the Italian where it had been published in *Aut Aut* a year earlier. That was when I started thinking about this term, governmentality. I'm certainly not a Foucault expert; even today I haven't read all the lectures; I certainly did not listen to the lectures at that time. I was simply trying to think about alternative ways of investigating political power. This term—governmentality—seemed to me to be incredibly suggestive because it placed this question within the activities of a whole domain of experts; that whole heterogeneous set of practices in which people's conduct is conducted under an authority towards certain ends. In my take in this term, it required one to focus on analysing the multifarious ways that authorities—parents, teachers, doctors, social workers—try to conduct the conduct of others. And then, from that prior analysis, one could ask how some of those authorities at different times are designated political and get linked up to a state apparatus, have their powers formalised through legislation and get enmeshed in a whole complex set of administrative structures and processes. Governmentality seemed to me to be a way of thinking about all those ways of conducting the conduct of individuals and collectives. It opened up ways of investigating historically how those authorities gained legitimacy and how they tried to govern in practice. That's how I came to governmentality.

Working with Peter Miller, I then tried to think through what governmentality might mean. On the one hand, there were certain mentalities. But we were conscious of the problems associated with writing histories of mentalities, so we called them 'rationalities', or styles of thought. Working with approaches from the analytics of discourse, especially in the French tradition of the history of science, we could then start to analyse how they constituted their objects, how they made divisions between different objects such as the mad and the sane, or the legal and the illegal, how they could speak with authority, and where, in what settings for forms, did they speak. But the point about governing is that it has to lash up a style of thought, on the one hand, and a set of technologies for doing something, on the other. So, there were rationalities and technologies, human technologies. We drew upon Ludwick Fleck (1979) for the notion of 'styles of thought'. We could begin to think about, to anatomise, how those human technologies work. Again, we drew inspiration from Foucault, from *Discipline and Punish*, about the spaces and micro-spaces, toe organization of time, space, gazes, the little techniques like interviews and examinations, the methods of record keeping and the practices that entailed and so forth. As you can see, our relationship to Foucault's essay on governmentality was a pretty loose one. Many of the concepts that we developed had a loose affiliation with those developed by Foucault in his studies of psychiatry, medicine and so forth. But others such as governing at a distance, translation mechanisms and so on, we either borrowed from elsewhere or made those up ourselves.

AM: If we stick with the metaphor of a conceptual toolkit then some of the conceptual language—certainly the sensibility—was derived from Foucault, but there were new tools that you had borrowed from elsewhere or made yourselves. It seems to me that you're describing a craftsman's toolkit that includes standard tools but also others that were modified for a specific task and perhaps only used once.

NR: There was certainly not a standardised set of tools for governmentality research. The tools were ways of thinking about how you take something apart and remake our understanding of a problem. As I said, we borrowed lots of ideas from elsewhere. Our thinking about 'rationalities' was informed by the idea of 'styles of thought' which is not a particularly Foucauldian notion—we took it up from Ludwik Fleck. Of course, it was also inflected by Hacking's work on styles of reason. But it was also influenced by James Tully's work on philosophy in its context. Philosophy is always about ontology but it is always, in important ways, tied up with practical problems. We also borrowed from science and technology studies, especially Latour's ideas about translation. And, as your craft metaphor suggests, we tinkered with these borrowed tools for our own purposes. This was a pretty inventive process. On the one hand, there was all that empirical work leading us towards that way of thinking. On the other hand, I was involved in conventional politics until that point, as a Marxist and as a member of the Communist Party. I had been the branch secretary, in Bloomsbury, of the British Communist Party; I was very engaged in the debates about Eurocommunism and *Marxism Today* under Martin Jacques; and with Stuart Hall trying to understand cultures of capitalism. There was a big Gramscian movement but the notion of 'Thatcherism' that is so associated with Hall and *Marxism Today*—or was at that time—implied too much coherence, too much singularity in that project. Also, the Gramscian approach developed in the UK largely by those from the Centre for Cultural Studies at the Unviersity of Birmingham, didn't seem to be able to generate any new ways of thinking about the challenges to the welfare state that were coming from left, right and centre. From the right, with the idea that the growing unproductive 'public sector' of the bloated welfare state was living on the surplus created by the productive part of the economy, and that as the proportion of the former grew in relation to the revenues generated by the latter, that there was going to be a fiscal crisis of the state. From liberals, talking about the huge expansion of discretionary powers under the welfare state that violated individual rights. Or, from the left, people like Alfred Hirschmann who talked about the paradoxical effects of the welfare state: that it hadn't reduced inequality but had enshrined certain modes of inequality and certain forms of clientism. I was coming from a left-wing tradition of critique of the welfare state, especially around medicine and health: again, the vast bureaucratic machine that produced clientism and tensions between the authorities and those over whom they exercised authority. The welfare state managed capitalism without challenging capitalism—I certainly didn't feel any allegiance to any of the ways of governing that we called welfare as they had taken shape over the previous three decades. But the left didn't have ways of understanding what was going on or thinking about how you might make things different. There was a lot of nostalgia about the welfare state, and this was largely how the left responded to Thatcher: people forgot that they had spent the last thirty years criticising the structures of the welfare state. So there was a conjunctural—as we used to say—incentive to try and find the conceptual tools that would not only help one to understand forms of political power beyond the state *in general* but also to understand in a more practicable way what was going on in these transformations of the present—that is to say the 1980s in Britain and Europe, and to some extent in the US, Australia and New Zealand. Our view was that it was first necessary to describe them before one could criticise them. We came in for a great deal of criticism for saying that these new ways of governing were actually 'productive'—by which we meant that it had been the right rather than the left that had turned their critiques practical and effective; that had devised new ways of governing. Some people took this to mean that we were advocates of these new ways of governing but that was not at all what we meant. Rather, we argued that it was about time that the left became a bit more inventive in devising new ways of governing.

AM: At one point, Foucault argues that what we need are new forms of so-cialist governmentality. And, there were some elements of that in *Marxism Today* in terms of flexibility and a return to skilled manufacturing. But even that could be read as something of a look back to a world of meaningful work that was being lost.

NR: Paul Hirst suggested that we need to think of a kind of socialist asso-ciationalism, arguing—quite rightly—that it was only in the early twentieth century that socialism became synonymous with the state. There were traditions of associationalism that did survive and that one might want to revive as a different way to govern. It is very sad that Pal died before he could really develop these ideas to the full, and gather others around him to take them forward.

AM: Let me pick away at one thing. Time and again, you insist that you are engaged in an empirical project. That these empirical projects have modest ambitions and that where you use concepts these are valued for their practicality rather than their theoretical coherence. Concepts are tools and where some tools are used repeatedly—such as governing at a distance—this is precisely because they have demonstrated their us-ability, their empirical value. There is always an insistence that this is not a theoretical exercise but certainly with 'Political Power Beyond the State' you provided others a ready-made way of thinking that—para-doxically—reduces their incentive to be inventive.

NR: Partly, the insistence that 'this is not a theory' is because I wanted to get away from the industry of commentary on Michel Foucault that I didn't find interesting or helpful in any way to deal with the issues that I wanted to think about. The most productive thing to do, in my view, is not to do commentary, nor to manufacture large theories, but to create concepts that can do some work. Peter and I wanted to de-velop concepts that could biting into a problem and rendering it think-able, see how a practice of government really worked, the thoughts that it embodied, the techniques it used, the subjectivities it created. Then one could begin to think of ways of changing thinking changing techniques, changing subjectivities, creating practicable alternatives. I would like to think that 'Political power Beyond the State' was inventive in terms of its concepts. But what began to happen was that people began to extract a kind of analytical machine from it: a kind of analytic of governmentality that you could then apply to almost any question that you might want to ask. At a certain point in this trajectory, especially when I was managing editor of *Economy & Society*, we were inundated with papers on governmentality: governing this, governing that, governing the other. It seemed to be that you could simply apply this theory to almost anything. Now, this was in part because the concepts and analytic methods were useful—they did provide a way of taking a complex problem space and rendering it thinkable. But what transpired was almost the application of a ready-made analytical machine. As we discussed earlier, we invented this way of thinking to answer the specific questions that interested us. Increasingly, we felt that others should also invent their own concepts specific to *their* problems, especially in regions of the world that didn't have the same genealogy as the advanced democracies, where the configuration of forces was very different. There were similarities between what was going on in the former *strong* states, the Nordic states for instance; there were similarities with the United States despite the fact that many disavowed the fact that there was every anything called a welfare state in the US—so we were certainly not arguing that people should not approach these issues drawing on our own ideas. But more generally we felt that 'governmentality' been ossified into an automatic machine for generating analyses and that the life had been wrung out of it. Once we started to get text books on governmentality, university courses on governmentality and so forth, I felt that I had said as much as I could about this approach. Basically, we had worked on this approach for over a decade and decided that we had done what we could and that it was up to others to take it forward.

Of course, we were in part responsible for the way things developed. As a hermeneutic exercise, in our early papers, we tried to sketch out three different families of governmentality: liberalism, welfarism and advanced liberalism. We tried to show that for those places and for that time there had been a family resemblance between ways of thinking about political power, between ways of thinking about what was legitimate; and legitimate ways of conducting conduct; ways of thinking about what fell under the state and what was the responsibility of the market; of what was civil society; and a sort of family of technologies of intervention. This was a hermeneutic exercise for us but I think it did two things. First, it over-emphasised the similarities of what was going on at any particular moment. It made it a lot easier for people to say, there was liberalism, then there was welfarism, and now there is neoliberalism. It encouraged a kind of epochal thinking that is not at all helpful and can lead to exactly the sort of totalising approach that we spent so long working against. In our defence, I would say that the labels were the outcome of an empirical work of investigation of how these families of governmentality worked. It was not that we started with the labels and then looked for examples of how that played out in practice.

This is linked to something else. I was also working with another good friend, Tom Osborne, and Tom and I developed this idea that there were two different styles of thought in social theory which we likened to electricians and painters and decorators. The electrician is interested in the wiring and switches and junction boxes and working out how that all combined together; all the messy and often tinkering business of making all those connections work. The painter and decorator likes to make a smooth surface and that's what gives him the greatest satisfaction. From our point of view, any analyst of governmentality—or anything else for that matter, needed to be more of an electrician and show the messy reality of what lies behind the apparently smoothly functioning system. So, we should be more of an electrician and less of a painter and decorator, if you like. If one relates that to the work that Peter and I did on governementalities, we wanted to show the messy realities but argue that they bore a family resemblance, for instance, rather the other way round, to start from the smooth surface of a finished concept and show how everything was a version of that. I suppose we had a very British way of thinking about governing as messy, if there was a machine, it was a Heath Robinson kind of machine: you improvise, take something that is already there, lash it together with something new and in the end it sort of works, but it clunks along, it never work perfectly. When people talk about neoliberalism as if it were this lean, sleek machine then they are absolutely starting from the wrong place: it's the putting together of many different things, some of which have come from elsewhere and were fashioned for quite different purposes. Because it's not this cold monster of neoliberalism it's this complex assemblage, there are sorts of weak points, there are little bits of that you might quite like, things that you might make useful but in another way. As a form of political thought instead of thinking of the cold monster of neoliberalism that we've got to oppose, destroy and replace entirely, you can then start to think in terms of what little bits might we make useful in some way, turn to *our* ends.

AM: Earlier you used the expression, 'handholds'—is that what you mean? Of course, you've got to be skilled to find handholds and strong to be able to use them. Do you mean to suggest this term intellectually and politically?

NR: Yes. I've been doing some work on the emergence on the idea of resilience because I've been working on bio-security then here in the UK initially and increasingly in the USA and elsewhere you see the idea of resilience gaining traction. In terms of bio-security, responses to every kind of threat—from terrorism, to floods to pandemics—are thought of in terms of resilience in the UK. In the United States, homeland security strategy is full of these references to resilience. Resilience is an intriguing as a way to think about threats. It's not about risk and risk prediction: you accept that horrible things are going to happen, that the state cannot provide complete, total protection to its citizens. Nor can its strategies of preparedness ward off all the dangers, the unknown unknowns. How do you produce a way of governing in the face of all those unknown unknown dangers which you cannot predict and therefore cannot prepare for? The answer is build resilience. Now, there's a lot of critique of this idea of resilience: that it's basically the state giving up on its responsibilities to protect the vulnerable, leaving the poor to their own devices and so forth. But actually I think that this idea of resilience, of communities developing their own capacities to withstand shocks, their capacities to deal with adversity in productive ways, provides some interesting handholds—to use that term—where you might use this idea of resilience to open up discussion of alternatives that might give more power to communities to manage their own affairs in a productive way. That's a little example of where you see something happening in the present and you don't immediately muster all your powers of critique against neoliberalism but think about how does that work; how is that put together; what are the liberating and enslaving possibilities—to borrow from Deleuze—and how might one work to intensify the liberating parts and mitigate the enslaving possibilities. He uses that phrase in his famous little postscript to *Societies of the Spectacle*, which is an oddly productive and provocative thing to read. I think you can also think about other ideas such as responsibility and the emergence of responsibilising strategies in a similar way. Responsibilising strategies that make individuals and communities responsible for crime control are clearly about shifting responsibility for the failure of other strategies of governing, but they also have some quite liberating dimensions that one might seek to intensify.

This all becomes important if you take the view, as I do, that to make a fairer society it is not a question of 'not being governed', but of 'governing differently'. If you are suspicious of the idea of revolution as a transformative moment, and realise that after any revolution, there is still the little mater of how to govern, then you have to look to use some of the techniques that are used to govern in the here and now as well as imagine what forms of governing might exist in a different future. This is a kind of Foucauldian politics. We need to be very sceptical about those general intellectuals who purport to have a comprehensive blueprint of a future society. Instead, 'intellectuals' should engage with those people working in particular domains, and think with them about how they might transform those domains, how they might be governed differently.

References

Cutler, A., Hindess, B. & Hirst, P. (1977), *Marx's Capital and Capitalism Today*, London: Routledge & Kegan Paul.

Deleuze, G. (1992), 'Postscript on the Societies of Control', *October* 59: 3–7.

Fleck, L. (1979), *Genesis and Development of a Scientific Fact*, Chicago: University of Chicago Press.

Foucault, M. (1967), *Madness and Civilisation: A History of Insanity in the Age of Reason*, London: Tavistock.

Foucault, M. (1977), *Discipline and Punish: The Birth of the Prison*, London: Penguin.

Hirschman, A. (1982), *Shifting Involvements: Private Interests and Public Action*, Princeton, NJ: Princeton University Press.

Hirst, P. (1993), *Associative Democracy: New forms of Economic and Social Governance*, Cambridge: Polity.

Miller, P. & Rose, N. (1990), 'Governing Economic Life', *Economy & Society* 19/1: 1–31.

Rose, N. (1985a), *Governing the Soul: The Shaping of the Private Self*, London: Free Association.

Rose, N. (1985b), *The Psychological Complex*, London: Routledge & Kegan Paul.

Rose, N. (1996), *Inventing Ourselves: Psychiatry, Power and Personhood*, Cambridge: Cambridge University Press.

Rose, N. & Miler, P. (1992), 'Political Power Beyond the State: Problematics of Government', *British Journal of Sociology* 43/2: 173–205.

Tully, J. (2002), 'Political Philosophy as a Critical Activity', *Political Theory* 30/4: 533–555.

Name Index

Subject Index

Printed in the United States
by Baker & Taylor Publisher Services